Basel Abbas & Ruanne Abou-Rahme//Nora Al-Badri//
Allora & Calzadilla//Doug Ashford//Judith Baca//Ute
Meta Bauer//Dave Beech//Franco 'Bifo' Berardi//Tania
Bruguera//Christoph Brunner//Judith Butler//Amílcar
Cabral//Elias Canetti//Jessica A. Cooley//Douglas
Crimp//Jodi Dean//Chto Delat//Gilles Deleuze//
T.J. Demos//Nika Dubrovsky//Süreyyya Evren//Mark
Fisher//Catherine Flood//Ann M. Fox//Andrea Fraser//
Matthew Fuller//Nan Goldin//David Graeber//Gavin
Grindon//Félix Guattari//Guerrilla Girls//Global Ultra
Luxury Faction//Gulf Labor//Stuart Hall//David Harvey//
Tom Holert//Brian Holmes//Darcus Howe//Immigrant
Movement International//Sanja Iveković//Amar
Kanwar//Lina Khatib//Leslie Labowitz//Suzanne
Lacy//Carrie Lambert-Beatty//Aude Launay//Marc
James Léger//Liberate Tate//Lucy Lippard//Achille
Mbembe//Yates McKee//MTL Collective//Chantal
Mouffe//Sethembile Msezane//Zanele Muholi//Antonio
Negri//Jan Nikolai Nelles//Roberto Nigro//Not An
Alternative//Katarzyna Pabijanek//Vivian Paulissen//
Michael Rakowitz//Gerald Raunig//Oliver Ressler//
Adam Rolston//Martha Rosler//Anca Rujoiu//Salman
Rushdie//Gregory Sholette//Stephanie Smith//Tidal
Magazine//Françoise Vergès//Peter Weiss//Eyal
Weizman//Deborah Willis

Activism

Whitechapel Gallery
London
The MIT Press
Cambridge, Massachusetts

Edited by Afonso Dias Ramos and Tom Snow

ACTIVISM

Documents of Contemporary Art

Co-published by Whitechapel Gallery
and the MIT Press

First published 2023
© 2023 Whitechapel Gallery Ventures Limited
All texts © the authors or the estates of the authors,
unless otherwise stated

ISBN 978-0-85488-314-1 (Whitechapel Gallery)
ISBN 978-0-85488-315-8 (Whitechapel Gallery
e-book)
ISBN 978-0-262-54656-0 (The MIT Press)
ISBN 978-0-262-37651-8 (The MIT Press retail
e-book)
ISBN 978-0-262-37650-1 (The MIT Press library
e-book)

A catalogue record for this book is available from
the British Library

Library of Congress Control Number: 2022947463

Whitechapel Gallery   10 9 8 7 6 5 4 3 2 1
The MIT Press   10 9 8 7 6 5 4 3 2 1

Commissioning Editor: Anthony Iles
Project Editor: Evie Tarr
Publications Assistant (MA Placement):
Nastia Svarevska
Design by SMITH
Gemma Gerhard, Justine Hucker,
Allon Kaye, Claudia Paladini
Printed and bound in Turkey

Cover, Sethembile Msezane. *Chapungu – The Day
Rhodes Fell* (2015). Photo: Courtesy of the Artist

Whitechapel Gallery Ventures Limited
77–82 Whitechapel High Street
London E1 7QX
whitechapelgallery.org

Distributed to the book trade (UK and Europe only)
by Thames & Hudson
181a High Holborn
London, WC1V 7QX
+44 (0) 20 7845 5000
sales@thameshudson.co.uk

The MIT Press
Cambridge, MA 02142
mitpress.mit.edu

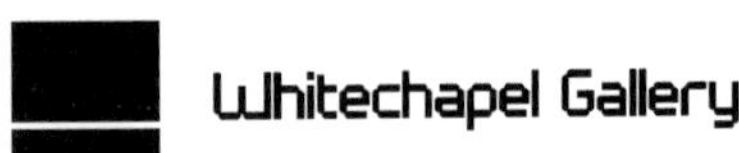
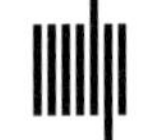

Documents of Contemporary Art

In recent decades artists have progressively expanded the boundaries of art as they have sought to engage with an increasingly pluralistic environment. Teaching, curating and understanding of art and visual culture are likewise no longer grounded in traditional aesthetics but centred on significant ideas, topics and themes ranging from the everyday to the uncanny, the psychoanalytical to the political.

The Documents of Contemporary Art series emerges from this context. Each volume focuses on a specific subject or body of writing that has been of key influence in contemporary art internationally. Edited and introduced by a scholar, artist, critic or curator, each of these source books provides access to a plurality of voices and perspectives defining a significant theme or tendency.

For over a century the Whitechapel Gallery has offered a public platform for art and ideas. In the same spirit, each guest editor represents a distinct yet diverse approach – rather than one institutional position or school of thought – and has conceived each volume to address not only a professional audience but all interested readers.

From
the
very
outset,
our
STUDYING
was
REBELLION.

Peter Weiss, 'The Aesthetics of Resistance', 1975 (see pages 24–28)

Afonso Dias Ramos and Tom Snow

Introduction//Contemporary Activism and the Politics of Art

From the alter-globalisation protests at the turn of the century, to the 2011 mass uprisings across the Arabic-speaking world, global Occupy demonstrations, and the ongoing Black Lives Matter and Rhodes Must Fall campaigns, social movements in recent decades have reshaped the way artists work politically across the world. Far from simply supplying protest groups with a visual identity or taking shelter in art institutions to articulate a critique, artists have contributed to and taken part in campaigns for social justice by developing and sharing strategies for collective organisation, creative and radical pedagogy, agitational street theatrics and mediatised counter-spectacles. At the same time, artists have turned their attention to interrogating endemic injustices within the representative politics of cultural institutions, increasingly challenging their historical ties to colonial regimes and current affiliations with corporate oligarchy, linked to economic precarity and urban gentrification. Given the relentless dismantling of public funding, and the wider expediency of culture and corporate whitewashing of neoliberal institutions globally, it seems appropriate, if not imperative, to ask whether institutions have ever adequately assimilated the multiple concerns of activist politics and the wider aesthetics of political art. By reconsidering the changing meaning of activism at this juncture, the overarching question that frames this anthology is whether contemporary art's most radical politics takes place outside, against, or in spite of conventional sites of display, such as museums, biennials, and galleries. Activism as defined throughout this book is, therefore, not simply reliant on staging interventions in the way narratives are presented and framed to the public, which is the aim of many critical art practices. Rather, it is also defined by the kind of collective proposals and egalitarian demands that seek expression through the forms that it takes, the alliances it makes and the media it mobilises. As such, this volume retraces ways that art's political stakes are being reconfigured from the outside, foregrounding the collective endeavour to reinvent a politics of aesthetics and likewise to reassess and trouble the hegemonic paradigms of art's mainstream and institutional life.

Politically-engaged artists have consistently led the way in cutting-edge material and discursive innovations that have redefined accepted conventions of artistic practice. Lucy Lippard's essay 'Trojan Horses' (1984), included in this volume, is often cited as the earliest instance of the word activism entering art criticism, compounding both creative practices and political organising. Since then, 'activism' has rapidly become one of the most ubiquitous and predictable terms within contemporary art. Indiscriminately used, its meaning now risks appearing more nebulous than ever, having spawned endless derivations and neologisms in the last decades, used and abused in blockbuster shows, generic surveys or gallery re-hangs to cover just about any sort of artistic action or institutional activity.

Consider, in this regard, Hal Foster's description of conceptual dematerialisations and diversifications in the discursive reach of art since the 1960s as a crisis in 'pluralism,' or representational abnegation, owing in part to institutional ambivalence towards the political ideas that art practices readily engage.[1] Miwon Kwon has further noted the easily commodifiable critical gestures of 'nomadic' artists, lamenting cultural reification and amorphous stereotyping in the age of neoliberal globalisation.[2] Conversely, Terry Smith pointed to the ever-increasing role of mega institutions and international exhibitions in reconfiguring histories of modern and contemporary art; bringing together ways of working outside Eurocentric traditions of painting and sculpture, challenging equally reductive notions of canonisation and classification.[3] Yet, the subsumption of potentially radical gestures usually occurs at a temporal and geographical distance. While this book is not only concerned with the limits or possibilities of cultural spaces, it is worth noting that institutions are often less keen to ingratiate themselves with politically challenging proposals when located too close to home. That is, sufficiently removed to immediately compromise the ethical rhetoric that multiple cultural sites are obliged to adopt owing to the artistic concerns and aesthetic discourses they inevitably implicate.

A further question raised throughout the texts in this volume, therefore, relates not merely to pedestrian appropriations or spurious co-optation of radical discourses – highly problematic though such instances remain – but rather to campaigns for social justice through tactics for self-organisation and creative disruptions geared towards mobilising solidarity *in situ*. Said otherwise, the writings selected in this anthology spotlight the capacity for closely interrogating the contemporaneity of art; meaning its relation to both the material and immaterial circumstances in which it takes place, resulting frequently in estrangement or even withdrawal from established cultural infrastructures and a reinvestment in direct action.

We may, in this instance, sense Peter Bürger's influential yet arguably monolithic interpretation of the historical avant-garde as a failed political programme, proceeded by the neo-avant-garde's institutionalisation and negation of 'genuinely avant-gardiste intentions.'[4] Yet, as Douglas Crimp pointed out at the beginning of the 1990s, in a text also included here concerning ACT UP and Gran Fury protest graphics, artists working with live activist cultures were often considered 'too rooted in movement politics' to be taken seriously by institutions that simultaneously sought affiliation with recent politically subversive groups. Crimp pointed to the reluctance of MoMA during an exhibition surveying current political prints to address the systemic and de-humanising prejudices associated with HIV and AIDS-related illnesses in close proximity. For Crimp, 'critical postmodernism', involving the 'promise of breaking out of the museum and marketplace to take on new issues and find new audiences' had itself become 'a sanctioned, if still highly contested, art world product'. Such institutionalisations, however, had limits, evident in the exclusion of HIV and AIDS discourses from inside the contemporary museum's walls.

Artists have, then, consistently engaged in activist discourses, mobilising their skills in social movements, regularly participating in civil and social rights campaigns whilst simultaneously boycotting cultural institutions and exerting significant pressure on them. Indeed, recent protest movements have come into conflict with cultural institutions, in many cases simultaneously foreshadowing directly agitational initiatives as those led by the collectives Gulf Labor and Decolonize This Place. As Yates McKee pointed out, recent movements demonstrated that exhibiting in galleries does not adequately represent the way politically-engaged artists work, or the critical discourses which they engage. Associated aesthetic practices have taken 'the avant-garde dialectic of "art and life" to a new level of intensity', thus challenging Bürger's chronological assessment head-on. After all, the avant-garde is not simply an empty signifier today, but remains subject to perpetual actualisation, continually re-emerging as a strategy for renewal.

As Gregory Sholette points out in these pages, a non-institutionalised 'dark matter' of cultural producers has long existed outside the parameters of institutional spaces. Rather than suggesting that developments in the 1960s prepared the ground for artists to depart from the gallery space and take to the streets in the twenty-first century[5], the texts collected here underscore the centrality of activism in redefining aesthetic practices in conjunction with social and political thought. Nor are we preoccupied with dominant editorial directives that foreground the voices of well-established global super curators in commissioned essays, such as Hou Hanru, Carolyn Christov-Bakargiev, Hans-Ulrich Obrist and Nicolas Bourriaud, who view quasi-utopic or relational art in the museum as amelioratory.[6] For its part, the hangover from Bourriaud's influential concept of 'relational aesthetics' – flawed by the assumption that art's dematerialisation evades commodification by restoring the social bond of community[7] – has been such that activism has, in our view, often been

ART NEEDS TO BE POLITICAL – OR LET ME SAY THAT <u>MY ART IS POLITICAL.</u> IT'S NOT FOR SHOW. IT'S NOT FOR PLAY.

Zanele Muholi, 'Faces and Phases: In Conversation with Deborah Willis', 2015 (see pages 78–80) misunderstood as lacking in antagonism and organised agitational strategy. Even Claire Bishop, whose authoritative critique of relational aesthetics is widely read yet far less implemented, has argued as a result that art's involvement in politics might be limited to throwing institutional limitations and contradictions into stark relief.[8] Accordingly, this volume traces practices and texts that reject or interrogate institutional conservatisms, collectively staking a claim for the specificity of activism as a concept representing cutting-edge developments in serious contemporary art practice, particularly where institutional legitimacy is on the wane.

In putting the texts together, we became aware of a distinct centre of gravitation forming around New York City. This was, of course, an unintentional oversight, but one which must nevertheless be acknowledged given the disproportional hold that this part of the world has had in articulating some of the most engaging discussions and positions on this topic. Yet, the texts in this reader have been selected with a view to encompass a varied range of different geopolitical contexts and subject positions, across linguistic divides and historical moments. Nor are we singularly concerned with theory-led, art-historical assessments. Throughout, artists' writings, statements, and interviews shed light on the practicalities of working with and as activists, as much as they articulate key discursive proposals sometimes in direct response to a field of study and debate that has all too often reproduced tired clichés—of simply 'raising awareness' or 'activating' viewers—prominent in the general literature on the topic. As editors we strove to resist the common temptation of surveys on art and activism to include everything at once, within sweeping historical panoramas that do not adequately account for the important developments underway and the radical edge of current artistic practices, whose use of the concept of 'activism' is rarely distinguished from 'protest', 'critique', 'participation', or 'community'.

There are, of course, blind spots; things we would have liked to include but could not, owing to a lack of suitable literature on certain practices or evolving theoretical positions, essays too long and dense to be realistically included in a reader of this nature, or simply our inability to locate them. To give just one example: we would have liked to feature Ai Weiwei's work. Though his practice as an activist likely jars with many of the positions taken here, we were still open to including a persuasive position that contextualised his artworks beyond their symbolic or monumental status. As interesting as many of the conversations with this artist are, particularly in biographical regard, there is a shortage of critical literature that is not simply commentary accepting of his work's stature.[9] What this process has shown us, however, is how much work remains to be done in thinking through the place(s) of activism and its visual culture in the literature concerning contemporary art, even as this critical task seems more urgent today than ever before. Indeed, as Sholette recently pointed out, 'the prevailing desire by artists to transform their practices into a form of highly focused protest is the most prominent – and in many ways the most perplexing – constituent of contemporary art today'.[10]

Activism opens with a prelude that includes two foundational texts about political struggles over the meaning of culture and emancipation, in the form of passages from Peter Weiss's 1975 novel *Aesthetics of Resistance* and a speech made by Amílcar Cabral in 1970 at Syracuse University. This is followed by four sections, each dealing with crucial aspects concerning the problem of activism in contemporary art, as well as a coda. In their diverse approaches to activism, each section touches on key debates not only in the contemporary art world, institutional frameworks and public history, but as part of, and in response to, the most pressing social and political struggles of the present time around the globe. Indeed, resurgent campaigns for decolonial reckoning, ecological justice, gender equality, indigenous rights and antiracist pedagogies, indicate that the role of activism in contemporary art practice urges the sort of critical reassessment that these texts aim to facilitate.

'Ideology and Dissent' takes as its point of departure the issue of hegemonic ideologies and dissenting cultural practices. Some of the indispensable texts included in this section provide solid grounding for situating an expanded definition of activism and art and conceptualising this relationship within the wider field of social and political struggle. Whilst no strict consensus is identifiable throughout the texts, there are traceable developments and influences legible throughout. For instance, landmark feminist approaches to the patriarchal aesthetic world discussed by Suzanne Lacy and Leslie Labowitz might be identifiable in Stuart Hall's insistence on reinventing visual and filmic languages in the campaign for civil rights in the UK and the Commonwealth, as much as Zanele Muholi's perspectives on photographic queer space and visual activism, as the means to effect changes on the ground. Other writings have been selected in order to address particular historical moments and critical topics, striking potential dialogues with the issues of migration, citizenship and precarity under late capitalism, such as Tania Bruguera and the Immigrant Movement International; part of an art project that also functioned as refugee support centre, community centre and legal advice network, to change the status of migrants as delinquents, in addition to organisational strategies that actively aim to combat violent and exclusionary political realities, from Sanja Ivekovic's work with shelters for domestic abuse victims to Carrie Lambert-Beatty's discussion concerning abortion rights and *Women on Waves* provision of women's health care in mobile clinics.

Concerns cross over between sections as much as direct dialogues are discernible within each of them. 'Institutions and Disruption' foregrounds the disputed terrain of the institution in ways that might be reflected in Crimp's regarding the AIDS and HIV crisis or Chantal Mouffe's Gramscian proposal in the previous section. The second section of the book directly discusses the ethics of institutional engagement and its possibilities, in ways that might be seen to move beyond the more familiar approach of institutional critique and its strategy to reveal the biases of conventional museum representation and operations. Whilst Martha Rosler warns against regression to well-worn institutional gimmicks, Chto Delat propose that museums now act as 'depositories and laboratories' which decline to compromise with the symbolic agendas of capitalism and should instead aim at revising the notion of a knowledge commons. The refusal to view capitalism as totality, or as the only method of cultural and intellectual valuation available currently, is shared by the arts collective Not An Alternative, which is later debated by Mark Fisher and Franco 'Bifo' Berardi in the final section. 'Institutions and Disruption' also includes discussions of direct and unsanctioned museum interventions which proved to be transformational, including texts by Liberate Tate written prior to the gallery ending their sponsorship deal with BP after a six-year campaign of creative disobedience, alongside Nan Goldin and PAIN (Prescription Addiction Intervention Now) who also called for major cultural institutions to sever ties with the Sackler Trust owing to their involvement with the opioid epidemic, leading the Metropolitan Museum of Art, Tate Galleries, Victoria and Albert Museum, London's National Gallery and National Portrait Gallery, the Serpentine Galleries, and the Guggenheim to refuse to continue philanthropic dealings with the pharmaceutical-derived fortune of the Sackler family. Questions are also raised here about the institution's waning capacity to determine what is and is not considered contemporary art. Liberate Tate certainly regarded their performances as art, but Tate refused to credit their actions in the decision to end relations with BP.[11] Yet as MTL Collective asks, what would liberation of a cultural institution proper actually look like? In addition, that is, to confronting corporate strategies to finesse their public image, despite destructive ecological practices and alleged tax breaks, Decolonize This Place question literal museum foundations erected on colonised lands. In Jessica A. Cooley and Ann M. Fox's crip manifesto, they call for an interrogation of 'bodily normalcy,' defying the narrative whereby the external forces in society come to 'rescue' people with disabilities, whilst Françoise Vergès relates prescriptive notions of universalism to lasting colonial attitudes, using the lens of antiracism to denounce art institutions as social structures that seek to subdue and absorb any dissent by appropriating the vocabulary of activist protest.

Our third section 'Occupy Aesthetics' focuses on writings concerning the c.2011 uprisings across the Arabic-speaking world and global Occupy protest movements. This concise section draws together texts that reckon with the significance of activism's new visual culture in the occupation of highly visible urban centres and their extension across digital media. In addition to Khatib's discussions of graffiti mural in Tahrir Square and Basel Abbas and Ruanne Abou-Rahme's reflection on the 'living archive,' Dave Beech surveys the way artists boycotted major biennial exhibitions at this moment, whilst Global Ultra Luxury Faction (G.U.L.F.) contextualise their actions around museums in line with the anti-state capitalist concerns of large-scale occupational encampments. David Harvey stresses the urban space as a battleground to exercise the potential of a collective *right to the city* against capitalism and the commodification of services and facilities, while Judith Butler develops the concept of public space, taking on the 2011 protest movements to claim that politics is defined by people appearing collectively in physical proximity or joint voicing.

The final section, 'Ecology and the Commons', focuses on debates concerning common space and its articulation in an age of ecological crises, foregrounding the ways in which recent struggles have reconfigured dichotomies between public and private spheres. There are a number of paired texts here, including Elias Canetti's continuously relevant mediations on the nature of gathered crowds from 1960, followed by Jodi Dean's reflection on his text. Félix Guattari's classic *Three Ecologies*, written in 1989, lays the groundwork for what is now commonly referred to as an intersectional approach to ecology, encompassing the 'ethico-political' interrogation of broadcast media and the ecosophic necessity in unpacking the relations between 'the environment, social relations and human subjectivity' in the context of a ubiquitous market system. Christoph Brunner, Roberto Nigro, and Gerald Raunig update Guattari's reflections in a way that warns against misappropriations of eco-art as simply 'green' art. That is, merely symbolising environmental concerns rather than addressing them, or perhaps more aptly greenwashing in a way that we unfortunately witness in major institutions currently. In broad and specific terms T.J. Demos, Catherine Flood and Gavin Grindon, Amar Kanwar, and Allora & Calzadilla discuss ways of displacing neocolonial exploitation of the natural environment, yet each share approaches that are unconventional to traditional forms of art-making and institutionalised politics alike. Relatedly, Judith Baca and Sethembile Msezane – two continents and almost two decades apart – discuss the heated controversies surrounding the standing monuments to colonial figures and corporate art mediating the experience of public space, both enacting a plea for greater daily consciousness and analyzing the forging of radical yet rational solidarities.

Our volume ends with a coda taking the form of a letter written by Michael Rakowitz to an 'encyclopedic museum curator,' offering to collaborate with curators of an undisclosed major global museum collection. Rakowitz offers to gift his artwork to the museum in exchange for the return of cultural heritage removed from Iraq around the turn of the twentieth century. This letter not only reflects our prelude but, for us, also synthesises several of the pressing concerns negotiated in this collection by presenting a workable – though relatively modest – proposal to push the present against the historical grain.

1   Hal Foster, *Recodings: Art, Spectacle, Cultural Politics* (Seattle: Bay Press, 1985) 13–32.

2   Miwon Kwon, 'One Place after Another: Notes on Site Specificity,' in *October*, vol. 80 (Spring 1997) 85–110.

3   Terry Smith, *Contemporary Art: World Currents* (London: Lawrence King Publishing, 2011).

4   Peter Bürger, *Theory of the Avant-Garde*, trans. Michael Shaw (Minneapolis: University of Minnesota Press, 1984) 58.

5   Peter Weibel, (ed.), *Global Activism – Art and Conflict in the 21st Century* (Cambridge and Karlsruhe: MIT Press and ZKM, 2014).

6   Steven Henry Madoff (ed.), *What about Activism?* (Berlin: Sternberg Press, 2019).

7   For instance, Stewart Martin, 'Critique of Relational Aesthetics' in *Third Text*, vol. 21, no. 4 (July, 2007) 369–386.

8   Claire Bishop, 'Antagonism and Relational Aesthetics,' in *October*, vol. 110 (Fall 2004) 51-79.

9   Ai Weiwei, 'Conversation with Tim Marlow,' [2018] in *Conversations: Ai Weiwei* (New York: Columbia University Press, 2021).

10   Gregory Sholette, *The Art of Activism and the Activism of Art* (London: Lund Humphries, 2022) 12.

11   See Tom Snow, 'Art as Activism', in *Art Monthly*, no. 472 (June 2019) 6–10.

we are at a moment
when the principles of
institutional critique
are being pushed
to a breaking point
and opening onto
something radically
new and radically old
at the same time.

MTL Collective, 'From Institutional Critique to Institutional Liberation?
A Decolonial Perspective on the Crises of Contemporary Art', 2018 (see pages 123–125)

The time has gone when, IN AN ATTEMPT TO PERPETUATE THE DOMINATION OF PEOPLE, culture was considered to be the prerogative of privileged peoples or nations.

Amílcar Cabral, 'National Liberation and Culture', 1970 (see pages 28–29)

PRELUDE

Peter Weiss
The Aesthetics of Resistance//1975

[...] And thus, on the twenty second of September, nineteen thirty-seven, a few days before my departure, we stood in front of the altar frieze, which had been brought here from the castle mountain of Pergamum to be reconstructed, and which, painted colourfully and lined with forged metals, had once reflected the light of the Aegean sky. Heilmann indicated the dimensions and location of the temple, as the temple, still undamaged by sandstorms or earthquakes, pillage or plunder, had shown itself on a protruding platform, on the terraced hill of the residence, above the city known today as Bergama, sixty-five miles north of Smyrna, between the narrow, usually dried-out rivers Keteios and Selinos, gazing westward, across the plain of Caicus, toward the ocean and the isle of Lesbos, a structure with an almost square ground plan, one hundred twenty by one hundred thirteen feet and with a perron sixty-five feet wide, the whole thing dedicated by Eumenes II, to thank the gods for helping him in his war – the construction having begun one hundred eighty years before our era and lasting for twenty years, the buildings visible from far away, included among the wonders of the world by Lucius Ampelius in his *Book of Memorabilia*, second century AD, before the temple sank into the rubble of a millennium. And has this mass of stone, Coppi asked, which served the cult of princely and religious masters of ceremony, who glorified the victory of the aristocrats over an earthbound mix of nations – has this mass of stone now become a value in its own right, belonging to anyone who steps in front of it. It was no doubt highbred figures who trod barbaric mongrels underfoot here, and the sculptors did not immortalise the people who were down in the streets, running the mills, smithies and manufactories, or who were employed in the markets, the workshops, the harbour shipyards; besides, the sanctuary on the thousand-foot-high mountain, in the walled district of the storehouses, barracks, baths, theatres, administration buildings and palaces of the ruling clan, was accessible to the populace only on holidays; no doubt, only the names of some of the master artists were handed down, Menecrates, Dionysades, Orestes, and not the names of those who had transferred the drawings to the ashlars, had defined the intersections with compasses and drills, and had practiced expertly on some veins and shocks of hair, and nothing recalled the peons who fetched the marble and dragged the huge blocks to the oxcarts, and yet, said Heilmann, the frieze brought fame not only for those who were close to the gods but also for those whose strength was still concealed, for they too were not ignorant, they did not want to be enslaved forever, led by Aristonicus they rebelled at the end of the construction, rising up against the lords of the city. Nevertheless the work still incorporated the same dichotomy as at the time of its creation. Destined to emanate royal power, it could simultaneously be questioned about its peculiarities of style, its sculptural persuasiveness. In its heyday, before falling to the Byzantine Empire, Pergamum was renowned for its scholars, its schools and libraries, and the special writing pages of cured, fleshed, and buffed calfskin made the fruits of poetic invention, of scholarly and scientific investigation permanent. The silence, the paralysis of those fated to be trampled into the ground continued to be palpable. They, the real bearers of the Ionian state, unable to read or write, excluded from artistic activity, were only good enough to create the wealth for a small privileged stratum and the necessary leisure for the elite of the mind. The existence of the celestials was unattainable for them, but they could recognise themselves in the kneeling imbruted creatures. The latter, in crudeness, degradation, and maltreatment, bore their features. The portrayal of the gods in flight and of the annihilation of urgent danger expressed not the struggle of good against evil, but the struggle between the classes, and this was recognised not only in our present-day viewing but perhaps also back then in secret glimpses by serfs. However, the afterdays of the altar were likewise determined by the enterprising spirit of the well-to-do. When the sculptural fragments that had lain buried under the deposits of Near Eastern power changes came to light, it was once again the superior, the enlightened who knew how to use the valuable items, while the herdsmen and nomads, the descendants of the builders of the temple, possessed no more of Pergamum's grandeur than dust. But it was a waste of breath complaining, said Heilmann, for the preservation of the showpiece of Hellenic civilisation in a mausoleum of the modern world was preferable to its traceless entombment in Mysian detritus. Since our goal was to eliminate injustice, to wipe out poverty, he said, and since this country too was only going through a transition, we could imagine that this site would someday demonstrate the expanded and mutual ownership intrinsic in the monumentality of the formed work. And so, in the dim light, we gazed at the beaten and dying. The mouth of one of the vanquished, with the rapacious hound hanging over his shoulder, was half open, breathing its last. His left hand lay feeble on the forward-charging leather-shod foot of Artemis, his right arm was still raised in self-defence, but his hips were already growing cold, and his legs had turned into a spongy mass. We heard the thuds of the clubs, the shrilling whistles, the moans, the splashing of blood. We looked back at a prehistoric past, and for an instant the prospect of the future likewise filled up with a massacre impenetrable to the thought of liberation. Heracles would have to help them, the subjugated, and not those who had enough armour and weapons. Prior to the genesis of the figurations, there had been the bondage, the enclosure in stone. In the marble quarries on the mountain slopes north of the castle, the master sculptors had pointed their long sticks at the best blocks while eyeing the Gallic captives toiling in the sultry heat. Shielded and fanned by palm branches, squinting in the blinding sun, the sculptors took in the rippling of the muscles, the bending and stretching of the sweating bodies. The defeated warriors, driven here in chains, hanging from ropes on the rock faces, smashing crowbars and wedges into the strata of glittering, bluish white, crystalline-like limestone, and transporting the gigantic ashlars on long wooden sleds down the twisting paths, were notorious for their savagery, their brutal customs, and in the evenings the lords with their retinues passed them timidly when the stinking prisoners, drunk on cheap rotgut, were camping in a pit. Up in the gardens of the castle, however, in the gentle breeze wafting up from the sea, the huge bearded faces became the stuff of the sculptors' dreams, and they remembered ordering one man or another to stand still, opening his eye wide, pulling his lips apart to view his teeth, they recalled the arteries swelling on his temples, the glistening nose, zygomas and forehead emerging from the cast shadows. They could still hear the lugging and shoving, the stemming of shoulders and backs against the weight of the stone, the rhythmic shouts, the curses, the whip cracks, the grinding of sled runners in the sand, and they could see the figures of the frieze slumbering in the marble coffins. Slowly they scraped forth the limbs, felt them, saw forms emerge whose essence was perfection. With the plundered people transferring their energies into relaxed and receptive thoughts, degradation and lust for power produced art. Through the noisy maelstrom of a school class we pushed our way into the next room, where the market gates of Miletus loomed in the penumbra. At the columns flanking the gates, which had led from the town hall of the port to the open emporium, Heilmann asked whether we had noticed that inside, in the altar room, a spatial function had been inverted, so that exterior surfaces had become interior walls. In facing the western perron, he said, we had our backs to the eastern side, the rear of the temple, that is, in its merely rudimentary reconstruction, and the unfolded southern frieze stretched out to the right while the relief on the northern cornice ran to the left. Something the viewer was to grasp by slowly circling it was now surrounding him instead. This dizzying procedure would ultimately make us understand the Theory of Relativity, he added when, moving a few centuries deeper, we walked along the clay-brick walls that had once stood in the cluster of Nebuchadnezzar's Babylonian towers, and we then suddenly stepped into an area where yellowing leaves, whirring sunspots, pale-yellow double-decker buses, cars with flashing reflections, streams of pedestrians and the rhythmic smashing of hobnailed boots demanded a readjustment in our bearings, a new indication of our whereabouts. [...]

Inseparable from economic advantage was the superiority of knowledge. Ownership involved greed, and the advantaged tried as long as possible to block the road to education for the have-nots. The privileges of the ruling class could not be eliminated until we gained insight into the conditions and acquired fundamental knowledge. We kept getting repulsed over and over because our ability to think, deduce and conclude was insufficiently developed. This state of affairs began changing with the realisation that the upper classes essentially opposed our thirst for knowledge. Ever since, our most important goal was to conquer an education, a skill in every field of research, by using any means, cunning and strength of mind. From the very outset, our studying was rebellion. We gathered material to defend ourselves and prepare a conquest. Seldom haphazardly, mostly because we continued with the things we understood, we moved from one object to the next, fending off weariness and familiar perspectives as well as the constant argument that we could not be up to the strain of self-education at the end of a workday. While our numb minds often had to squeeze out of a void and relearn nimbleness after monotony, we did not want paid labour to be either derogated or despised. In rejecting the opinion that it was a special achievement for people like us to deal with artistic, scientific and scholarly problems, we wished to maintain ourselves in work that did not belong to us. [...]

When stumbling upon a text or a painting in a magazine, a museum, we would usually test it to see if could be used in the political struggle, and we accepted it if it was openly partisan. But then again we also stumbled on things that did not reveal an immediate political impact and yet had disturbing and, we felt, important qualities. If books or paintings of this sort, especially when decried as degenerate by the new rulers, were removed from the public collections, then we felt all the more strongly about including them in the registers of sabotage acts and revolutionary manifestations. We had already been impressed by Surrealism when [Max] Hodann, in Haeckel Hall, proceeding from numerous questions about the origins of neuroses, depressions and obsessions, pointed out the links between social conditions and illness motives, the dream impulses, and explained their repercussions in an art that followed the unhampered torrent of inspirations. This kind of expression, transcending logic, acknowledging all exotic, terrifying things in order to thrust forward to the causes of personal behaviour, was right up our alley in our search to find ourselves. After all, we too distrusted anything that was definite and solid, and beneath the envelope of legitimacies we saw the manipulations that were destroying many of us. Dadaism likewise evinced some of our tendencies, it had spit into the elegant parlours, it had toppled the plaster busts from their pedestals and shredded the garlands of petty bourgeois self-aggrandisement, that was fine with us, we endorsed the ridiculing of dignity, the deriding of holiness, but we had no time for the call for a total annihilation of art, people who were sated with culture could afford such slogans, but we wanted to take over the cultural institutions left unscathed and see which of their contents could be made serviceable for our craving to learn. […]

Peter Weiss, extracts from *The Aesthetics of Resistance, Volume I* (1975), trans. Joachim Neugroschel (Durham and London: Duke University Press, 2005) 7–11, 44–45, 47–48.

Amílcar Cabral
National Liberation and Culture//1970

[…] Culture, whatever may be the ideological or idealistic manifestations of its character, is thus an essential element in the history of a people. It is perhaps the product of history as the flower is the product of a plant. Like history, or because it is history, culture has as its physical base the forces of production and the means of production. It plunges its roots into the material reality of the soil of the environment in which it grows, and reflects the organic nature of society but being all the same capable of being influenced by exterior factors. If history allows us to know the nature and the causes of the imbalances and conflicts (economic, political and social) which characterise the evolution of a society, culture teaches us what have been the dynamic syntheses, structured and established by the mind of society for the solution of these conflicts, at each stage in the evolution of this same society in the quest for survival and progress.

As with the flower in a plant, it is in culture that you find the capacity (or responsibility) for the production and the fertilising of the seed which ensures the continuity of history, ensuring at the same time, the perspectives of the evolution and of the progress of the society in question. It is therefore seen that imperialist domination being the negation of the true historical process of the oppressed people, it must necessarily be the negation of its cultural processes. We understand further why the practice of imperialist rule, like all other foreign rule, demands for its own security, cultural oppression and a direct or indirect attempt to control the essential aspects of the culture of the oppressed people.

The study of the history of liberation struggles shows that in general, they are preceded by an increase in cultural phenomena which progressively crystallise into an attempt, successful or not, to assert the cultural personality of the oppressed people in an act of rejection of that of the oppressor. Whatever may be the state of subjection of a nation to foreign rule and the influence of economic, political and social factors in the furtherance of this domination, it is generally in culture that the seed of protest, leading to the emergence and development of the liberation movement, is found.

A nation which frees itself from foreign rule, will only be culturally free if, without a complex and without underestimating the importance of positive contributions from the oppressors' culture and of other cultures, it recaptures the commanding heights of its own culture, which derives sustenance from the living reality of its environment and equally rejects the harmful influences which any kind of subjection to foreign cultures involves. Thus one sees that if imperialist domination necessarily practices cultural oppression, national liberation is necessarily an act of culture.

Nowadays it has become quite commonplace to assert that each nation has its own culture. The time has gone when, in an attempt to perpetuate the domination of people, culture was considered to be the prerogative of privileged peoples or nations and, by ignorance or bad intention, culture was confused with technology, or with the colour of the skin or shape of the eyes. Liberation movements, representatives and defenders of the culture of the people, have to be conscious of the fact that whatever may be the material conditions of the society that it represents, that society is the bearer and creator of culture. The liberation movement must besides achieve a mass character, the popular character of the culture, which is not, and cannot be the prerogative of one or of certain sectors of the society.

In the detailed analysis of the social structure that all liberation movements should be capable of making in coming to grips with the imperatives of the struggle, the cultural characteristics of each sector of society have a supremely important place. For, though culture has a mass character, it is nevertheless not uniform, it does not develop equally in all sectors of the society. The attitude of each social group when faced with the struggle is dictated by its economic interests, but it is also profoundly influenced by its culture. One could even say that it is the differences in the levels of culture which explain the different reactions of individuals in the same socioeconomic group to the liberation movement. And it is here that the full importance of culture for each person is reached: understanding of, and integration with his environment, identification with the fundamental problems and aspirations of the society, and acceptance of the possibility of change in the direction of progress. […]

Amílcar Cabral, extract from 'National Liberation and Culture' (1970), *Transition*, no. 45 (1974) 13-14.

Activist art
is not only
'oppositional',
although it is
usually critical
in some sense

IDEOLOGY AND DISSENT

Lucy Lippard
Trojan Horse: Activist Art and Power//1984

Maybe the Trojan Horse was the first activist artwork. Based in subversion on the one hand and empowerment on the other, activist art operates both within and beyond the beleaguered fortress that is high culture or the 'art world'. It is not a new art form so much as it is a massing of energies, suggesting new ways for artists to connect with the sources of energy in their own experience. Today, in 1984, there is a renewed sense of the power of culture to affect how people see the world around them. Activist art – sometimes called 'the movement for cultural democracy' – then provides 'a developing, shared consciousness whose impact we can't predict ... a kind of consensus in practice that is now at a stage of consciousness-raising and organizing'.[1] […] Much activist art is innovative and expansive and the mainstream could learn from it, just as activists learn from the mainstream.

The movement for cultural democracy is a critique of the homogeneity of the corporate, dominant culture, which serves very few of us while affecting all of us. We see this culture melting (or microwaving) down the multiracial, multicultural differences that are [the USA's] greatest strength and its greatest hope for understanding and communicating with the rest of the world before we destroy it. Thus, art reflecting lived experience in different constituencies will differ. This is both an advantage and a disadvantage as the Black, Latin, and Asian art communities know well.

Cultural democracy is a right just like economic and political democracy, the right to make and to be exposed to the greatest diversity of expression. It is based on a view of the arts as communicative exchange. A true cultural democracy would encourage artists to speak for themselves and for their communities, and it would give all of us access to audiences both like and unlike ourselves. We have learned from Amílcar Cabral that self-expression is a prerequisite for self-empowerment. This doesn't mean that everyone has to make art any more than creating a politically aware populace means everyone has to become a politician. It means simply that the power of art is curtailed unless it is understood in the broadest sense and accepted as a possibility by everyone.

Activist art is confined to no particular style and is probably best defined in terms of its functions, which also cover a broad span. It does not, for the most part, limit itself to the traditional art media: it usually abandons frames and pedestals. It is an art that reaches *out* as well as *in*. To varying degrees it takes place simultaneously in the mainstream and outside of accepted art contexts.

In practice, activist art might include teaching, publishing, broadcasting, filmmaking, or organising – in or out of the art community. It often incorporates many different media within a single, long-term project. Most activist artists are trying to be synthesisers as well as catalysts; trying to combine social action, social theory, and the fine arts tradition, in a spirit of multiplicity and integration, rather than one of narrowing choices.

Activist art is not only 'oppositional', although it is usually critical in some sense. As an art of contact, it is often hybrid, the product of different cultures communicating with each other. Activist artists do not expect, say, to change Ronald Reagan's values (if he has any), but to oppose his views of war and de-humanism by providing alternative images, metaphors, and information formed with humour, irony, outrage, and compassion, in order to make heard and seen those voices and faces hitherto invisible and powerless.[…]

Activist art is, above all, process-oriented. It has to take into consideration not only the formal mechanisms within art itself, but also how it will reach its context and audience and why. For example, Suzanne Lacy's feminist dinner/organising/performance/media events culminate in recognisable 'art pieces', but in fact the real work includes the yearlong organising and workshops that led up to it, as well as film and documentation that may follow. These considerations have led to a radically different approach to artmaking. Tactics, or strategies of communication and distribution, enter into the creative process, as do activities usually considered separate from it, such as community work, meetings, graphic design, postering. The most impressive contributions to current activist art are those that provide not only new images and new forms of communication (in the avant-garde tradition), but also delve down and move out into social life itself, through long-term activities. […]

Two frequent criticisms of activist art run as follows: 'Art can't change anything, so if you care about politics you should be a politician instead of an artist'. (This plays in tandem with another act called, 'It's not art, it's sociology'.) Next comes, 'Social-change art is rendered useless when co-opted by exhibitions and sales within the mainstream art world.'

Activist artists are not as naive as their critics. Few labour under the illusion that their art will change the world directly or immediately. Rudolf Baranik has pointed out that art may not be the best didactic tool available, but it can be a powerful partner to the didactic statement, speaking its own language (and, incidentally, sneaking subversively into interstices where didacticism and rhetoric can't pass). With the deepening and broadening of activist art practice in the United States during the past five years, this partnership is receiving more consideration from political groups as well as from the mainstream. It is also crucial to remember that grassroots activism begins at home. We tend to forget that organising within the art community is also 'effective'. Artists alone can't change the world. Neither can anyone else, alone. But we can choose to be part of the world that is changing. There is no reason why visual art should not be able to reflect the social concerns of our day as naturally as novels, plays, and music. [...]

If the first ingredient of art's power is its ability to communicate what is seen – from the light on an apple to the underlying causes of world hunger – the second is control over the social and intellectual contexts in which it is distributed and interpreted. The real power of culture is to join individual and communal visions, to provide 'examples' and 'object lessons' as well as the pleasures of sensuous recognition. Ironically, those artists who try to convey their meanings directly are often accused of being propagandists, and their accessibility is thus limited to those not afraid of taking a stand. The ability to produce visions is impotent unless it's connected to a means of communication and distribution. [...]

Much activist work is collaborative or participatory and its meaning is directly derived from its use-value to a particular community. The needs of a community provide artists with both outlets and boundaries. While straddling the fence between mainstream and outreach is a way of avoiding co-optation, it's not a comfortable position. Accessibility to 'a broader audience' is a conscious if not often realised component of activist art. It takes years to develop formally effective ways to exchange powers with one's chosen audience. As many have discovered, it is impossible just to drop into a 'community' and make good activist art. The task is specialised (though not in the same ways high art is) and it demands discipline and dedication (as high art does). To be out of touch, unanalytical, or uninformed is disastrous (maybe this too, in a different arena, goes for high art).

The intricately structural quality that characterises activist art results from the complexity of the position these artists find themselves in, fraught as it is with economic, aesthetic, and political contradictions. Community or political work can and often does restrict the artist's own need to go further out, or further in, to experiment past the bounds of immediate necessity. The burnout rate among fine artists working with groups is high because the rewards for such activities are seen as entirely separate from the development of the art and are less likely to be appreciated by peers within the art world.

On the other hand, I have yet to see an artist who ventured out of the art world to work in unfamiliar contexts come back empty-handed. Such experience enriches *any* art. Leaving the safety of one's home base – the context in which one was trained to act – one learns a great deal not only about the world, but about oneself, one's art and imagery, and their communicative effects. New symbols can emerge from these new experiences. An art that takes on activism as its driving force must emphasise clarity of meaning and communication. But this does not mean it has to be simplistic, which implies a condescending approach toward the audience. In addition, what may appear simple or stereotyped to one audience may be rich and meaningful to another that is more involved in specific issues. […]

The degree to which an activist art is integrated with the artist's beliefs is crucial to its effectiveness. Much well-meaning progressive and activist art does not truly reflect the artist's lived experience, and often the artist's lived experience bears little resemblance to that of most other people. Work with tenants organisations, feminist, radical, or solidarity groups, labour unions, or in the cultural task forces of the many small left parties, or with environmental, pacifist and anti-nuclear groups offers ways to connect with those who are interested. Another option is to see the changing self as a symbol of social change, using personal histories (not necessarily one's own) to illuminate world events and larger visions. In this process local, ethnic, gender and class identifications can augment individual obsessions. The extraordinary Senegalese film *Jom* shows the *griot* (storyteller, historian, shaman, artist) as the backbone of daily political consciousness in the community, the source of continuity through which power is maintained or lost.

I like to keep reminding myself that the root of the word radical is the word 'root'. Grassroots then means not only propagation – spreading the word – but is based on the fact that each blade of grass has its own roots. Power means to be able – the ability to act vigorously with 'strength, authority, might, control, spirit, divinity'. And the word 'craft' comes from Middle English and means strength *and* power, which later became 'skill'. Neither the word 'art' nor the word 'culture' bear these belligerent connotations. Art originally meant 'to join or fit together', and 'culture' comes from cultivation and growth. An artist can function like a lazy gardener who cuts off the weeds as a temporary holding action. Or s/he can go under the surface to the causes. Social change can happen when you tear things up by the roots, or – to collage metaphors – when you go back to the roots and distinguish the weeds from the blossoms and vegetables… the Trojan horses from the four horses of the apocalypse.

1 Arlene Goldbard and Don Adams, 'From the Ground Up: Cultural Democracy as a National Movement', in *Upfront*, no. 8 (Winter, 1983–84) 6.

Lucy Lippard, extracts from 'Trojan Horse: Activist Art and Power', in *Art After Modernism, Rethinking Representation*, ed. Brian Wallis (New York: New Museum of Contemporary Art, 1984), 341–347, 355–356, 357–358.

Chantal Mouffe
Artistic Activism and Agonistic Spaces//2007

[...] I do not see the relation between art and politics in terms of two separately constituted fields, art on one side and politics on the other, between which a relation would need to be established. There is an aesthetic dimension in the political and there is a political dimension in art. This is why I consider that it is not useful to make a distinction between political and non-political art. From the point of view of the theory of hegemony, artistic practices play a role in the constitution and maintenance of a given symbolic order or in its challenging and this is why they necessarily have a political dimension. The political, for its part, concerns the symbolic ordering of social relations, what Claude Lefort calls 'the *mise en scène*', 'the *mise en forme*' of human coexistence and this is where lies its aesthetic dimension.

The real issue concerns the possible forms of critical art, the different ways in which artistic practices can contribute to questioning the dominant hegemony. Once we accept that identities are never pre-given but that they are always the result of processes of identification, that they are discursively constructed, the question that arises is the type of identity that critical artistic practices should aim at fostering. Clearly those who advocate the creation of agonistic public spaces, where the objective is to unveil all that is repressed by the dominant consensus are going to envisage the relation between artistic practices and their public in a very different way than those whose objective is the creation of consensus, even if this consensus is seen as a critical one. According to the agonistic approach, critical art is art that foments dissensus, that makes visible what the dominant consensus tends to obscure and obliterate. It is constituted by a manifold of artistic practices aiming at giving a voice to all those who are silenced within the framework of the existing hegemony.

In my view this agonistic approach is particularly suited to grasp the nature of the new forms of artistic activism that have emerged recently and that, in a great variety of ways, aim at challenging the existing consensus. Those artistico-activist practices are of very different types, from a variety of new urban struggles like 'Reclaim the Streets' in Britain or the 'Tute Bianche' in Italy to the 'Stop advertising' campaigns in France and the 'Nike Ground-Rethinking Space' in Austria. We can find another example in the strategy of 'identity correction' of the Yes Men who appearing under different identities – for instance as representatives of the World Trade Organization – develop a very effective satire of neoliberal ideology. Their aim is to target institutions fostering neoliberalism at the expense of people's well-being and to assume their identities in order to offer correctives. For instance the following text appeared in 1999 in a parody of the WTO website:

> The World Trade Organization is a giant international bureaucracy whose goal is to help businesses by enforcing 'free trade': the freedom of transnationals to do business however they see fit. The WTO places this freedom above all other freedoms, including the freedom to eat, drink water, not eat certain things, treat the sick, protect the environment, grow your own crops, organize a trade union, maintain social services, govern, have a foreign policy. All those freedoms are under attack by huge corporations working under the veil of 'free trade', that mysterious right that we are told must trump all others.

Some people mistook this false website for the real one and the Yes Men even managed to appear as WTO representatives in several international conferences where one of their satirical interventions consisted for instance in proposing a telematic worker-surveillance device in the shape of a yard-long golden phallus.

I submit that to grasp the political character of those varieties of artistic activism we need to see them as counter-hegemonic interventions whose objective is to occupy the public space in order to disrupt the smooth image that corporate capitalism is trying to spread, bringing to the fore its repressive character. Acknowledging the political dimension of such interventions supposes relinquishing the idea that to be political requires making a total break with the existing state of affairs in order to create something absolutely new. Today artists cannot pretend any more to constitute an avant-garde offering a radical critique, but this is not a reason to proclaim that their political role has ended. They still can play an important role in the hegemonic struggle by subverting the dominant hegemony and by contributing to the construction of new subjectivities. In fact this has always been their role and it is only the modernist illusion of the privileged position of the artist that has made us believe otherwise. Once this illusion is abandoned, jointly with the revolutionary conception of politics accompanying it, we can see that critical artistic practices represent an important dimension of democratic politics. This does not mean, though, as some seem to believe, that they could alone realise the transformations needed for the establishment of a new hegemony. As [Ernesto Laclau and I] argued in *Hegemony and Socialist Strategy* a radical democratic politics calls for the articulation of different levels of struggles so as to create a chain of equivalence among them. For the 'war of position' to be successful, linkage with traditional forms of political intervention like parties and trade-unions cannot be avoided. It would be a serious mistake to believe that artistic activism could, on its own, bring about the end of neoliberal hegemony.

Chantal Mouffe, 'Artistic Activism and Agonistic Spaces', extract from *Art & Research: A Journal of Ideas, Contexts and Methods*, vol. 1, no. 2 (Summer 2007) 3–4. (Footnotes omitted).

Suzanne Lacy with Leslie Labowitz
Feminist Artists: Developing a Media Strategy for the Movement//1981

> Strong feminist art might or might not be obviously political. By virtue of its expression of a repressed cultural experience, it will always in fact be political, as long as women's experience is not widely acknowledged in our society. The purpose of feminist art (and contrary to the myth of functionless art, it does have a purpose) is to provide information about women's way of seeing, to invite an exchange with its audience on the issues within the work and put forth a vision of a feminist culture. Concerned with communication above all else, feminist art cannot rest on prior assumptions or conventions about the nature of art. Its shape will be as radical as its contents.
> – Suzanne Lacy, *Frontiers: A Journal of Woman Studies*

In the early seventies, women artists gathered together to share stories of their oppression as women and as artists. At first they talked of their loss of employment and grant and exhibition opportunities and their exclusion from the dialogue of art through publication of their work. Later it became evident that this erasure of women artists had effects far more profound than simple economic disparity. In hiding the accomplishments of women artists from the past and present, the patriarchy was essentially controlling a powerful tool in the building of culture. Now we look out on a world created almost solely by the imagination of men; if we close our eyes, we can begin to see the 'look' of a world created by women. To truly understand what it means for a society to exist without visual images by women is to begin to envision why that power has been robbed from us, and what role art making might play in social revolution. Any change in the structure of a society will be accompanied by a change in our visual, as well as verbal, culture.

In 1973 the artist Judy Chicago, with the designer Sheila de Bretteville and the art historian Arlene Raven, founded the Woman's Building in Los Angeles.

At the Feminist Studio Workshop, an educational program for women artists and writers, they began using performance art as a teaching strategy. Performance, a combination of theatre and visual art, allowed women to directly and immediately express their life stories to each other. As they shared their experiences through consciousness-raising groups, women artists looked for ways to put these feelings and analyses into their artwork. Two themes stood out: the importance of revealing women's experiences, ideas and activities through art; and the use of art forms to generate situations where people would interact in human ways.

Feminist artists became guides in rituals developed intuitively by women looking for new ceremonies to formalise relationships and culture. These artists were collaborative, inviting their audiences to participate with them in making art. They began to dream of making their images and performances visible to a large grassroots audience. Many designed performances and graphics that used public forums such as billboards, buses and trains, and the media. Maria Karras photographed women from different ethnic backgrounds in Los Angeles, and put posters of their pictures and their bilingual messages on buses throughout Los Angeles. Mother Art, a group of four performing mothers of small children, did installations and performances in laundromats. The Waitresses performed wildly funny skits in restaurants, relating the oppression of women in that occupation. The Feminist Art Workers combined educational and consciousness-raising techniques with performance art and toured the country performing for feminist conferences and meetings. Susan Mogul installed in a Hollywood drugstore a life-sized photo cutout of a waitress waiting to be discovered, videotaping 'hopefuls' from the feminist community at the small soda fountain. Feminist art became increasingly pragmatic, public, and action-oriented, developing its own theories and strategies.

Particularly when it came to protesting images of women in the media, or creating new and authentic images, artists found they had skills to offer their political sisters. Within popular culture we are constantly presented with images of women as victims. Along with feminist activists, women artists are exploring how these images affect our lives and how we can create alternatives. Trained to analyse the structure and manipulate the content of an image, artists can help to restructure our visual reality. Artists can demystify image making and help women understand how media manipulates. To learn how images are made, even to learn to make them oneself, can be a powerful affirmation.

In 1977 Leslie had just returned from Germany, where she worked with feminist groups. Suzanne had been teaching performance and organising at the Woman's Building. We began to work together immediately, creating large performances which took place throughout the city, involving hundreds of people. From the beginning, our work combined performance and conceptual art ideas with feminist theory, community organisation, media analysis and activist strategies. We formed Ariadne: A Social Art Network of women in the arts, politics, media, and women's community. Through Ariadne we developed a media strategy that was carefully planned, concrete, action-oriented, and easily available. For the past three years we have collaboratively produced large-scale public performance events in Los Angeles, San Francisco, and Las Vegas on the issues of rape and the violent images of women in record advertising, news, and pornography.

Ariadne's media interventions fall into two categories: the 'media performance' and the 'public informational campaign'. The first is a one-time event designed specifically for TV newscasts and aimed at controlling the content of the event as it is distributed through the media. These events cannot take the place of person-to-person contact through community organising or long-term media education, but they serve as a very exciting and useful way to 'tag' or identify an issue. Creating a successful media event is one part of an overall strategy to influence public opinion, and needs to be followed up with the in-depth and complex information people need to make informed choices.

The second type of project, the public informational campaign, consists of several different kinds of media coverage over an extended period of time around a specific issue. In addition to media, we use art performances, exhibitions, lectures, self-defence classes, and speak-outs to reach people on a direct level, reinforcing the radio interviews, talk shows, TV newscasts, and feature articles and announcements in newspapers and magazines. Such a campaign builds public interest; it educates and organises the community.

Our audience for both the media performances and the public campaigns is the grassroots community in which we work, and the broader public reached through mass media. When these artworks are successful, they become in effect public rituals. Since the beginnings of the women's liberation movement, feminist artists have been doing rituals, most of which have been private or enacted for a small community. Now that we are speaking out on important issues, public ritual offers a feminist art approach to larger audiences. Our intentions with these performances have been to interrupt the consistent flow of media images and messages that perpetrate the myth of woman as victim with positive and active images of women.[1] [...]

1   As a result of our success with media coverage, Leslie Labowitz and I developed this 'how to' guide for artists and activists. Although simplistic within the total context of our analysis and

practice, it represents the logistical and practical thinking that made this work effective in the public realm. The first draft, for *Heresies Magazine*, was authored by Labowitz. We redrafted it together and published it in *Fight Back* by Cleis Press (1981), in *Cultures in Contention* by Real Comet Press (1985), and elsewhere since that time.

Suzanne Lacy with Leslie Labowitz, extract from 'Feminist Artists: Developing a Media Strategy for the Movement' (1981) in *Leaving Art: Writings on Performance, Politics, and Publics, 1974-2007* (Durham and London: Duke University Press, 2010) 83–86.

Salman Rushdie, Stuart Hall and Darcus Howe
Exchange on Black Audio Film Collective's *Handsworth Songs*//1987

Salman Rushdie, Songs Doesn't Know the Score (1987)

[...] Down at the Metro cinema, in Soho, there's a new documentary starting a three-week run. *Handsworth Songs*, made by Black Audio Film collective. The 'buzz' about the picture is good. *New Socialist* likes it, *City Limits* likes it, people are calling it multi-layered, 'original', imaginative, its makers talk of speaking in metaphors, its director John Akomfrah is getting mentioned around town as a talent to watch.

Unfortunately, it's no good, and the trouble does seem to be one of language.

Let me put it this way. If you see 'Handsworth', what do you see? Most Britons would see fire, riots, looted shops, young Rastas and helmeted cops by night. A big story; front page. Maybe a *West Side Story*: Officer Krupke, armed to the teeth versus the kids with the social disease.

There's a line that *Handsworth Songs* wants us to learn. 'There are no stories in the riots'. It repeats, 'only the ghosts of other stories'. The trouble is, we aren't told the other stories. What we get is what we know from TV. Blacks as trouble; blacks as victims. Here is a Rasta dodging the boat; here are the old news-clips of the folks in the fifties getting off the boat, singing calypsos about 'darling London'.

Little did they know, eh? But we don't hear about their lives, or the lives of their British-born children. We don't hear Handsworth's songs.

Why not? The film's handout provides a clue. 'The film attempts to excavate hidden ruptures/agonies of "Race"'. It 'looks at the riots as a political field coloured by the trajectories of industrial decline and structural crisis.' Oh dear. The sad thing is that while the filmmakers are trying to excavate ruptures and work out how trajectories can colour fields, they let us hear so little of the much richer language of their subjects.

When Home Secretary Hurd visits Handsworth looking bemused, just after the riots, a black voice is heard to say: 'The higher monkey climb the more he will expose.' If only more of this sort of wit and freshness could have found its way into the film. But the makers are too busy 'repositioning the convergence of "Race" and "Criminality"', describing a living world in the dead language of race industry professionals. I don't know Handsworth very well, but I do know it's bursting with tales worth telling. Take a look at John Bishton and Derek Reardon's 1984 photo and text essay, *Home Front*. There are Vietnamese boat people in Handsworth where Father Peter Diem, a refugee himself, runs a pastoral centre to which they come for comfort.

There's an Asian businessman in Handsworth who made his pile by employing his fellow-Asians in sweatshops to make, of all things, the Harrington jackets beloved of the skinheads who were also, as it happened fond of bashing the odd Paki.

Here are two old British soldiers. One, namely Shri Dalip Singh, sits stiffly in his army tunic, sporting his Africa Star with pride; the other a certain Jagat Singh, is a broken old gent who has been arrested for drunkenness on these streets over 300 times. Some nights they catch him trying to direct the traffic.

It's a religious place, Handsworth. What was once a methodist chapel is now one of the many Sikh gurdwaras. Here is the Good News Asian Church, and there you see Rasta groundations, a mosque, Pentecostal halls, and Hindu, Jain and Buddhist places of worship. Many of Handsworth's songs are hymns of praise. But there's reggae, too, there are Toasters at blue dances, there are Punjabi *ghazals* and Two Tone bands.

These days, the kids in handsworth like to dance the Wobbler. And some of it denizens dream of distant 'liberations', nurturing, for example, the dark fantasy of Khalistan.

It's important, I believe, to tell such stories, to say, this is England: *Allahu Akbar* from the minaret of Birmingham mosque, the Ethiopian World Federation which helps Handsworth Rastas 'return' to the land of Ras Tafari. These are English scenes now, English songs.

You won't find them, or anything like them, in *Handsworth Songs*, though for some reason you will see plenty of footage about troubles in Tottenham and Brixton, which is just the sort of blurring you know the Harlem writers would have jumped on, no matter how right-on it looked.

It isn't easy for black voices to be heard, It isn't easy to get it said that the state attacks us, that the police are militarised. It isn't easy to fight back against media stereotypes. As a result, whenever somebody says what we all know, even if they say it clumsily and in jargon, there's a strong desire to cheer, just because they managed to get something said, they managed to get through.

I don't think that's much help myself. That kind of celebration makes us lazy.

Next time, let's start telling those ghost-stories. If we know why the caged bird sings, let's listen to her song.

Stuart Hall, Song of Handsworth Praise (1987)

Sir, I must take issue with the way Salman Rushdie attacked Black Audio Film Collective and its film *Handsworth Songs*, from his well-deserved but secure position in the literary firmament.

Of course, the film isn't perfect. Of course, a mere recital of the known contours of racism and oppression in the same, old, stale language does no one any good. Of course, black artists deserve something more from us than mere celebration for having managed to say anything at all.

What I don't understand is how anyone watching the film could have missed the struggle which it represents, precisely, to find a new language. The most obvious thing to me about the film is its break with the tired style of the riot-documentary.

For example, the way documentary footage has been retimed, tinted, overprinted so as to formalise and distance it; the narrative interruptions; the highly original and unpredictable sound-track; the 'giving voice' to new subjects; the inter-cutting with the 'ghosts of other stories.'

These new ways of telling bring *Handsworth Songs* into the line with *Passion of Remembrance* and, in a different way, *My Beautiful Laundrette*, in that distinctive wave of new work by third generation black artists, part of whose originality is precisely that they tell the black experience as an *English* experience.

For what reason, apart from making us look in new ways, does Salman Rushdie want these 'new languages'? He seems to assume that his songs are not only different but better, presumably because they don't deal with all that dreary stuff about riots and the police etc. He prefers colourful stories about experience, closer to 'the richer language of their subjects.'

I fully agree that there is no one 'black experience', and we need to confront its real diversity without forcing it into simplistic moulds. But subjects and experience don't appear out of thin air. The counterposing of 'experience' to 'politics' is a false and dangerous dichotomy.

Black Audio may have been guilty of mixing its metaphors when it spoke of 'a political field coloured by trajectories of industrial decline and structural crisis'. But it seems to be struggling harder for a language in which to represent Handsworth as I know it than Salman's lofty, disdainful, and too-complacent 'Oh dear'.

Darcus Howe, The Language of Black Culture (1987)

Sir, I want to take issue with Stuart Hall's attack on Salman Rushdie's critical piece on the Black Audio collective's film, *Handsworth Songs*.

I write neither from Rushdie's 'well-deserved but secure position in the literary firmament' nor from, dare I say it, Stuart Hall's equally well-deserved but secure position in the academic firmament.

I have been an activist in the black movement for over 20 years, organising and developing political, cultural and artistic thrusts which have emerged from within our black communities and continue to do so today.

For some time now my activist colleagues and I have been moaning in print about the absence of critical tradition in the field of black arts and culture. We recognise that such an absence is a point of greater weakness. Without it we are left with nothing but cheerleaders on the one hand and a string of abuses on the other.

Enter Salman Rushdie with a well written and thoughtful piece of criticism which serves the dual function of a critique of the film itself, while at the same time laying the foundations of a critical tradition. It is most welcome.

Hall's main objection is that Rushdie misses the fact of the struggle for a new language which the film represents. Rushdie does nothing of the sort. He simply says that the attempt to shape a new language does not work, and I agree with him. In the best critical tradition he goes to suggest what he thinks would work. And I am certain that the filmmakers will take that on board. If they don't we are in a sorry state indeed.

Finally, I could find not a trace of loftiness, disdain nor complacency in Rushdie's critique. His is a useful and timely intervention, a far cry from the patronising 'ten out of ten for struggling' approach.

Salman Rushdie, extract from 'Songs Doesn't Know the Score', (review) *The Guardian* (12 January, 1987); Stuart Hall, 'Song of Handsworth Praise', (letter) *The Guardian* (15 January, 1987) and Darcus Howe, 'The Language of Black Culture', (letter) *The Guardian* (19 January, 1987).

The implicit promise of breaking out of the museum and marketplace to take on new issues and find new audiences has gone largely unfulfilled.

Douglas Crimp with Adam Rolston, 'AIDS Activist Graphics: A Demonstration', 1990

Douglas Crimp with Adam Rolston
AIDS Activist Graphics: A Demonstration//1990

[...] That simple graphic emblem – SILENCE=DEATH printed in white Gill sanserif type underneath a pink triangle on a black ground – has come to signify AIDS activism to an entire community of people confronting the epidemic. This in itself tells us something about the styles and strategies of the movement's graphics. For SILENCE=DEATH does its work with a metaphorical subtlety that is unique, among political symbols and slogans, to AIDS activism. Our emblem's significance depends on foreknowledge of the use of the pink triangle as the marker of gay men in Nazi concentration camps, its appropriation by the gay movement to remember a suppressed history of our oppression, and, now, an inversion of its positioning (men in the death camps wore triangles that pointed down: SILENCE=DEATH's points up). SILENCE=DEATH declares that silence about the oppression and annihilation of gay people, *then and now*, must be broken as a matter of our survival. As historically problematic as an analogy of AIDS and the death camps is, it is also deeply resonant for gay men and lesbians, especially insofar as the analogy is already mediated by the gay movement's adoption of the pink triangle. But it is not merely what SILENCE=DEATH says, but also how it looks, that gives it its particular force. The power of this equation under a triangle is the compression of its connotation into a logo, a logo so striking that you ultimately *have* to ask, if you don't already know, 'What does that mean?' And it is the answer we are constantly called upon to give to others – small, everyday direct actions – that make SILENCE=DEATH signify beyond a community of lesbian and gay cognoscenti.

Although identified with ACT UP, SILENCE=DEATH precedes the formation of the activist group by several months. The emblem was created by six gay men calling themselves the Silence = Death Project, who printed the emblem on posters and had them 'sniped' at their own expense.[1] The members of the Silence = Death Project were present at the formation of ACT UP, and they lent the organisation their graphic design for placards used in its second demonstration – at New York City's main post office on 15 April, 1987. Soon thereafter SILENCE=DEATH T-shirts, buttons and stickers were produced, the sale of which was one of ACT UP's first means of fundraising.

Nearly a year after SILENCE=DEATH posters first appeared on the streets of lower Manhattan, the logo showed up there again, this time in a neon version as part of a window installation in the New Museum of Contemporary Art on lower Broadway. New Museum curator Bill Olander, a person with AIDS and member of ACT UP, had offered the organisation the window space for a work about AIDS. An ad hoc committee was formed by artists, designers, and others with various skills, and within a few short months *Let the Record Show*, a powerful installation work, was produced. Expanding SILENCE=DEATH's analogy of AIDS and Nazi crimes through a photomural of the Nuremberg trials, *Let the Record Show* indicted a number of individuals for their persecutory, violent, homophobic statements about AIDS – statements cast in concrete for the installation – and, in the case of then president Ronald Reagan, for his six-year-long failure to make any statement at all about the nation's number-one health emergency. The installation also included a light-emitting diode (LED) sign programmed with ten minutes of running text about the government's abysmal failure to confront the crisis.[2] *Let the Record Show* demonstrated not only the ACT UP committee's wide knowledge of faces and figures detailing government inaction and mendacity, but also its sophistication about artistic techniques for distilling and presenting the information. If an art world audience might have detected the working method of such artists as Hans Haacke and Jenny Holzer in ACT UP's installation, so much the better to get them to pay attention to it. And after taking in its messages, who would have worried that the work might be too aesthetically derivative, not original enough? The aesthetic values of the traditional art world are of little consequence to AIDS activists. What counts in activist art is its propaganda effect; stealing the procedures of other artists is part of the plan – if it works, we use it.

ACT UP's ad hoc New Museum art project committee regrouped after finishing *Let the Record Show* and resolved to continue as an autonomous collective – 'a band of individuals united in anger and dedicated to exploiting the power of art to end the AIDS crisis.' Calling themselves Gran Fury, after the Plymouth model used by the New York City police as undercover cars, they became, for a time, ACT UP's unofficial propaganda ministry and guerrilla graphic designers. Counterfeit money for ACT UP's first-anniversary demonstration, WALL STREET II; a series of broadsides for New York ACT UP's participation in ACT NOW's spring 1988 offensive, NINE DAYS OF PROTEST; placards to carry and T-shirts to wear to SEIZE CONTROL OF THE FDA; a militant *New York Crimes* to wrap around *The New York Times* for TARGET CITY HALL – these are some of the ways Gran Fury contributed to the distinctive style of ACT UP. Their brilliant use of word and image has also won Gran Fury a degree of acceptance in the art world, where they are now given funding for public artworks and invited to participate in museum exhibitions and to contribute 'artist's pages' to *Artforum*.[3]

But, like the government's response to the AIDS activist agenda, the art world's embrace of AIDS activist art was long delayed. Early in 1988 members of the three ACT UP groups Gran Fury, Little Elvis, and Wave Three protested at the Museum of Modern Art (MOMA) for its exclusion of AIDS activist graphics. The occasion was an exhibition organised by curator Deborah Wye called 'Committed to Print: Social and Political Themes in Recent American Printed Art'. Work in the show was divided into broad categories: gender, governments/ leaders, race/culture, nuclear power/ecology, war/revolution, economics/class struggle/the American dream. The singleness of 'gender' on this list, the failure to couple it with, say, 'sexuality', already reveals the bias. Although spanning the period from the 1960s to the present, 'Committed to Print' included no work about either gay liberation or the AIDS crisis. When asked by a critic at the *Village Voice* why there was nothing about AIDS, the curator blithely replied that she knew of no graphic work of artistic merit dealing with the epidemic. AIDS activists responded with a handout for museum visitors explaining the reasons for demonstrating:

- We are here to protest the blatant omission from 'Committed to Print' of any mention of the lesbian and gay rights movement and of the AIDS crisis.
- By ignoring the epidemic, MOMA, panders to the ignorance and indifference that prolong the suffering needlessly.
- By marginalising 20 years of lesbian and gay rights struggles, MOMA makes invisible the most numerous victims of today's epidemic.
- Cultural blindness is the accomplice of societal indifference. We challenge the cultural workers at MOMA and the viewer of 'Committed to Print' to take political activism off the museum walls and into the realm of everyday life.

The distance between downtown and uptown New York – and between its constituent art institutions – was rarely so sharply delineated as it was with MOMA's blindness to SILENCE=DEATH, for it was only a few months earlier that Bill Olander had decided to ask ACTUP to design *Let the Record Show*, after having seen the ubiquitous SILENCE=DEATH poster the previous year: 'To me', he wrote, 'it was among the most significant works of art that had yet been inspired and produced within the arms of the crisis.' For more traditional museum officials, however, a current crisis is perhaps less easy to recognise, since they 'see' only what has become distant enough to take on the aura of universality. The concluding lines of MOMA curator Wye's catalogue essay betray this prejudice: 'In the final analysis it is not the specific issues or events that stand out. What we come away with is a shared sense of the human condition: rather than feeling set apart, we feel connected.'[4] The inability of others to 'feel connected' to the tragedy of AIDS is, of course, the very reason we in the AIDS activist movement have had to fight – to fight even to be thought of as sharing in what those who ignore us nevertheless presume to universalise as 'the human condition'.

But there is perhaps a simpler explanation for MOMA's inability to see SILENCE=DEATH. The political graphics in 'Committed to Print' were, it is true, addressed to the pressing issues of their time, but they were made by 'bona fide' artists – Robert Rauschenberg and Frank Stella, Leon Golob and Nancy Spero, Hans Haacke and Barbara Kruger. A few collectives were included – Group Material and Collaborative Projects – and even a few ad hoc groups – Black Emergency Cultural Coalition and Artists and Writers Protest Against the War in Vietnam. But these were either well-established artists' organisations or groups that had been burnished by the passage of time, making the museum hospitable to them. The Silence = Death Project (whose AIDSGATE poster had been printed in the summer of 1987) and Gran Fury (who by the time of the MOMA show had completed their first poster, AIDS: 1 IN 61) were undoubtedly too rooted in movement politics for MOMA's curator to see their work within her constricted aesthetic perspective; they had, as yet, no artistic credentials that she knew of.

The distance between downtown and uptown is thus figured in more ways than one. For throughout the past decade postmodernist art has deliberately complicated the notion of 'the artist' so tenaciously clung to by MOMA's curator. Questions of identity, authorship, and audience – and the ways in which all three are constructed through representation – have been central to postmodernist art, theory, and criticism. The significance of so-called appropriation art, in which the artist forgoes the claim to original creation by appropriating already-existing images and objects, has been to show that the 'unique individual' is a kind of fiction, that our very selves are socially and historically determined through preexisting images, discourses, and events.

Young artists finding their place within the AIDS activist movement rather than the conventional art world have had reason to take these issues very seriously. Identity is understood by them to be, among other things, coercively imposed by perceived sexual orientation or HIV status; it is, at the same time, wilfully taken on, in defiant declaration of affinity with the 'others' of AIDS: queers, women, Blacks, Latinos, drug users, sex workers.[5] Moreover, authorship is collectively and discursively named: the Silence = Death Project, Gran Fury, Little Elvis, Testing the Limits (an AIDS activist video production group), DIVATV (Damned Interfering Video Activist Television, a coalition of ACT UP video-makers), and LAPIT (Lesbian Activists Producing Interesting Television, a lesbian task group within DIVA). Authorship also constantly shifts: collectives' memberships and individual members' contributions vary from project to project.

Techniques of postmodernist appropriation are employed by these groups with a sly nod to art world precursors. In a number of early posters, for example, Gran Fury adopted Barbara Kruger's seductive graphic style, which was subsequently, and perhaps less knowingly, taken up by other ACT UP graphic producers. In the meantime, Gran Fury turned to other sources. Their best-known appropriation is undoubtedly the public service announcement on San Francisco (and later New York) city buses produced for 'Art Against AIDS on the Road', under the auspices of the American Foundation for AIDS Research. Imitating the look of the United Colors of Benetton advertising campaign, Gran Fury photographed three stylish young interracial couples kissing and topped their images with the caption KISSING DOSEN'T KILL: GREED AND INDIFFERENCE DO. The punch of the message, its implicit reference to the risk of HIV transmission, and its difference from a Benetton ad derive from a simple fact: of the three kissing couples, only one pairs boy with girl. If their sophisticated postmodern style has gained art world attention and much-needed funding for Gran Fury, the collective has accepted it only hesitantly, often biting the hand that feeds. Their first poster commission from an art institution was discharged with a message about art world complacency: WITH 42,000 DEAD, ART IS NOT ENOUGH. Familiar with the fate of most critical art practices – that is, with the art world's capacity to co-opt and neutralise them – Gran Fury has remained wary of their own success. Such success can ensure visibility, but visibility *to whom?*

For AIDS activist artists, rethinking the identity and role of the artist also entails new considerations of audience. Postmodernist art advanced a political critique of art institutions – and art itself as an institution – for the ways they constructed social relations through specific modes of address, representations of history, and obfuscations of power. The limits of this aesthetic critique, however, have been apparent in its own institutionalisation: critical postmodernism has become a sanctioned, if still highly contested, art world product, the subject of standard exhibitions, catalogues, and reviews. The implicit promise of breaking out of the museum and marketplace to take on new issues and find new audiences has gone largely unfulfilled. AIDS activist art is one exception, and the difference is fairly easy to locate.

The constituency of much politically engaged art is the art world itself. Generally, artists ponder society from within the confines of their studios; there they apply their putatively unique visions to aesthetic analyses of social conditions. Mainstream artistic responses to the AIDS crisis often suffer from just such isolation, with the result that the art speaks only of the artist's private sense of rage, or loss, or helplessness. Such expressions are often genuine and moving, but their very hermeticism ensures that the audience that will find them so will be the traditional art audience.[6]

AIDS activist artists work from a very different base. The point of departure [...] is neither the studio nor the artist's private vision, but AIDS activism. Social conditions are viewed from the perspective of the movement working to change them. AIDS activist art is grounded in the accumulated knowledge and political analysis of the AIDS crisis produced collectively by the entire movement. The graphics not only reflect that knowledge, but actively contribute to its articulation as well. They codify concrete, specific issues of importance to the movement as a whole or to particular interest within it. They function as an organising tool, by conveying, in compressed form, information and political positions to others affected by the epidemic, to onlookers at demonstrations and to the dominant media. But their primary audience is the movement itself. AIDS activist graphics enunciate AIDS politics to and for all of us in the movement. They suggest slogans (SILENCE=DEATH becomes 'We'll never be silent again'), target opponents (*The New York Times*, President Reagan, Cardinal O'Connor), define positions ('All people with AIDS are innocent'), propose actions ('Boycott Burroughs Wellcome'). Graphic designs are often devised in ACT UP committees and presented to the floor at the group's regular Monday night meetings for discussion and approval. Contested positions are debated, and sometimes proposed graphic ideas are altered or vetoed by the membership. In the end, when the final product is wheat-pasted around the city, carried on protest placards, and worn on T-shirts, our politics, and our cohesion around those politics, become visible to us, and to those who will potentially join us. Sometimes our graphics signify *only* internally, as when an ACT UP affinity group went to TARGET CITY HALL wearing T-shirts silk-screened with a photograph of the actress Cher. The group adopted the movie star's name as a camp gesture, and each time someone asked what it meant, CHER became an acronym for whatever could be concocted on the spot: anything from 'Commie Homos Engaged in Revolution' to 'Cathy Has Extra Rollers'.

ACT UP's humour is no joke. It has given us the courage to maintain our exuberant sense of life while every day coping with disease and death, and it has defended us against the pessimism endemic to other Left movements, from which we have otherwise taken so much. The adoption of the name CHER for an affinity group makes this point. A tradition of Left organising, affinity groups are small associations of people within activist movements whose mutual trust and shared interests allow them to function autonomously and secretly, arrive at quick decisions by consensus, protect one another at demonstrations, and participate as units in coordinated acts of civil disobedience. ACT UP's affinity groups function in all of these ways, but our affinities, like our identities, are complexly constituted. Because being queer is an identity most of us share, one of our happiest affinities is camp. ACT UP graphics reflect that part of our politics too. [...]

1   [Footnote 2 in source] 'Sniping' is a means of ensuring that posters pasted on hoardings will remain there for a specific time period without being covered over by anyone else's posters. In New York City, 'snipers' are usually paid by promoters to put up rock concert advertisements and to replace them if they are torn down or pasted over.

2   [3] For a more complete description of *Let the Record Show*, see the introduction to Douglas Crimp (ed.), *AIDS: Cultural Analysis/Cultural Activism* (Cambridge: MIT Press, 1988) 7–12.

3   [4] Gran Fury, 'Control', Artforum, no. 28 (October 1989) 129–30. 167–68.

4   [7] Deborah Wye, *Committed to Print: Social and Political Themes in Recent American Printed Art* (New York: Museum of Modern Art, 1988) 10.

5   [8] 'I am a member of the gay community and a member of the AIDS community. Furthermore, I am a gay member of the AIDS community, a community that some would establish by force, for no other end but containment, toward no other end but repression, with no other end but our deaths – a community that must, instead, establish *itself* in the face of this containment and repression. We must proudly identify ourselves as a coalition.' (Gregg Bordowitz, writing about the Testing the Limits video collective, in 'Picture a Coalition', *AIDS: Cultural Analysis/Cultural Activism*, op. cit., 195.

6   [9] Individual artists' aesthetic responses to AIDS have not always been genuine or moving; sometimes they are exploitative and damaging. To take a notorious example, Nicholas Nixon's serial photographic portraits of people with AIDS (PWAs) reinforce mainstream media stereotypes of PWAs as isolated, despairing victims. When the photographs were shown at the Museum of Modern Art in the fall of 1988, ACT UP members protested, demanding NO MORE PICTURES WITHOUT CONTEXT. Part of the context excluded from Nixon's pictures, of course, is everything that kills people with AIDS besides a virus – everything that AIDS activists, PWAs among us, are fighting.

Douglas Crimp with Adam Rolston, extracts from 'AIDS Activist Graphics: A Demonstration', in *AIDS Demo Graphics*, (Seattle: Bay Press, 1990) 15–23. (Some footnotes omitted).

Gregory Sholette
Dark Matter: Activist Art and the Counter-Public Sphere//2003

[…] Cosmologists describe *dark matter*, and more recently *dark energy*, as large, invisible entities predicted by the Big Bang theory. So far, dark matter has been perceived only indirectly, by observing the motions of visible astronomical objects such as stars and galaxies. Despite its invisibility and unknown constitution, however, most of the universe, perhaps as much as 96% of it, consists of dark matter. This is a phenomenon sometimes called the 'missing mass problem' . Like its astronomical cousin, *creative dark matter* also makes up the bulk of the artistic activity produced in our post-industrial society. However, this type of dark matter is invisible primarily to those who lay claim to the management and interpretation of culture – the critics, art historians, collectors, dealers, curators and arts administrators. It includes informal practices such as home-crafts, makeshift memorials, internet art galleries, amateur photography and pornography, Sunday-painters, self-published newsletters and fanzines. […]

What can be said of dark matter in general is that, either by choice or circumstance, it displays a degree of autonomy from the critical and economic structures of the art world and moves instead within, or in between, the meshes of the consciousness industry. But this independence is not risk free. Increasingly inexpensive technologies of communication, replication, display and transmission that allow informal and activist artists to network with each other have also made the denizens of this shadowy world ever more conspicuous to the very institutions that once sought to exclude them. In short, dark matter is no longer as *dark* as it once was. Yet, the art world, and global capital, can do little more than immobilise specific, often superficial aspects of this shadow activity by converting it into a fixed consumable or brand. However, even this cultural taxidermy comes at a cost to the elite, contemporary art world because it forces into view the latter's arbitrary value structure. In terms of combat therefore, the double-edged hazards brought on by increasing and decreasing visibility are essential to comprehend. […]

Least available for appropriation by the culture industry is not the slack look of dark matter, but its semi-autonomous and do-it-yourself mode of production and exchange. Zines, for example, are frequently belligerent, self-published newsletters that, as cultural historian Stephen Duncombe argues, do not offer:

Just a message to be received, but a model of participatory cultural production and organization to be acted upon. The message you get from zines is that you should not just be getting messages, you should be producing them as well. This is not to say that the content of zines – whether anti-capitalist polemics or individual expression –is not important. But what is unique, and uniquely valuable, about the politics of zines and underground culture is their emphasis on the practice of doing it yourself.[1]

Duncombe draws an explicit connection between this reflexivity of the zinester and Walter Benjamin's concept of the author as a producer. Applying Benjamin's analysis to the case of zines, it is exactly their position within the conditions of production of culture that constitutes an essential component of their politics. In an increasingly professionalised culture world, zine producers are decidedly amateur. In producing cheap, multiple-copy objects, they operate against the fetishistic archiving and exhibiting of the high art world and the for-profit spirit of the commercial world. And by their practice of eroding the lines between producer and consumer they challenge the dichotomy between active creator and passive spectator that characterises our culture and society.

Indeed, with satiric titles such as *Temp Slave*, *Dishwasher*, *Welcome to the World of Insurance* and simply *Work*, zines produced by service workers offer an instance of what [Oskar] Negt and [Alexander] Kluge term the 'contradictory nature of the public horizon', at least in so far as they represent a sporadic moment of resistance, rather than a means of sustained opposition.[2]

The zine aesthetic and its tactics of recycling and satire bear a certain resemblance to far more self-consciously politicised art-related collectives including: Temporary Services, Las Agencias, WochenKlausur, Collectivo Cambalache, the Center for Land Use Interpretation, the Stockyard Institute, Ne Pas Plier, Take Back the Streets, Mejor Vida, RTMark, the Critical Art Ensemble, Ultra Red, the Surveillance Camera Players, the Center for Tactical Magic, Radical Software Group and the Institute for Applied Autonomy. All work within some aspect of public space, and many ascribe their approach as that of tactical media, an activist deployment of new media technology. Yet, the groups mentioned here are difficult to categorise within most definitions of art because their engagement extends well into the public sphere and involves issues of fair housing; the treatment of unemployed people, 'guest' workers and prisoners; as well as global politics; biotechnology; and even access to public space itself.[3] Groups such as Temporary Services, Las Agencias, WochenKlausur, Take Back the Street, Ne Pas Plier, the Surveillance Camera Players, the Stockyard Institute and Mejor Vida design participatory projects in which objects and services are made to be given away or used up in public settings or street actions. Other groups, including most notably RTMark use technology to encourage 'the intelligent sabotage of mass-produced items.' RTMark exists entirely online and its website invites workers, students and other disenfranchised individuals to collaborate with them by purchasing 'shares' of RTMark stock. Because the group is a legally registered corporation, it has successfully used limited liability rules to shield its members from personal lawsuits. The list of those who have sought to censor the group because of its 'intelligent sabotage' includes major record companies, toy manufacturers and even the World Trade Organization.[4] And, unlike the lone, disaffected rebel worker, RTMark's collective approach raises sabotage to the level of ideological critique, much in the manner proposed by Negt and Kluge.

This same typically humorous reappropriation and do-it-yourself, zine aesthetic is also evident in the work of Las Agencias, an informally structured collective of artists and activists now primarily based in Barcelona but who have collaborated on projects in Madrid, Tarifa, Boston and Milan. Similarly to RTMark, Las Agencias appropriates both the technology and appearance of the consciousness industry, but it also works directly in the streets and barrios to unsettle normative ideological structures and reveal the contradictions and false tranquillity of the bourgeois public sphere. Carefully planned group actions have supported local squatters and migratory 'guest' workers, while the group has also designed campaigns against gentrification and militarism. But perhaps the work most crucial to my argument is Las Agencias' creative subversion of the riot police during street demonstrations and the group's tactical assault upon *lifestyle* marketing by global corporations. Take for example the group's line of apparel designed for use in demonstrations and street actions. These colourful, 'ready to revolt' designs contain hidden pockets that allow the wearer to conceal materials for buffering the blows of police batons or to conceal cameras for documenting abuse by the constabulary. Expanding upon the group's intervention into the couture industry is a more recent project entitled *Yomango*: a word that is slang for shoplifting. Mockingly playing off the retailing strategy of the Mango clothing label that markets itself to young, European professionals, Las Agencias has developed its own 'lifestyle' campaign that integrates a range of 'anti-consumer' products and services with everyday acts of customer sabotage. Specially adapted clothing and shopping bags are available on the Las Agencias label designed for 'disappearing' products out of the retail outlets of global emporiums. Las Agencias also provides workshops on how to defeat security systems through orchestrated teamwork that, on one occasion, to mark the Argentinean riots of December, 2001, took the form of a choreographed dance. For Las Agencias, shoplifting is a type of civil disobedience in which reflexive kleptomania is directed against the homogenising and instrumentalising effect of global capital.

For a time, all of Las Agencias' tactics – including counter-couture, anti-war graphics, strategy lessons, street actions and communication systems – came together in the *Show Bus* (2001): a brightly painted, motor coach equipped with display and networking technologies and topped off by a rooftop platform for public speaking and live performances. With its windows refitted for rear-view projecting of live internet feeds, the *Show Bus* was a combination of mobile organising space and self-contained agitation apparatus. It also made a conspicuous target for reactionary forces. The *Show Bus* was demolished and set alight one night by unknown forces, thus forcing the group to reconsider the conspicuousness of this approach. Nevertheless, the *Show Bus* was a concrete manifestation of counter-public space in so far as it brought together numerous otherwise fragmented forms of resistance while remaining networked to street culture and yet relatively autonomous with regard to the high art world. And it is important to add a final note about the cunning of Las Agencias in relationship to the art industry. By 2002, the group had gained enough notoriety for a liberal-minded curator to solicit their participation in the Torino Art Biennial. The members met and agreed to bring their *Yomango* campaign into the 'white box' of the institutional art museum. But they elected to do so in the form of an 'installation' that replicated an actual retail franchise. Within this simulated storefront the audience would be invited to practice shoplifting as well as attend workshops on civil disobedience and activism. Furthermore, all of the shopliftable practice products were themselves to be procured from nearby retail chains prior to the exhibition's opening. The organisers of the biennial, upon hearing about Las Agencias' plans to essentially 'squat' their exhibition, acted to evict the group.

However, on other occasions, the group has managed to 'leverage' art world funds provided by a museum and use this money to carry out political actions in non-art-related public spaces. Nevertheless, this catty interplay between art activists and art institutions underscores the opportunities as well as potential risks of moving this type of dark matter into greater visibility within the public sphere. And, to the extent that Las Agencias focuses on the process and organisation of creative work itself, rather than the production of objects, its 'art' is difficult for the art world to appropriate. With group activity divided between theorising, creating posters, designing clothes, organising and carrying out actions and giving workshops, as well as networking with other activists and artists, it is simply not possible for the formal institutions of the art world to represent the full extent of Las Agencias' 'work'. No art objects exist that could summarise group identity and, unlike individuals artists such as Joseph Beuys, the group has so far avoided making fossils and souvenirs of their work for museums and collectors. In addition, because its audience participates in the making of the work and its meaning, it is difficult to imagine what aspect of the group's work would appeal to conventional art collectors. At least to date, the legitimisation of collective authorship has been avoided by the culture industry, most likely because it undermines artistic values as defined by collectors, who expect art works to be the product of one individual with one clearly articulated artistic vision. Finally, and most important to my argument, groups such as Las Agencias, Temporary Services and RTMark have adopted forms of creative expenditure and gift giving more typically found within the informal arts that are fundamentally hostile to the functioning of the formal art industry economy. It is my contention that such acts of expenditure without the expectation of a specific return on investment is aimed at building egalitarian social relations rather than optimising one's position within a market.[5] And it is this adaptation, rather than any formal resemblance to dark matter, that draws these oppositional practices into dark matter's gravitational field and away from the hegemony of the elite art world. [...]

1   [Footnote 35 in source] Stephen Duncombe, *Notes from Underground: Zines and the Politics of Alternative Culture* (London and New York: Verso, 1997) 129.

2   [37] Oskar Negt and Alexander Kluge, *Public Sphere and Experience: Toward an Analysis of the Bourgeois and Proletarian Public Sphere* (Minneapolis: University of Minnesota Press, 1993) 171.

3   [38] 'Tactical media are what happens when the cheap "do it yourself media" made possible by the revolution in consumer electronics and the expanded forms of distribution (cable, satellite and internet) are exploited by groups and individuals who feel aggrieved or excluded by the wider culture', Geert Lovink, David Garcia, 'The ABC of Tactical Media', (2002), (http://subsol.c3.hu/subsol_2/contributors2/garcia-lovinktext.html).

4   [40] The WTO even attempted to prosecute the group over a website the group created parodying the global juridical agency that not only sowed confusion, but spread detailed information about the WTO's neoliberal brand of global profiteering, (www.corpwatch.org/article.php?id=2671).

5   [44] Georges Bataille, 'The Notion of Expenditure', in *Visions of Excess: Selected Writings 1927–1939* (Minneapolis: University of Minnesota Press, 1985). See also Bruce Barber and Jeff Dayton-Johnson, 'Marking the Limit: Re-framing a Micro-economy for the Arts', *Parachute*, no. 106, April, May, June 2002, 27 and 39; and Ted Purves, *What We Want Is Free: Generosity and Exchange in Recent Art*, (Albany: State University of New York Press, 2014).

Gregory Sholette, extracts from 'Dark Matter: Activist Art and the Counter-Public Sphere', (2003) in *Delirium and Resistance: Activist Art and the Crisis of Capital* (London: Pluto Press, 2017), 184–202, 189, 190–191, 196–200. (Some footnotes omitted).

Oliver Ressler
From Reaching Heiligendamm: In Conversation with Marc James Léger//2008

[...] In 2007 Ressler was a participant in the international art project *Holy Damn It: 50,000 Posters against G8*. This affinity group assembled ten artists and artist groups who produced posters to be distributed for free among groups mobilising against the G8 summit in Heiligendamm, Germany (6–8 June, 2007), and at lead-up demonstrations in Rostock. Proceeds from the sale of a limited number of copies were reserved for legal aid to arrested demonstrators. Concurrently, a number of artists committed to the de-escalation of antagonism between protesters and police participated in a group exhibition titled *Art Goes Heiligendarnm, Art Goes Public*, a project organised by Adrienne Goehler for the city of Rostock (24 May–9 June, 2007). In the context of increased police intimidation and defamation campaigns against global-resistance movements in Germany, *Holy Damn It* refused to participate in this exhibition and publicly criticised its legitimisation of G8 politics. [...]

Oliver Ressler The initial idea for *Holy Damn It* came from Petra Gerschner and Michael Backmund. They proposed the production of a series of posters as an artistic intervention to be used in the course of the mobilisation against the G8. The first meeting took place in September 2006 in Graz, Austria, on the occasion of an exhibition at the Forum Stadtpark. Five of the ten artists and groups who would eventually produce one poster each participated in this meeting. From that point on we were all of us invested in making the project possible. We proposed other participants, raised some money, created the webpage, and tried to build a network of exhibition and presentation sites in order to distribute the posters as widely as possible with our limited budget.

When we started organising *Holy Damn It*, we did not know about *Art Goes Heiligendamm*. After making contact with our group, *Art Goes Heiligendamm* offered to present the ten posters. We later had a dispute due to dissatisfying e-mail conversations with its organisers. When we realised that they were not interested in discussing the problematic political aims of their project with us, we decided to make our contrasting political agendas public.

Marc James Léger Art Goes Heiligendamm's proposed 'third way', not to mention its stated motifs of 'intercultural communication' and 'cultural translation', seem like laudable goals. At the same time, these themes, which are academically respectable, seemed to almost naively return to a moralistic argument that the two sides do not represent good and evil, black and white, thus setting up a simple dichotomy to 'deconstruct' as one wishes. But the problem is not so simple, considering that the conditions in which the questions themselves can be posed are so heavily weighted by the discourse of neoliberal global capitalism. Tell me more about your collective response to the premises of *Art Goes Heiligendamm*.

Ressler The project description of *Art Goes Heiligendamm* and the interviews with the curator, Adrienne Goehler, make it obvious that they seek to functionalise art in order to mediate between the conflicting parties gathered around the G8 summit. The instrumentalisation of art is nothing particularly new, but what really disturbed me was the number of interesting, politicised artists who accepted the invitation to participate in such a project. While in Rostock and Heiligendamm, I spent my time at the blockades and demonstrations against the G8, which were a great example of collective intelligence. My experiences were so intense and rich during the week I was there that I did not want to spend my time visiting a show like *Art Goes Heiligendamm*.

While my knowledge about the exhibition mainly comes from the webpage, I assumed that there was no real need to see a show whose subtitle, 'Art Interventions on the Occasion of the G8 Summit 2007', already brings the failure of the curatorial concept to the point. How can you talk about an intervention when your show is located in an old shipyard building thirty or forty kilometers away from the G8 summit in Heiligendamm, and while at the same time more than ten thousand activists managed to delegitimise the official summit directly with three days of blockades in the banned 'red zone'?

Sometimes I think it is necessary to express precisely what side you are on. Concerning the struggle between the movement and the G8, with its neoliberal politics of exclusion, I think that the majority of cultural workers are on the side of the movement and don't have to look for 'third ways'. I think that in certain cases polarisation is necessary in order to make visible different political viewpoints and ideals. Those people who don't want to express 'yes' or 'no' – to the G8 in particular or the hegemonic system of power in general – de facto contribute to the continuation of the present conditions. […]

Léger Tell me about the poster distribution campaign itself. Were you in close contact with other affinity groups?

Ressler Individuals and groups could order the posters for free from our webpage. Petra Gerschner and Michael Backmund were in close contact with a variety of different organisations and affinity groups. They participated in several coordinating meetings for the mobilisation and political conferences against the G8 summit, and also used these opportunities to spread information about our project and to make the posters available to thousands of people. I think that *Holy Damn It* can really be seen as a kind of embedded art project, a part of the mobilisation, and not as a project that simply deals with the issues. The widespread awareness of our project within the movement also led to the use of our poster images in many of the left magazines and leaflets mobilising against the G8. They used the *Holy Damn It* posters as images to be printed along with texts. Many activists and groups ordered posters from our webpage and distributed them. Through these different strategies, we reached a circulation of more than one hundred thousand. In additionthere were numerous publications of our posters in left or liberal daily, weekly, and monthly magazines, for example, *Publik*, the largest union newspaper of the German union ver.di [Vereinte Dienstleistungsgewerkschaft, or United Services Union]. […]

Léger I would like to ask you more about the conjuncture of art and activism and how this relates to what we could hesitantly call contemporary avant-garde practice. To my mind, what makes *Holy Damn It* and your work avant-garde is its interventionist character. Many years ago, Krzysztof Wodiczko identified some 1960s and 1970s interventionist work as 'Situationist Cultural Avant-Garde' and 1980s artists like Barbara Kruger, Alfredo Jaar, and Dennis Adams as 'Critical Public Art'. Wodiczko further defined this type of work as

> critical-affirmative action on everyday life and its institutions ... critical collaboration with institutions of mass and public media, design, and education in order to raise consciousness ... to win time and space in information, advertising, billboards, lightboards, subways, public monuments and buildings, television cable and public channels, etc.[1]

In many ways the work that you do is similar to some of these artists, and we could also find some precursors among the historical avant-gardes, in particular the agitational work of the Russian Constructivists. But the situation has changed dramatically. In the 1980s it was possible to imagine reversing the effects of the first wave of neoliberalism, but now, after thirty years of policy changes, the situation within capitalist democratic countries has been exacerbated. Yet the discourse on public art sometimes seems to have become increasingly relativistic, with the emphasis placed on community art in a way that is compatible with corporate interests, or at least nonthreatening to them. In contrast, when you make interventionist work, you are categorically oppositional and you assume the responsibility of dealing with and presenting confrontational work and ideas. How do you see your work, or the kind of work that is represented by *Holy Damn It*, in relation to critical art practice in general?

Ressler Of course my artistic practice is influenced by the kind of political art you describe. There are several different artists I am interested in, at least with regard to certain aspects of their work. Often it happens that I appreciate the formal presentation of a project but don't agree with the way it addresses its message – or the other way around. I see my work as operating differently from certain types of work that are usually labelled 'political'. For instance, I think that the pathos of Alfredo's work is absolutely unbearable, in particular his aestheticised presentation of suffering in works related to the genocide in Rwanda. The form of Barbara Kruger's work interested me a great deal when I was still a student. I liked the way she combined short messages in huge fonts with images, but most of her projects since the late 1980s, at least the ones that I have seen, seem to repeat and alter the visual language she is already famous for. Besides that, her critical potential does not seem to go beyond a critique of mass culture. I think that Barbara Kruger is probably already too much involved in the commercial art market since she does not even reject doing an advertising campaign for a company like Selfridges Department Stores.

So 'critical public art' can even lead toward 'incorporated advertisement art'. Martha Rosler has made the distinction between a general criticism, around which the art world and the criticised institutions have learned to collude over the years, and a concrete criticism that is more difficult to absorb. The majority of political artists seem to prefer the concept of a general criticism; the artist gets bestowed the prestigious attribute of being an art-world rebel, while at the same time the way s/he expresses criticism does not hurt the art market, private collectors, and major museums. So the show can go on.

The early works of Hans Haacke have some importance for me. Haacke always tried to keep a distance from his subject, which is significant for the classical approach of criticism. In comparison, several of my projects are not carried out from the position of a neutral observer, but by someone who is personally involved in the struggles or clearly positions himself on one side. In my artistic practice in the last few years I have tried to avoid focusing too much on criticism and have focused more on alternative economic models and modes of organisation. Maybe this also fits in with what you call the 'categorically oppositional' in my work. At least it has to be clear that I don't work in order to be oppositional, but to highlight some of the important ideas and experiences that take place in our world. For example, I realised two films in collaboration with Dario Azzellini on the political changes in Venezuela. One of them, *5 Factories – Worker Control in Venezuela*, was also presented as part of the film program at the counter-summit in Rostock. The largest project I have been working on so far is the [thematic installation] project *Alternative Economics, Alternative Societies*. It now consists of sixteen video interviews with political analysts, economists, and historians, and deals with proposals for the organisation of alternative societies.

The poster I made for *Holy Damn It* could also be seen in this way – using art to address and support political struggles that represent alternative ways of organising that could one day lead to the existence of alternative societies on a larger level. The poster not only points to the possibility and capacity of the multitude to block a summit, to show the media and those in power that they are ready to fight against militarised neoliberalism; it also addresses positive things that are worth fighting for. The text proposes 'a democratization of society, social welfare, dismantling [of] capitalism and the creation of free space.' The poster uses direct language that can easily be read. For a piece of art, it is pretty antielitist since the content is not hidden somewhere behind aesthetically designed surfaces. The extremely successful blockades at the G8 summit in Heiligendamm will also be the starting point for a new video on the movement of the movements, which I am currently working on in collaboration with the Australian artist Zanny Begg. The video *What Would It Mean to Win?* will be released in 2008. […]

Léger How do you see yourself opposing neoliberalism in its cultural aspects? In other words, how do you take the modes and relations of production and consumption into account in a way that does not leave people comfortable with the idea of art on one side and politics on the other? Can politics become the general category that subsumes the specific artistic aspect of a work, and do you think this can be done from within the art world?

Ressler Even when they are presented in major shows, as we have seen in recent years, political artistic practices are still marginalised to some extent. If you visit the major art fairs, political art is almost invisible. This may not be the worst obstacle, but it can become a problem when it comes to funding the production of new work. Funding in Europe very often comes from the state or region, or from foundations, and is usually only available for a few artists. I think that funding is the aspect that most directly influences a political art project. To supply only certain artists with production funds functions as a form of invisible censorship within neoliberal capitalism.

Ignoring this problematic dependency for a moment, I really think that art has the potential to intervene in the political sphere. I am interested in dissolving this artificial barrier between art and politics, and I think that art can be used as a tool to intervene in political debates. It is clear that such a practice cannot be undertaken only within the usual sites for the presentation of art, but also has to consider other means such as performance, art in inner-city spaces, posters, video activism, and magazine editing. [...]

1   [3] Krzysztof Wodiczko, 'Strategies of Public Address: Which Media, Which Publics?' in *Discussions in Contemporary Culture*, no. 1, ed. Hal Foster (Seattle: Bay Press, 1987), 44–45.

Oliver Ressler and Marc James Léger, extracts from 'From Reaching Heiligendamm: An Interview with Oliver Ressler', in *Art Journal*, vol. 67, no. 1 (2008), 101–102, 103, 103–108, 111.

Brian Holmes
Eventwork: The Fourfold Matrix of Contemporary Social Movements//2012

Art into life: Is there any more persistent utopia in the history of vanguard expressions?

Shedding its external forms, its inherited techniques, its specialised materials, art becomes a living gesture, rippling out across the sensible surface of humanity. It creates an ethos, a mythos, an intensely vibrant presence; it migrates from the pencil, the chisel or the brush into ways of doing and modes of being. From the German Romantics to the Beatnik poets, from the Dadaists to the Living Theater, this story has been told again and again, each time with a startling twist on the same underlying phrase. At stake is more than the search for stylistic renewal; it's about transforming your everyday existence.

Theory into revolution: Is there any more ardent desire for the future of leftist thinking?

The fundamental demand of the thinkers and rioters of May 68 was also 'change life' (*changer la vie*). But from a revolutionary viewpoint, the consequences of intimate desire should be economic and structural. Situationist theory had no meaning without immediate communisation. 'Marx, Mao, Marcuse' was a slogan for the streets. The self-overcoming of art was understood as just one part of a programme to vanquish class divides, transform labour relations and put alienated individuals back in touch with one another.

The 60s were full of wild fantasies and unrealised potentials; yet significant experiments were undertaken, with consequences extending up to the present. Campus radicalism gave new life to educational alternatives, resulting in large-scale initiatives like the University Without Walls in the United States or the Open University in Britain. The counter-cultural use of hand-held video cameras led to radical media projects like Paper Tiger Television, Deep Dish TV and Indymedia. Politics itself went through a metamorphosis: autonomous Marxism gave rise to self-organised projects all across Europe, while affinity groups based on Quaker conceptions of direct democracy took deep root in the US, structuring the anti-nuclear movement, becoming professionalised in the NGOs of the 80s, then surging back at full anarchist force in Seattle. Since the AIDS movements, activism regained urgency and seriousness, grappling with concrete and progressively more complex issues such as globalisation and climate change. Yet, society still tends to absorb the transformations, to neutralise the inventions. [...] The question is how to change the forms in which we are living. [...]

Absorbing all this historical experience, social movements have expanded to include at least four dimensions. Critical research is fundamental to today's movements, which are always at grips with complex legal, scientific, and economic problems. Participatory art is vital to any group taking its issues to the streets, because it stresses a commitment to both representation and lived experience. Networked communications and strategies of mass-media penetration are another characteristic of contemporary movements, because ideas and directly embodied struggles just disappear without a megaphone. Finally, social movement politics consists in the collaborative coordination or 'self-organisation' of this whole set of practices, gathering forces, orchestrating efforts and helping to unleash events and to deal with their consequences. These different strands interweave, condense into gestures and events, and disperse again, creating the dynamics of the movement. A fourfold matrix replaces any single, easily definable initiative.

No doubt the complexity of this fourfold process explains the rarity of effective interventionism. But that's the challenge of political engagement. What has to be grasped, if we want to renew our democratic culture, is the convergence of art, theory, media and politics into a mobile force that oversteps the limits of any professional sphere or disciplinary field, while still drawing on their knowledge and technical capacities. This essay tries to develop a concept for the fourfold matrix of contemporary social movements. The name I propose for it is *eventwork*. [...]

As living conditions deteriorate in the capitalist democracies, one pressing question is how artists, intellectuals, media makers, and political organisers can come together to help change the course of collective existence. The answer lies in a move across institutional boundaries and modernist norms. Each of the separated disciplines needs to define the paradox of eventwork – and thereby open up a place for itself, beyond itself, in the fourfold matrix of contemporary social movements.

Let's go straight to the most impressive example of eventwork in the late 60s, which unfolds not in New York or London or Paris, but in Argentina. This was the moment of the country's industrial take-off, when an expanding middle class enjoyed close links to cultural developments in the metropolitan centres. In capitalist societies, utopian longings often accompany periods of economic growth, because the abundance of material and symbolic production promises real use values. But since mid-1966 Argentina was under the grip of a military dictatorship, which repressed individual freedoms and imposed brutal programs of economic rationalisation. Under these conditions, a circle of self-consciously 'vanguard' artists in Buenos Aires and Rosario began to sense the futility of the rapid cycles of formal innovation that had marked the decade of pop, op, happenings, minimalism, performance and conceptualism. They became keenly aware that inventions designed to shatter bourgeois norms were being used as signs of prestige and intellectual superiority by the elites, to the point where, as León Ferrari wrote, 'the culture created by the artist becomes his enemy.'[1] Therefore these artists began an increasingly violent break with the gallery and museum circuits that had formerly sustained their practices, using transgressive works, actions and declarations to curtail their own participation in officially sanctioned shows.

By mid-summer of 1968 they decided to organise an independent congress, the 'First National Meeting on Avant-Garde Art'. The goal was to define their autonomy from the elite cultural system, to formulate their social ideal – a Guevarist revolution – and to plan the realisation of a work that would embody their aims. In this work, the aesthetic material, as Ferrari explained, would no longer be articulated according to formal innovations, but instead with clearly referential and immediately graspable 'meanings' (*significados*) which themselves would be subjected to transgressive profanation, in order to generate a powerful denunciation of existing social conditions. Echoing Ferrari's approach in the language of semiotics and information theory, another contributor to the meeting, Nicolás Rosa, insisted that 'the work is experimental when it proceeds to the *rupture of the cultural model*.' This rupture was to be frank, direct and irreversible, enacted in a visual, verbal and gestural language that would allow anyone to participate. It would also be disseminated in the mass media. Situated outside the elite institutions and linked to the social context of its realisation, the work would 'produce an effect similar to that of political action', in the words of the artist Juan Pablo Renzi, who had drafted the framing text for the meeting. And because 'ideological statements are easily absorbed', Renzi continued, the revolutionary work 'transforms the ideology into a real event from within its own structure.' Such was the theoretical program that led to *Tucumán Arde*, or 'Tucumán is Burning'.

What was meant by the title? The group sought to denounce the process of restructuring that had been imposed on the sugar industry in the province of Tucumán, resulting in widespread unemployment and hunger for the workers. Beyond Tucumán itself, they wanted to reveal the larger program of economic rationalisation being carried by the national bourgeoisie under dictatorial command, in line with US and European interests. To do so would require the production of 'counter-information' on the strictly semiotic level, using factual analysis to oppose the government propaganda campaign that surrounded the restructuring. So the artists collaborated with students, professors, filmmakers, photographers, journalists and a left-wing union, engaging in a covert fact-finding mission which they disguised as a traditional cultural project. In the course of two trips they visited fields and factories, circulated questionnaires, interviewed, filmed, and photographed workers and their families, putting their preliminary analysis to the test of experience. This on-site research was the first phase of the project, culminating in a press conference where they ripped the veil from their activities and explained the real purpose of their work, hoping – in vain, as it turned out – to raise a scandal and push their messages out into the mass media.

An effective denunciation would also require the production of what the artists called an 'over-informational circuit' (*circuito sobreinformacional*) which would operate on the perceptual level, in order to overcome the persuasive power of the official propaganda both quantitatively and qualitatively. For the second phase they formulated a multilayered exhibition strategy, beginning with teaser campaigns that introduced potential publics to the words 'Tucumán' and 'Tucumán Arde' through posters, playbills, cinema screens and graffiti interventions. They then created two multimedia exhibitions in union halls in Rosario and Buenos Aires, attempting in both cases to use not a single room but the entire building. They deployed press clippings and images from the government propaganda campaign and contrasted these to economic and public-health statistics as well as diagrams indicating the links between industrial interests, local and national officials, and foreign capital. They displayed documentary photographs, projected films, delivered speeches and circulated a critical study prepared by the collaborating sociologists. At roughly half-hour intervals the lights were cut, dramatising the kinds of infrastructural failures that were typically endured by people in the provinces. Bitter coffee was served to give the public a taste of the hunger affecting a cane-growing region where food and sugar itself, was in chronically short supply.

The exhibition strategy was a success. The opening in Rosario on 3 November attracted over a thousand people on the first night, resulting in a prolongation of the show for two weeks instead of one. It was restaged in Buenos Aires on 25 November, this time including the covertly produced 'Third Cinema' film, *La Hora de los Hornos* (*The Hour of the Furnaces*, 1968), by Octavio Getino and Fernando Solanas, whose projection was halted every half hour for immediate discussion. The level of courage implied by this process, under conditions of military rule, is difficult to imagine. The show in Buenos Aires was censored on its second day by threats against the union, exposing the repressive character of the regime and inviting a further radicalisation of the country's cultural producers.

Because of its collective organisation, its experimental nature, its investigatory process, its tight articulation of analytic and aesthetic means, its oppositional stance and its untimely closure, *Tucumán Arde* has become something of a myth in Argentina and abroad. The American critic Lucy Lippard, who would later be active in the Art Workers Coalition, repeatedly claimed that she had been radicalised by her meeting with members of the group on a visit to Argentina in October 1968. The French journal *Robho* devoted a dossier to the work in 1971, emphasising its break with bourgeois art and its revolutionary potentials. In its more recent reception, which has included a large number of shows and articles from the late 1990s on, the project has been linked to 'global conceptualism', and to an interventionist form of media art based on semiotic analysis. This attention from the museum world testifies to an intense public interest in a process that emphasised common speech, direct action and a break with bourgeois cultural forms. But that same attention opens up the questions of absorption, banalisation and neutralisation. In the most thoroughly documented analysis, the Argentine art historian Ana Longoni vindicates the aims of the project by asking the obvious disciplinary question: 'Where's the vanguard art in *Tucumán Arde*?' She responds: 'If *Tucumán Arde* can be confused with a political act, it is because it *was* a political act. The artists had realised a work that extended the limits of art to zones that did not correspond, that were external.'[2]

So what was achieved by the move to these zones external to art? At a time when institutional channels were blocked and the modernising process had become a dictatorial nightmare, the project was able to orchestrate the efforts of a broad division of cultural labour, capable of analysing complex social phenomena. It then disseminated the results of this labour through the expressive practices of an event, in order to produce awareness and contribute to active resistance. What resulted was a change in the finality, or indeed the use-value, of cultural production. As one statement indicates, the project was conceived 'to help make possible the creation of an *alternative culture* that can form part of the revolutionary process.'[3] Or as the *Robho* dossier put it, 'The extra imagination found in *Tucumán Arde*, if compared for example to the usual agitation campaign, comes expressly from a practice of, and a preliminary reflection on, the notions of event, participation and proliferation of the aesthetic experience.'[4] That's a perfect definition of eventwork.

Its effectiveness comes from a perceptual, analytic and expressive collaboration, which lends an affective charge to the interpretation of a real-world situation. Such work is capable of touching people, of involving them, not through a retreat to the exalted dreamland of a white cube, but instead within the everyday complexity of life in a technocratic society, where the most elusive possibility is that of shared resistance to the vast, encroaching programs of government and industry. My question is how to extend that resistance into the present, how to make it last past each singular event. […]

1   [Footnote 4 in source] León Ferrari, 'The Art of Meanings' (1968) in Inés Katzenstein, ed., *Listen Here Now! Argentine Art of the 1960s: Writings of the Avant-Garde* (New York: MoMA, 2004) 312.

2   [9] Ana Longoni and Mariano Mestman, *Del Di Tella a Tucumán Arde*, (Buenos Aires: Eudeba, 2010) 216.

3   [10] 'Frente a los acontecimientos políticos….', unsigned document in the archive of Graciela Carnevale (2 pages), apparently a sketch for a broadside to be distributed at the Rosario exhibition.

4   [11] 'Dossier Argentine: Les fils de Marx et de Mondrian', *Robho*, no. 5-6, (1971) 16.

Brian Holmes, 'Eventwork: The Fourfold Matrix of Contemporary Social Movements', in Nato Thompson (ed.), *Living As Form. Socially Engaged Art from 1911–2011*, (New York: Creative Time Books, 2012) 73–78. (Some footnotes omitted).

Sanja Iveković
Women's House: In Conversation with Katarzyna Pabijanek//2009

Katarzyna Pabijanek [...] My first question concerns the *Women's House (Sunglasses)* project you started in 1998. It has just been shown at the Muzeum Sztuki in Łódź (*Practice Makes the Master*, curated by Magdalena Ziółkowska). Could you say something about the background of the project and, especially, about its current Polish version?

Sanja Iveković The series produced for the show is a collaboration with the Federation for Women and Family Planning, titled *Women's House (Sunglasses)* and is indeed a part of a bigger project. *Women's House* deals with violence against women, an issue that was still a hidden issue in Croatia when I started to work on this topic. I myself learned about it at the Centre for Women's Studies (founded in 1995) where I was teaching contemporary women's art. Some of the courses at the Centre were taught by women-activists who established the Autonomous Women's House – the first shelter for women victims of domestic violence in Eastern Europe. The House started in Zagreb in 1989 when a group of women squatted in an empty apartment and turned it into the shelter. I visited the shelter and it turned out to be an eye-opening experience for me. I decided to do an art project that would make this issue visible to the general public. I also wanted to develop a new type of work, one in which women who experienced violence were not just my artwork's subjects but rather its active participants. It took me some time to find a method that would be easy, fast and cheap so that that the piece could be produced by the women in the shelter themselves. In the end I opted for a process that included a workshop in which we produced plaster casts of the women's faces, along with short life stories the wrote themselves. Then the 'masks' and texts were installed in accordance with specific exhibition spaces, either indoors or outdoors.

Pabijanek And how did you decide to turn your project into an international cycle of events, one that triggered a wide-ranging interrogation of women's rights?

Iveković I consider *Women's House* a work in progress, a long-term project. It was first exhibited at Manifesta 2 – The European Biennial of Contemporary Art in Luxembourg in 1998 – and since then I have collaborated on the project with the Autonomous House in Zagreb, the Fraenhaus in Luxembourg, the Bangkok

Emergency Home in Bangkok, Safe House in Peje, Kosova, Casa per le donne in Genova, the Center for Women and Children in Belgrade, VieJa in Utrecht, Mor Çatı in Istanbul, and Federation for Women and Family Planning in Polish cities. The project started in Croatia and the war in former Yugoslavia clearly comprised the background of my interest in these stories. The sex industry in Bangkok is the background for the stories of the women there, but there is also the perhaps unexpected level of domestic violence in the wealthy liberal democracy of Luxembourg. You may say that the project bears witness to the continued and unceasing level of violence against women in our societies, West and East, North and South. Each case may have its own 'local' character, but the 'universal' is the violence. Violence against women is regrettably a 'universal' – not in the sense of a 'transcendent' characteristic – since the reasons for this violence vary hugely – but in terms of a common 'universal' condition that women inevitably experience in patriarchal societies. We know that violence against women is not confined to any class, race or creed. In this work I wanted to redraw the 'universal' in such a way that, even though we are witnessing particular cases we are forced to reflect on the values in our own culture and society rather than merely distancing ourselves from this problem as something that happens to 'others' or in 'other cultures'.

Pabijanek How did you move from using the casts of real women's faces to using anonymous images appropriated from advertisements? How important is it for you to use the appropriated image instead of images of women who actually were victims of domestic violence? How is this related to the attempt to take these women out of the private space and make their experience public?

Iveković I am very conscious of the context in which I am exhibiting. In the context of the museum or a gallery space, I find the installation to be the most appropriate form. The plaster 'masks', placed on pedestals and accompanied by the texts of the women's stories, consciously mimic the installations one still finds in ethnographical or historical museums, where artefacts from different cultures are displayed. My motivation is to re-introduce real women from our society, who are often treated in a way as the 'Other', into public discourse. By situating this installation in a museum, I also question the role of the museum as an institution more generally, and the ways in which it functions. Though art galleries and museums are also public places, I find the mass media to be the most suitable vehicle by way of which to involve the general public. The media's role in shaping dominant cultural representations should never be underestimated. That's why it is important for me to use other media, such as posters, advertisements and billboards. I appropriate media images because my intention is to subvert the assumptions implied in the discourse of the mass media using its own language. This is not a new strategy, of course. It has been used by activists and artists for a long time. In the 90's, when I became intensely involved in the activities of women's NGOs in Croatia, I helped create a number of campaigns which were conceived by a coalition of women's groups that involved producing posters, leaflets, and TV commercials. My experience as a graphic designer definitely did help me here.

Pabijanek Producing material that is distributed outside the gallery space makes the works more democratic and accessible. What kind of feedback have you received on these pieces?

Iveković Well, it is difficult to say. It is not a performance, there is no round of applause at the end to let you know whether it's working or not, and if so how well. In the case of *Sunglasses* it is not so easy to measure the feedback. Some people like it, others will criticise it. Being an artist who tries to also be an activist, I am eager to disseminate the message that there is violence against women, that there are legal problems related to this, and that something must be done about this. On the other hand, as an artist, I cannot allow myself to be conditioned by the feedback. I strongly believe in what I am doing, otherwise I wouldn't do it. I have found that aesthetics are inseparable from politics. I must say that on a few occasions I had to disagree with the activists who commissioned a work from me. They thought that my proposals would not 'work', because my visuals were too 'ambiguous' or they didn't contain enough straightforward information, while I considered some of the material they produced not visually interesting at all. The position of an artist differs from that of an activist, but rather than separating the two activities, we can see them as circles of human activity that overlap in a relatively small area, and that is the area in which I try to do most of my work. [...]

Pabijanek The rationale behind the project as a whole and behind the previous versions (in Croatia, Italy, Thailand and Turkey) was to tackle the issue of violence against women. However, in Poland, you decided to talk about abortion. Why this change? You know that the problem of domestic violence exists here as well. Does your decision to replace domestic violence with abortion imply that you perceive the lack of access to safe and legal abortion as a kind of violence?

Iveković I come from an ex-communist country and at the time when Croatia won its independence and democracy was established, the first government was a right-wing conservative government, and one of its first tasks was to illegalise abortion. I remember myself being part of the coalition of women's groups who started a fierce and hard fought campaign against its initiative in 1995. We were working days and nights trying to collect the signatures on our petition. Under communism, legal abortion was a basic right and we had never considered the possibility of losing it. Having personally experienced this terrible moment when the threat of losing this right was real, and being aware of the situation in Poland, I felt compelled to deal with abortion for the work that was being produced there. This is the way I normally operate; in every country where I am invited to work, I try to take the local socio-political context and use it as material for my work. But to return to the question if a lack of access to abortion is violence: yes, I do think it is, there's no doubt about it. The illegalisation of abortion is a violation of the basic human rights enshrined in the CEDAW and other UN documents. The right to a free choice is a basic right of all women. [...]

Pabijanek Why do you involve social organisations in your projects? What kind of influence does this have on your work and its dissemination?

Iveković I collaborate with activist organisations because I think that they offer efficient models of production that can expand the rather confining borders of the art world. It's not only a matter of empowerment, but also of the wish to encourage a fertile dialogue between activities that, lamentably, generally remain quite far removed from one another – art and activism. I try to be critical towards my own role, so I refrain from giving my view on issues I don't know much about, preferring instead to leave their presentation to those who are immersed in them. But I am also ready to fight for a visual language of my own, the one I consider best suited to give shape to the project, in order to establish communication with the public and create greater visibility for a given project. I started my artistic career in 1971 and my art naturally changed over time. In the 70s, when I was living in the former Yugoslavia, I produced various works dealing with the power structures typical of the kind of socialist society I was living in. By 1989 everything had changed and I felt that new modes of operation should be introduced into my art practice. It was challenging for me to think about art that could be still critical but also participatory. Instead of being limited by traditional ways of merely illustrating the political context, I was searching for the method that would have the strongest possible impact on real life. [...]

Sanja Iveković and Katarzyna Pabijanek, extracts from '"Women's House": Sanja Iveković Discusses Recent Projects (Interview)' in *Art Margins*, (20 December, 2009) (https://artmargins.com/qwomens-houseq-sanja-ivekovic-discusses-recent-projects-interview/)

Carrie Lambert-Beatty
Twelve Miles: Boundaries of the New Art/Activism//2008

[...] In 1999, a Dutch physician named Rebecca Gomperts formed a non-governmental organisation called Women on Waves. Its first action was to turn a shipping container into a fully functional, mobile gynaecological clinic. Then, in 2001, Gomperts and her group began strapping the unit to rented ships and sailing to countries that criminalise abortion. Their plan: to dock, take aboard local women, and sail them twelve miles out to sea. Twelve miles is, in most cases, the limit of a nation's territorial waters. Beyond that line, Gomperts had realised, the ship's doctors could offer all the advice and treatment available in a liberal nation like the Netherlands, including abortion. For it is Dutch law that governs a ship registered in the Netherlands afloat in international waters. So far, boats bearing the clinic have embarked for Ireland (2001), Poland (2003), and Portugal (2004), bringing the Netherlands to the shores – or at least to twelve miles from the shores – countries where abortion, information on abortion, and even contraception are difficult to access.[1]

For Gomperts and Women on Waves, abortion is a human rights issue, and their project is powered by its urgency. United Nations studies make it clear that criminalising abortion does not eliminate or even radically reduce its rates; what it does accomplish is an increase in unsafe abortion. [...]

Women on Waves responds to such calls with a fully functional medical clinic, two physicians and a nurse, an almost entirely female crew, and networks of local volunteers, all backed by years of planning and research. In port it offers legal and medical workshops, sex education, and contraception; on the way out to sea it gives sonograms and counselling; and in international waters it provides the abortion pill to women who want it. Its missions have been controversial enough to earn its doctors and volunteers not only bombardment with eggs and paint but also court cases and even death threats; it was radical enough in its challenge to national sovereignty to move the Portuguese government to launch warships to protect its populace from the feminist invasion. As a result, Women on Waves has spurred debate on abortion law where such debates had not occurred for years. Its visits galvanised the local groups of activists that invited the abortion boat to each country, and more such pro-choice groups were formed in its wake.[2] A Polish government survey in 2003 found that popular support for liberalising abortion law had gone up 12% in a year and cited the Women on Waves visit that summer as a source of the change. Meanwhile, the media has swarmed to a project that is as photogenic as it is controversial, allowing Women on Waves to raise awareness and spark debate worldwide.

This project demands serious study as an innovative and deeply controversial instance of feminist activism. And yet the focus on feminist art practices […] offers an opportunity to mark something about Women on Waves that very few reports on the project have noted: that it is also a remarkable case of the intersection of activism and art.

[…] Women on Waves is moored to the artistic in a surprising number of ways. Start with the act of radical imagination at the core of the project: the idea that the dominion of one nation-state over the bodies of its women could be evaded by a short trip on a boat registered in another. Outrageous in its simplicity as well as its implications (what's next, one wonders: cannabis cruises? euthanasia yachts?), using international waters as a refuge for women's rights, in particular, unfurls into a poetic series of associations. It literalises the metaphor of waves that we use to describe generations of feminism and links it to old images that associate dangerous female power and the sea – from sirens and mermaids to the female pirates Anne Bonny and Mary Read. Meanwhile it takes on the traditional associations of women and ships, invariably referred to as 'she'. In the eighteenth century, shipwrecks were even called miscarriages.

But you need not take such interpretive journeys to discover what Women on Waves calls 'the art part of activism'. You need only know that the shipping container/clinic was designed by the well-known Dutch artist Joep van Lieshout, who dubbed it the *A-Portable*, and that his design was made public in a show at the Witte de With Center for Contemporary Art in Rotterdam. It might help to realise that while in port Women on Waves held workshops on its ships not only for lawyers and doctors but also for artists and writers, or that it has been featured in exhibitions like Ute Meta Bauer's Women Building in Portugal and in a dedicated show at the Mediamatic art space in Amsterdam. It has also appeared in *Artforum* and was counted by art critic Claire Bishop among examples of new political art. If you were in Venice in the summer of 2001 and noticed a strange blue box afloat on a raft at the Arsenale, you also know that the portable abortion clinic was represented in that year's Venice Biennale.

From the alternative and local to the established and eminent, then, art institutions have been remarkably willing to accept and support this particular activist project. And this activist project has been remarkably interested in using art to enable and extend its mission. In 2003 Gomperts and the Dutch artist and critic Willem Velthoven began exhibiting a series of installations that, in part, documented the abortion boat trips. In a video projection called *Sea*, for instance, the voices of women who called the boat's hotline in 2001 play over images of the open ocean. But the installations went beyond documentation, using the language and spaces of contemporary art to promote the project's vision of a normalised and safe abortion policy for all women. For instance, a display of specially designed minidresses on hangers, each bearing on one side a red circle and on the other the text 'I had an abortion' in one of the languages spoken in Europe, links the dangers of unsafe abortion to the need to destigmatise the procedure. This display nods to Man Ray, who made and photographed a modernist mobile of coat hangers in 1920–21; to pro-choice agitprop in which the hanger symbolises illegal, back-alley abortions; and to the history of open letters like the famous 1971 French 'Manifesto of the 343' (*Nouvel Observateur,* 1971), in which prominent women fought stigmatisation by publicly proclaiming 'I had an abortion'.

The intersection with the modes, traditions, and institutions of art is neither coincidental nor incidental to Women on Waves. While she was in medical school, and before the stint as a ship's doctor for Greenpeace during which she came up with the idea for Women on Waves, the remarkable polymath Rebecca Gomperts (also a published novelist) completed a four-year art degree at Amsterdam's Reitsveld Academy, studying conceptual art. And while she no longer identifies as an artist, it was, in a very literal way, art that allowed her to put her idea into practice. The grant that provided the bulk of the money to construct Women on Waves' portable clinic did not come from the Dutch health ministry nor the World Health Organization, not from the International Planned Parenthood Federation nor Ipas nor the Feminist Majority Foundation. It came from the Mondriaan Foundation.

Given all this, it is not difficult to imagine making an argument for Women on Waves as art – specifically, to imagine slipping it into the category of activist art that has been used, since it began to be theorised by critics like Lucy Lippard in the 1980s, to hold open a space for the fusion of work that is symbolic with work that is social. It is likely the viability of this category that has allowed so many arts organisations and institutions to support Women on Waves – and indeed activist art was explicitly the topic of the workshop for artists held aboard the Women on Waves ship in Ireland in 2001. Yet I am not interested in arguing that Women on Waves *is* art of even this special kind. In fact, I fear that the activist art category, as important as it has been for legitimating, theorising, and promoting politically engaged practice, now somewhat obscures the nature of many of the most productive and provocative practices at the crossing of its terms. These projects do not hybridise art and activism so much they as they tactically play on their ambiguous separation – to which the apparent mismatch of Women on Waves' boat and the container atop it might be said to give visual form. Women on Waves is not art, nor is it not-art: rather it tacks between

art and politics in much the same way it moves between actual human rights
mission and media-political campaign, legality and piracy, fact and myth. [...]

1   [Footnote 2 in source] Along with Malta, these were at the time the only European nations in
which abortion was illegal. Portugal was among the most restrictive countries – one of the few to
actually prosecute women for having abortions – but under a new government 59% of voters in
February 2007 supported a referendum legalising abortion if performed during the first ten weeks of
pregnancy (the cutoff in other European countries ranges from twelve to twenty-four weeks).
Although low voter turnout was considered to invalidate the referendum, in March 2007 parliament
voted to enact the new, more liberal abortion regulation.
2   [5] Doctors for Choice and Lawyers for Choice were formed in Ireland in 2001.

Carrie Lambert-Beatty, extracts from 'Twelve Miles: Boundaries of the New Art/Activism', in *Signs*,
vol. 33, no. 2 (Winter, 2008) 309–316. (Some footnotes omitted).

Zanele Muholi
Faces and Phases: In Conversation with Deborah Willis//2015

Deborah Willis Let's begin with *Faces and Phases*. When and where did this project begin?

Zanele Muholi It started in 2006 and I dedicated it to a good friend of mine who died from HIV complications in 2007, at the age of twenty-five. I just realised that as black South Africans, especially lesbians, we don't have much visual history that speaks to pressing issues, both current and also in the past. South Africa has the best constitution on the African continent and, dare I say, world – when it comes to recognising LGBTI (Lesbian, Gay, Bisexual, Transgender, Intersex) persons and other sexual minorities. It is the only country on the continent that legalised same-sex marriage in 2006. I thought to myself that if you have remarkable women in America and around the globe, you equally have remarkable lesbian women in South Africa.

We should be counted and certainly counted on to write our own history and validate our existence. We should not feel that somebody owes us these liberties. So, it's another way in which I personally claim my full citizenship as a South African photographer, as a South African female in this space, as a South African who identifies as black, and also as a lesbian. I'm basically saying we deserve recognition, respect, validation, and to have publications that mark and trace our existence.

Willis That's a beautiful introduction to the project, which offers a wonderful way of reading bodies and faces and new identities. When's the first time you remember seeing a photograph, or knowing a photograph, of a black lesbian in South Africa?

Muholi The early images I remember are black-and-white images of apartheid-era South Africa. Most were captured by male photographers like Ernest Cole or Alf Kumalo. Early images I saw depicted black women crying, images of pain, of struggle. Before black lesbian imagery clouded my mind, the first images I remember are of domestic workers, which were captured mainly by men. I looked at the work of David Goldblatt, who I regard as one of the forefathers of photography in South Africa, and the work of Jürgen Schadeberg. Those are some of the male photographers who captured apartheid South Africa.

I was born at the height of apartheid. I learned about South African women photographers very, very late. A friend gave me a book called *Viewfinders: Black Women Photographers* (1993), which was produced in America. I liked that book very much.

Willis *Viewfinders* was written by the photographer Jeanne Moutoussamy-Ashe.

Muholi Yes, her book changed my life in so many ways. I just thought to myself that photography has to become a lifetime thing in which I deal with my own issues, my own personal issues. I quoted Joan E. Biren (JEB), an American photographer, in my thesis. Her work related to what I wanted to achieve, and it still means so much to me in ways that you won't believe. You look at Biren's images and you think that someone has done what I'm trying to capture now, except I'm doing it from a South African point of view.

I understood the South African struggle of being forcefully removed from your own space, a space you thought belonged to you, where women were regarded as working machines. My mom was a domestic worker and the images of domestic workers, and the images of women crying, struggling, with children on their backs, those became my daily consumption.

Willis Did you start off by photographing your mother, early on?

Muholi I photographed my mom very, very late, around the time she started getting ill. It's often very difficult for us to confront our own issues. I mention in my film *Difficult Love* (2010) that it's a pity we don't tend to look at ourselves and our immediate spaces and how the outside world becomes familiar and easier for us to deal with than our own personal issues. She had cancer of the liver, and she passed on in 2009. But I do have images that I took of her.

Willis How did she feel about the photographs?

Muholi She was always quite supportive of what I was trying to achieve, and I was out to my mom. I delayed the whole process of photographing her and missed her as a beautiful young woman. Looking at our family album, of images that were either dated, without the photographer's name, or that had some strange names at the back, you think, Who has taken those images? What was their intention? Why are they not captured in this and that way?

The photograph that I eventually took later was of her wearing a church uniform. She was sick but allowed me to take that particular photograph. But I regret very much not having photographed her in her coffin. She looked so beautiful. But that meant negotiating with my family members, who didn't understand the importance of documentation, so I let go of that photograph. In my imagination, I have this beautiful woman who did not look sick in her coffin.

Willis Your photography has been described as work that 'mourns and celebrates'. What do you think about such labelling?

Muholi It depends on the context. I'm reclaiming photography as a black female being. I'm calling myself a visual activist, whether I am included in a show or not, whether I am published or not. That's my stance as a person, before anything else, before my sexuality and gender, because photography doesn't have a gender.

Ernest Cole, for instance, captured the men in the mines. The mineworkers were humiliated to nothing, captured naked, discounted to nothing, nameless. He showed an unjust system that dehumanised workers. All we see, all we remember, are those black men and their bodies facing the wall. That was visual activism, but at that time people did not regard it as anything of that sort, even if people at that time were killed and forcibly removed. Today, lesbians in South Africa are brutally murdered. 'Curative rape' is used on us. That forces me to redefine what visual activism is. If I were to reduce myself to the label 'visual artist', it would mean that what I'm doing is just for play, that our identities, as black female beings who are queer or are lesbian, is just art. Art needs to be political – or let me say that my art is political. It's not for show. It's not for play. [...]

Zanele Muholi and Deborah Willis, 'Zanele Muholi's Faces & Phases', *Aperture Magazine*, (April, 2015) 59-62.

Tania Bruguera and Immigrant Movement International
Migrant Manifesto//2011

We have been called many names. Illegals. Aliens. Guest Workers. Border crossers. Undesirables. Exiles. Criminals. Non-citizens. Terrorists. Thieves. Foreigners. Invaders. Undocumented.

Our voices converge on these principles:

1. We know that international connectivity is the reality that migrants have helped create, it is the place where we all reside. We understand that the quality of life of a person in a country is contingent on migrants' work. We identify as part of the engine of change.

2. We are all tied to more than one country. The multilaterally shaped phenomenon of migration cannot be solved unilaterally, or else it generates a vulnerable reality for migrants. Implementing universal rights is essential. The right to be included belongs to everyone.

3. We have the right to move and the right to not be forced to move. We demand the same privileges as corporations and the international elite, as they have the freedom to travel and to establish themselves wherever they choose. We are all worthy of opportunity and the chance to progress. We all have the right to a better life.

4. We believe that the only law deserving of our respect is an unprejudiced law, one that protects everyone, everywhere. No exclusions. No exceptions. We condemn the criminalisation of migrant lives.

5. We affirm that being a migrant does not mean belonging to a specific social class nor carrying a particular legal status. To be a migrant means to be an explorer; it means movement, this is our shared condition. Solidarity is our wealth.

6. We acknowledge that individual people with inalienable rights are the true barometer of civilisation. We identify with the victories of the abolition of slavery, the civil rights movement, the advancement of women's rights, and the rising achievements of the LGBTQ community. It is our urgent responsibility and our historical duty to make the rights of migrants the next triumph in the quest

for human dignity. It is inevitable that the poor treatment of migrants today will be our dishonour tomorrow.

7. We assert the value of the human experience and the intellectual capacity that migrants bring with them as greatly as any labour they provide. We call for the respect of the cultural, social, technical, and political knowledge that migrants command.

8. We are convinced that the functionality of international borders should be re-imagined in the service of humanity.

9. We understand the need to revive the concept of the commons, of the earth as a space that everyone has the right to access and enjoy.

10. We witness how fear creates boundaries, how boundaries create hate and how hate only serves the oppressors. We understand that migrants and non-migrants are interconnected. When the rights of migrants are denied the rights of citizens are at risk.

Dignity has no nationality.

Immigrant Movement International
November 2011

Tania Bruguera and Immigrant Movement International, 'Migrant Manifesto', (2011) (http://immigrant-movement.us/wordpress/migrant-manifesto/).

THE POSITION OF AN ARTIST DIFFERS FROM THAT OF AN ACTIVIST, BUT RATHER 'THAN SEPARATING THE TWO ACTIVITIES. WE CAN SEE THEM AS CIRCLES OF HUMAN ACTIVITY THAT OVERLAP

EVERYONE IN POSITIONS OF POWER

CURATORS, CRITICS, COLLECTORS, THE ARTISTS THEMSELVES

PASSED THE BUCK.

Guerrilla Girls, 'Guerrilla Girls Bear/Bare All', 1995

INSTITUTIONS AND DISRUPTION

Guerrilla Girls
Guerrilla Girls Bear/Bare All//1995

Q. […] How did the Guerrilla Girls start?

Käthe Kollwitz In 1984, The Museum of Modern Art in New York opened an exhibition titled 'An International Survey of Painting and Sculpture'. It was supposed to be an up-to-the minute summary of the most significant contemporary art in the world. Out of 169 artists, only 13 were women. All the artists were white, either from Europe or the US. That was bad enough, but the curator, Kynaston McShine, said any artist who wasn't in the show should rethink 'his' career. And that really annoyed a lot of artists because obviously the guy was completely prejudiced. Women demonstrated in front of the museum with the usual placards and picket line. Some of us who attended were irritated that we didn't make any impression on passersby.

Meta Fuller We began to ask ourselves some questions. Why did women and artists of colour do better in the 1970s than in the 1980s? Was there a backlash in the art world? Who was responsible? What could be done about it?

Q. What did you do?

Frida Kahlo We decided to find out how bad it was. After about 5 minutes of research we found that it was worse than we thought: the most influential galleries and museums exhibited almost no women artists. When we showed the figures around, some said it was an issue of quality, not prejudice. Others admitted there was discrimination, but considered the situation hopeless. Everyone in positions of power curators, critics, collectors, the artists themselves passed the buck. The artists blamed the dealers, the dealers blamed the collectors, the collectors blamed the critics, and so on. We decided to embarrass each group by showing their records in public. Those were the first posters we put up in the streets of SoHo in New York .

Q. Why are you anonymous?

GG1 The art world is a very small place. Of course, we were afraid that if we blew the whistle on some of its most powerful people, we could kiss off our art careers. But mainly, we wanted the focus to be on the issues, not on our personalities or our own work.

Lee Krasner We joined a long tradition of (mostly male) masked avengers like Robin Hood, Batman, The Lone Ranger and Wonder Woman.

Q. Why do you call yourselves 'girls?' Doesn't that upset a lot of feminists?

Gertrude Stein Yeah. We wanted to be shocking. We wanted people to be upset.

Kahlo Calling a grown woman a girl can imply she's not complete, mature, or grown-up. But we decided to reclaim the word 'girl', so it couldn't be used against us. Gay activists did the same thing with the epithet 'queer'.

Q. Why are you Guerrillas?

Georgia O'Keeffe We wanted to play with the fear of guerrilla warfare, to make people afraid of who we might be and where we would strike next. Besides, 'guerrilla' sounds so good with 'girl'.

Q. Isn't calling yourselves the Conscience of the Art World a little pretentious?

Eva Hesse Of course. Everyone knows artists are pretentious!

GG1 Anyway, the art world needs to examine itself, to be more self-critical. Every profession needs a conscience! [...]

Q. If the art world is so corrupt and disgusting, why do you want to be part of it?

Kollwitz We don't all want a piece of the pie. We are a diverse group, different ages, different races, different sexual orientations and different levels of art world success. Some of us want to blow up SoHo, some have already had museum retrospectives. What we do agree on unanimously is that women and artists of colour deserve a piece of the pie and shouldn't be prevented from getting a big piece, if that's what they're after.

Violette LeDuc People who attack us for wanting a piece of the pie usually have most of it. They wouldn't attack a woman in another field like a law graduate who wants to be a partner in a firm, or a Supreme Court Judge. [...]

Q. Doesn't the mask keep you from taking responsibility for the charges you make? Isn't that cowardly?

Rosalba Carriera Actually, what started off as a lark, as a way of doing something constructive with our anger, has become a big responsibility to a huge audience. We didn't ask for it but we're trying to live up to it. None of us has ever profited from being a Girl.

Ana Mendieta Give us a break. Was the Lone Ranger a coward?

Q. Has anyone ever tried to expose who you really are?

Paula Modersohn-Becker One guy threatened us. But the thought of millions of angry, spear-carrying feminists on his case was more than he could bear.

Liubov Popova A number of years ago, two guys put up a poster with their photos, claiming to be the Guerrilla Girls. Some weird career strategy!

Q. Have you made a difference?

Emily Carr We've made dealers, curators, critics and collectors accountable. And things have actually gotten better for women and artists of colour. With lots of backsliding.

Frida Kahlo Just last year, Robert Hughes, who in the mid 80s claimed that gender was no longer a limiting factor in the art world, reviewed a show of American art in London for *Time* and said, 'You don't have to be a Guerrilla Girl to know that there weren't enough women in the show.' That's progress, even though Hughes reneged on a promise to apologise in this book for his past insensitivity.

Modersohn-Becker Mary Boone is too macho to admit we influenced her in any way, but she never represented any women until we targeted her.

Käthe Kollwitz Museum curators feel compelled to suck up to us on camera. They used to ignore us and hope wed just go away.

Stein The situation was pathetic. It had to change. And we were a part of that change.

Q. Has success ruined you?
33.3%: Yes.
33.3%: No.
The rest: Undecided.

Q. Where do you go from here?

All Back to that jungle out there. Back to work. [...]

Guerrilla Girls, extracts from 'Guerrilla Girls Bear/Bare All', *Confessions of the Guerrilla Girls*, (New York: HarperCollins, 1995) n.p.

Doug Ashford
Group Material: An Artwork Is a Person//2010

[...] Most of the members of Group Material were children during the rise of the civil rights, women's liberation, free love, gay power, and anti-war movements of the 1960s. Even if we were too young to directly witness the physical mobilisations that rejected state totality and corporate greed, the concomitant changes in ethos, fantasy, and feelings were tacitly embedded in our practice. Group Material understood that connected to the liberation movements against colonialism, patriarchy and capital were artist-led oppositions to the accepted hierarchies between institutions, audiences and artists themselves. The process of re-imagining ourselves through the rebellious inventing of art objects was, in many ways, a continuation of a larger political momentum.

In this way 60s activisms and 80s interpretive enactments were more than the socioeconomic conditions for Group Material's work: they were the foundations of its aesthetic action. Activist politics presented a moment of collective refusal, but in that refusal came an identification with others, known and unknown. The desire for political change produces conjecture on a number of fronts and conjecture necessitates affinity with others. Modelling a future by banding together amidst the interests of strangers is a legacy shared by the political imperatives of social organising and the methodological sensibilities of artists. [...]

Group Material's refutations were multiple and situation-specific. We said 'no' to the false neutrality of the museum that forbade the social context of relations between our imaginations, 'no' to the reduction of other public domains to corporatist management and blind consumption. We said 'no' to the sequestering of art as outside the purview of audiences and artists; we said 'no' to the disappearance of subaltern cultures under imperialism and we said 'no' to the supposed inevitable death of our friends to AIDS. Our set of refusals were shared with each other and with the many other individuals and groupings responding to social inequity at that time. We recognised that the politics of any group is made real in collecting seemingly unrelated refusals, showing how group action can generate new life into an individual […]

As Group Material's work matured, it became increasingly clear that in order to oppose the oblivion of the present, a form had to be invented through the visualisation of democratic process. How else could an authentic response to the imposed disaster of contemporary life be constructed? As artists we knew that the street and the symposia as forms of response were often beautiful – that collectively diverse declarations of justice have all the qualities of improvisation, comparison, proportion, absence, suggestion, and substitution. In many ways the practices that Group Material developed were un-theorised, suggested by the exigencies of the constituent matters of life over death: be they the formation of Central American independence movements facing American sponsored genocide or the activist response to official indifference to the AIDS epidemic. Our forms of exhibition and public practice reflected the need to invent a dynamic situation, a designed moment of reflection that could include discussion and present dissent. If such an apparatus of artistic presentation emerges from the framework of political assembly – the installation of art can begin to look and perhaps even act, like a forum. In calling the exhibition a forum we were excavating all its meanings: roundtable, caucus, public assembly, parliament, open framework, anarchic exchange and more. Making the artwork comparable to the apparatus of democracy did have an actual political effect; it acted as a ground for meetings, associations, transformations of artistic context and real probabilities for the constituents of those represented by and attending to the work. […]

In rereading the documents now collected in our archive, it becomes clear to me that the kind of work produced by Group Material simply had to be made – it happened, like the social activism it followed, out of desperation. Group Material thought then, and it was not unusual to have such ideas, that one could create meaning outside of the privatising influence of corporate culture by re-organising the actual experience of culture independently. The art projects we developed resembled the forms of the political vanguard by reflecting the modern notion that individuals have a right to bind themselves together to produce a context that might retain work and happiness. It is against the 1980s emergence of a right wing culture of physical control and spectacularised consistency that this generation of artworks and collective action need to be rethought: the false stability of religious fundamentalism, the mediagenic degradation of culture into profit, the relentless never-returning value of our labour, a historical amnesia that disintegrates capacities to read or even to speak to each other directly. These are the vicissitudes of 80s economic and political regression and they still weigh upon us, attempting to re-form us into an anti-culture of mutual repression. A repression no longer exclusive to the barrel of a gun – a repression designed through images.

Group Material saw that politics happens at the site of representation itself, not just where information is transferred, but rather at the place we recognise ourselves; where we have the sense that we are ourselves, feel a stability that is hailed and recognised by others. A radical representational moment may be collective but it also suggests that we can give ourselves over to a new vision through feeling, an experience linked to contemplation and epiphany. In this way no public description of another, in frame or in detail can be presented as neutral. So when Group Material asked, 'How is culture made and who is it for?' we were asking for something greater than simply a larger piece of the art world's real estate. We were asking that the relationships change between those who depict the world and those who consume it, and demonstrating that the context for this change would question more than just the museum: a contestation of all contexts for public life. In making exhibitions and public projects that sought to transform the instrumentality of representational politics, invoking questions about democracy itself, Group Material presented a belief that art directly builds who we are – it engenders us. This was an insistence that the representations found in art give rise to our sense of self and in the end encompass us as subjects. Accordingly we believed that the existing management of art, and of culture in general through the market, enforces a complex system of limiting notions of what makes 'us' us or 'me' me, what normalises and enacts the contours of fixed identity. The definitions of gender, race and power were, and still are, dependent on a visual system – images that make possible the recognition or misrecognition of ourselves, between ourselves.

The museum – like the city and the government that makes us in them – is always already in ruins. The anxiety of the proximity to power that art, and art's management implies, is therefore always part of art's production. The historical dynamism of the museum carries within it all the battles fought over the public domain since its modern inception. For Group Material the market-dominated context for culture in the 80s and its consolidation in the museum were presented to artists unfairly, as universalising opportunities steeped in false neutrality. The white walls that Group Material re-painted red critically reacted to institutions, critically insisting that they, not artists or audiences, were the producers of meaning. The prevailing notions of aesthetic pluralism at that time, the promotional levelling of all artistic forms onto consumption, the blandly humanist notions of equivalence in scholarship and public record – all partook in the deeply ideological construction of democracy as a kind of blanketing agreement, a blind consensus. If it is true that capitalism is the most creative form of production the earth has ever known, its reservoir of manufactured agreement strangely needed formal and physical protection.

And it still does. The threat felt by the status quo from art is a real threat. The moment of social unrest of the 60s, like the collectively designed exhibition, shows that you are closer to the ideas of others than you think. This is perhaps why the experience of an art that can concurrently untangle, remake, and re-tangle the ideas we have of ourselves is not easy to produce. The struggle to communicate even amongst those invested in a common project seems at times insurmountable. Manifest in this chronicle is the fact that Group Material created work in struggle with itself, with members often in debate and contention, producing artwork that manifested conflict. As part of the audience it is only logical our disagreement with the world would inspire dissent among ourselves. [...] If there is an emotional equivalency to the idea of creative dissensus, it can be found in the resolute presentation of dialogue in Group Material's process and installations. One of the most compelling memories of the work we did in forming the exhibition was the argument. There is not a single artistic product we made that did not come from discussion, opposition, and disagreement. Today, after many artists and many decades of aesthetic experimentation, dissensus can finally be proffered as the basis for imagining social and aesthetic action – it is an emotional invention of great beauty.

Group Material's self-assignment was to locate the dissensual feelings associated with activism, its emotional reverberations and actual evocations, into a realisable model or design. It meant we had to try to invent visual solutions that would be able to question themselves. By insisting that the presentation of art could approach the experience of dialogue and dissent we showed that when art addresses us as subjects in conversation, we can experience art as an array of personified encounters. We created a site where multiple and conflicting forms and histories cross over and through one another, mutating into paradoxical and unexpected notions of how we could define ourselves as humans. When artworks are engendered as persons in dialogue, the experience of art can make a rebellion.

Doug Ashford, extracts from 'An Artwork is a Person', in *Show and Tell: A Chronicle of Group Material*, ed. Julie Ault (London: Four Corners Books, 2010) 220–225.

The historical dynamism of
THE
MUSEUM
carries within
it all the battles
fought over
the public
domain since
its modern
inception.

Doug Ashford, 'An Artwork is a Person', 2010

Martha Rosler
Out of the Vox: Art's Activist Potential//2004

Art with a political face typically gains visibility during periods of social upheaval. 'Marxism and art' of the 70s and 'political art' of the 80s are among only the most recent examples. A good proportion of artists typically aim their work into the thick of things, but institutional gatekeepers try to manage the political dimension of art, blunting artists' partisanship into a universalised discourse of humanistic ideals and individualised expression. Virtually all avant-gardes and art-world insurgencies, from Constructivism to Dada to Abstract Expressionism and beyond, have suffered this reinterpretation.

But the game changed when curators with a bent toward geopolitics organised successive recent Documentas, confirming an international trend that legitimated some political expression in art, mostly work fitting the rubric of postcolonialism, but also collaborative and extra-institutional work, such as that of Park Fiction, Superflex, and Raqs Media Collective. (A commonly voiced witticism, however, was that to be a 'postcolonial artist', you had to move to Europe and become a market artist, and similar reframing problems attend most importations, whether from artists working long term in local communities or graffiti artists and skateboarders.)

Generally speaking, a lack of clear political alignments – 'artistic autonomy' – works well for most Western artists and their institutions. Who are we, after all? What are our allegiances? 'Embourgeoisement' – in home, health, family, and leisure – has for many supplanted bohemianism, making it harder to identify too strongly with the dispossessed, the dejected, and the disenfranchised, let alone with those whose labour is exploited. Fine! mutter those who observe how little use the organised left has had for artists. But the total freedom of the artist in Western society also ineluctably signals total irrelevance, just as obsessive interiority speaks of social disconnection and narcissism, if not infantilism. The collapse of utopianism as a horizon has often deprived art of a philosophical or ethical backstory, allowing curators to treat whimsical activities (tartly termed 'sponsored hobbies' by Russian curator Ekaterina Dyogot) as symbolic of autonomy, of artistic advance, or even of social transformation. Thin notions of communalism pass for social engagement, and weak interpretations of art as a gift freely given reduce the claims made for its socially transformative power to a therapeutic time-out for atomised individuals – the new postbourgeois subject performing self anew every day.

I am ambivalent about the return of 'political art' as a flat field of action or analysis. Fashionability makes it susceptible to dismissal. Much worse, artists are hailed as merry pranksters, as some curators actively celebrate the frivolously empty riff (by what might be termed the Monkees of the art world) on 60s collectivism. Conversely, there is a sad superficiality in reducing art's political possibilities to agitprop, ignoring the debates about the instrumentalisation of art between [Theodor] Adorno, [Bertolt] Brecht, [Walter] Benjamin, and others. This thought recently drove me – and, by odd chance, the young activist-artist reading group at 16 Beaver in New York – to revisit Adorno's 1962 article 'Commitment', in which art is called upon to provide a silence and reproach to the deformations of modernity: 'Today, every phenomenon of culture, even if a model of integrity, is liable to be suffocated in the cultivation of kitsch. Yet paradoxically in the same epoch it is to works of art that has fallen the burden of wordlessly asserting what is barred to politics.'

One stumbles over 'wordlessly asserting', over Adorno's expressed scorn for 'information theory' in art, since much today depends on direct information retailing. Especially since the Seattle protests of 1999, many activist artists find they can't be bothered with the art world and what art historian Chin-tao Wu has called its 'enterprise culture'. The end of socialism as a framework means that 'interventionism' looks to various inflections of anarchism (some much better theorised than others, some virulent toward art-world institutions of every stripe) or flies theory-blind. Electronic art forms have offered a moment of activism – as in 'tactical media' – and often provided sophisticated political analysis, available online, of course. ('The revolution will be webcast!' writes Geert Lovink.) Activists and hacktivists have stepped into the space vacated by video, whose expansively utopian and activist potential has been depoliticised, as 'video art', much like photography before it, was removed from wide public address by its incarceration in museum mausoleums and collectors' cabinets.

In the present context, the political work of the late 60s through 70s – now purged of exigency and brought out of the closet by the market – may be evaluated differently. This work may be tinged with nostalgia to young artists likely to have encountered it in art-history classes, but it offers a starting point and a history to connect with, an ur-moment that all trends in art like to locate. What initially seemed attractive for its look becomes more compelling for its commitment.

At its best, Conceptual and other post-Pop forms of art led to a tremendously productive encounter between artists and the 'life world', providing a space for deduction, exposition, and insight, as well as self-revelation and play. Play, including (postmodern) irony and parody and a subversion of officialdom, becomes more evident the closer one gets to the present – though it started with yippie guerrilla performances, as well as with musical groups like the Mothers of Invention, the Fugs, and Country Joe & the Fish. Artists' groups of the 60s and 70s were organised mostly around public actions, adopting the protest style of the day. West Coast women such as Suzanne Lacy and Leslie Labowitz or the Waitresses were more likely to engage in civic square performances. Many of the 80s collectives in New York set up ad hoc shadow commercial-gallery structures, while others like PAD/D, REPOhistory, and Group Material were operating here and there within established institutions and more public venues. Groups bridging different times and practices range from the Bread & Puppet Theater and the Zapatistas (not an art group, of course) to the Guerrilla Girls and Critical Art Ensemble (now caught in the Orwellian web of the Patriot Act). Among the more recent examples are attac, Ne Pas Plier, Las Agencias, subRosa, the Yes Men, ®™ark, Boat-People.org, Disobbedienti/Tute Bianche, and others operating as the dark matter of the counterpublic sphere, in the words of artist Greg Sholette. Media collectives include the long-lived Paper Tiger and Deep Dish and newer ones such as Whispered Media and the post-1999 Indymedias around the world, as well as pirate radio. (I am leaving out the robust community and public art movements in the US that have little interest in joining the more mandarin art world that, say, follows *Artforum* and does not accommodate their public actions and spectacles.) The practices of many such collectives – most of which would refuse the artist label – range from left-wing pranks to strategically deployed vandalism and criminality (such as Yomango's choreographed shoplifting). The globalisation of the social-justice movement, the diffuse sites of social labour, and new communication technologies have helped create communities that exist primarily through Listservs but finally wind up with feet on streets.

The question, then, is not, Is it art? but Whose art is it? And art for whom? The question is, What is art? If one is to believe, as I do, that art provides a different frame for interpreting experience (although clobbered in its reach by corporate media) and offers the possibility of intelligible political engagement, then the flattening of political art by trendiness or vital but short-term political exigencies is a missed opportunity. The new turn to Kantian aesthetics emanates mostly from people seeking to renovate a decrepit aestheticism and quash unruly 'politicised' practices, but some writers, such as Susan Buck-Morss, seem to be looking to [Immanuel] Kant, as Adorno did, to support a conviction that it offers a different way of knowing. I am no Kantian, so far. Adorno's brief for an art of imminent critique, of open-ended criticality, cannot fully define artists' practice. In a moment of unmistakable crisis in all dimensions, cultural, political, and economic, in the US and the rest of the world, artists once again, in all self-aggrandisement, seek to reorient their audiences, forming them into public constituencies. Let us try to figure out what art is beyond what the art world's present regression suggests.

Martha Rosler, 'Out of the Vox: Art's Activist Potential', *Artforum* (September, 2004) 218–219.

Chto Delat
A Declaration on Politics, Knowledge and Art on the Fifth Anniversary of the Chto Delat Work Group//2008

Our Principles: Self-Organisation, Collectivism, Solidarity

The Chto Delat platform unites artists, philosophers, social researchers, activists, and all those whose aim is the collaborative realisation of critical and independent research, publication, artistic, educational and activist projects.

All of the platform's initiatives are based on the principles of self-organisation and collectivism. These principles are realised through the *political coordination* of working groups – the contemporary analogue of soviets. The projects undertaken by any of these groups represent the entire platform and are closely coordinated with one another. At the same time, the existence of the platform creates a common context for interpreting the projects of its individual participants. We are likewise guided by the principle of solidarity.

We organise and support mutual assistance networks with all grassroots groups who share the principles of internationalism, feminism, and equality. [...]

Capitalism Is Not a Totality

We believe that capital is not a totality, that the popular thesis that 'there is nothing outside capital' is false. The task of the intellectual and the artist is to engage in a thoroughgoing unmasking of the myth that there are no alternatives to the global capitalist system. We insist on the obvious: *a world without the dominion of profit and exploitation* not only can be created but always already exists in the micropolitics and microeconomies of human relationships and creative labour.

We have to reveal this *joyous space of life* to the greatest number of people. The historical becoming of this economic, political, intellectual and creative emancipation is *communism*.

The Communist Decoding of Capitalist Reality

The person who is genuinely free, who lives in the fullness of their being, is a person who is alive to various sciences and disciplines, who critically examines themselves and the world. However, the narrow specialisation of scientific knowledge in capitalist society places knowledge in the service of the dominant class. Individual research serves private interests, while research of society, research based on the universality of critical utterance, is not supported institutionally.

We affirm that there is *only one form of knowledge* – knowledge that enables the discovery that the calling of human beings is *to be free with other human beings*. Critical knowledge should not be a commodity, and its maximally widespread distribution – enlightenment and education – is the cause of each intellectual and cultural worker. This synthesis of theory and practice, knowledge of the world and its transformation, we call the communist decoding of capitalist reality.

We repeat along with Marx: 'We do not say to the world: Cease your struggles, they are foolish; we will give you the true slogan of struggle. We merely show the world what it is really fighting for, and consciousness is something that it has to acquire, even if it does not want to.' ('Letter to Arnold Ruge, September 1843'.)

Faithfulness to the Intellectual and Artistic Avant-Gardes of the Twentieth Century

We recognise the importance of twentieth century avant-garde thought for the rethinking and renewal of the leftist philosophical and political tradition. We believe that in order for this renewal to happen we need a maximally open, non-dogmatic approach that presupposes a critical reception of ideas, concepts, and practices that have formed outside the framework of doctrinal Marxism. Our urgent task is to reconnect political action, engaged thought, and artistic innovation. [...]

The Tasks of Contemporary Art

Contemporary art that is produced as a commodity form or a form of entertainment is not art. It is the conveyor-belt manufacture of *counterfeits and narcotics* for the enjoyment of a 'creative class' sated with novelty. One of our most vital tasks today is unmasking the current system of ideological control and manipulation of people. The pseudo-creativity of this system is no more than the commodification not only of the fruits of their labour, but also of all forms of life.

We are convinced that genuine art is art that de-automates consciousness – first, that of the artist, then that of the viewer. And because art is an activity open to everyone, neither power nor capital can have a monopoly on the 'ownership' of art. One answer to the perennial debate on art's autonomy is the possibility that it can be produced independently of art institutions, whether state or private. In the contemporary conjuncture, the self-negation essential to art's development happens outside institutional practices. As a public form of the unfolding of each person's creative potential, the place of art during moments of revolutionary struggle has always been and always will be in the thick of events, on the squares and in the communes. At such moments, art takes the form of street theatre, posters, actions, graffiti, grassroots cinema, poetry, and music. Renewing these forms at this new stage in history is the task of the genuine artist.

What Is the Place of Revolutionary Art in a Time of Reaction?
Although mass movements for the transformation of society are *temporarily* absent, art's place is nevertheless still *on the side of the oppressed*. Its central task is the elaboration of new forms for the sensual and critical apprehension of the world from the perspective of collective liberation. Art should exist not for museums and dealers but in order to develop and articulate a new mode of 'emancipated sensuality.' It should become an instrument for seeing and knowing the world in the totality of its contradictions.

The museums and institutions of art should function as depositories and laboratories for the aesthetic exploration of the world. We should, however, shield them from privatisation, economisation, and subordination to the populist logic of the culture industry. That is why we believe that right now it would be wrong to refuse to work in any way with cultural and academic institutions – despite the fact that the *majority* of these institutions throughout the world are engaged in the flagrant propaganda of commodity fetishism and servile knowledge. The political propaganda of all other forms of human vocation either provokes the system's harsh rejection or the system co-opts it into its spectacle. At the same time, however, the system is not homogeneous – it is greedy, stupid and dependent.

Today, this leaves us room to use these institutions to advance and promote our knowledge. We can bring this knowledge to a wide audience without succumbing to its distortion.

That is why we need to develop clear criteria for deciding in which venues we can conduct our struggle, which projects should be boycotted and denounced, and with whom and on what conditions we can collaborate.

Our Basic Programme
In the current situation, we propose that self-governed collectives use the following basic program as their guide:

– Don't allow external factors to intervene as you develop your ideas and realise your projects. Don't give away exclusive rights to the distribution of your work. Don't directly or indirectly advertise the institutions of power and capital within your projects.

– Economic relations have to be built in a political way. You need to collectively demand that your labour be compensated fairly and with dignity. By entering into a working relationship with the institutions of power, you demonstrate their capitalistic, exploitative nature.

– Don't participate in projects whose results (symbolic capital, surplus value) can be instrumentalised for political ends that contradict the internal tasks of your collective's work.

– As you realise your project you should try to make your work as 'non-transparent' as possible. At the same time, you should strive to produce situations whose meaning can be fully manifested only outside the limited frame of concrete relations of production. This means that you should construe the use value of the work in such a way that institutions of power will be hard pressed when they try to convert it into exchange value.

At the same time, we insist on an uncompromising critique of and struggle against all institutions of culture that base their work on corruption and the primitive servicing of the interests of commercial structures, the state, and ideology. We must constantly 'slap' these dimwits and prostitutes 'on the wrist' and show them their shameful place in history. We will use all the means at our disposal to make this happen.

The Local Aspect of the Struggle

We demand, as a minimum, the abolition of tacit censorship and an end to all repression of political and cultural activity.

It follows from this demand that we need state and public support for social research projects and critical art practices in Russia that are independent of private interests. Avoiding the traditional choice between reformism and radicalism, we insist on the search for a specific, local configuration of demands and transformational programs. For a start we demand a few concrete things. Public funds should be transparently distributed for the support of research and art in the public space, as well for grassroots initiatives. They should also be used to support work based on the harsh criticism of contemporary institutions of power, both in culture and in politics. On the other hand, this is possible only as part of a radical social transformation that would undermine the entire system of authoritarian capitalism. In order to foster conditions for this transformation, we need *new forms of coordination* with all other fronts of the struggle – with workers, trade unions, environmentalists, feminists and anti-authoritarian activists. We have to propagate models of activist self-education and the politicisation of artistic and intellectual practices. These are the bases for a future broad consolidation of leftists and the hegemony of our ideas in society.

Chto Delat, extracts from 'A Declaration on Politics, Knowledge, and Art on the Fifth Anniversary of the Chto Delat Work Group', in *Chto Delat? Newspaper, #special issue: When Artists Struggle Together* (November, 2008).

Gilles Deleuze
In Conversation with Antonio Negri//1990

Gilles Deleuze [...] You see, we think any political philosophy must turn on the analysis of capitalism and the ways it has developed. What we find most interesting in Marx is his analysis of capitalism as an immanent system that's constantly overcoming its own limitations, and then coming up against them once more in a broader form, because its fundamental limit is *Capital* itself. *A Thousand Plateaus* sets out in many different directions, but these are the three main ones: first, we think any society is defined not so much by its contradictions as by its lines of flight, it flees all over the place, and it's very interesting to try and follow the lines of flight taking shape at some particular moment or other. Look at Europe now, for instance: western politicians have spent a great deal of effort setting it all up, the technocrats have spent a lot of effort getting uniform administration and rules, but then on the one hand there may be surprises in store in the form of upsurges of young people, of women, that become possible simply because certain restrictions are removed (with 'untechnocratisable' consequences); and on the other hand it's rather comic when one considers that this Europe has already been completely superseded before being inaugurated, superseded by movements coming from the East. These are major lines of flight. There's another direction in *A Thousand Plateaus*, which amounts to considering not just lines of flight rather than contradictions, but minorities rather than classes. Then finally, a third direction, which amounts to finding a characterisation of 'war machines' that's nothing to do with war but to do with a particular way of occupying, taking up, space-time, or inventing new spacetimes: revolutionary movements (people don't take enough account, for instance, of how the PLO has had to invent a space-time in the Arab world), but artistic movements too, are war-machines in this sense. You say there's a certain tragic or melancholic tone in all this. I think I can see why. I was very struck by all the passages in Primo Levi where he explains that Nazi camps have given us 'a shame at being human.' Not, he says, that we're all responsible for Nazism, as some would have us believe, but that we've all been tainted by it: even the survivors of the camps had to make compromises with it, if only to survive. There's the shame of there being men who became Nazis; the shame of being unable, not seeing how, to stop it; the shame of having compromised with it; there's the whole of what Primo Levi calls this 'gray area'. And we can feel shame at being human in utterly trivial situations, too: in the face of too great a vulgarisation of thinking, in the face of TV entertainment, of a ministerial speech, of 'jolly people' gossiping. This is one of the most powerful incentives toward philosophy, and it's what makes all philosophy political. In capitalism only one thing is universal, the market. There's no universal state, precisely because there's a universal market of which states are the centres, the trading floors. But the market's not universalising, homogenising, it's an extraordinary generator of both wealth and misery. A concern for human rights shouldn't lead us to extol the 'joys' of the liberal capitalism of which they're an integral part. There's no democratic state that's not compromised to the very core by its part in generating human misery. What's so shameful is that we've no sure way of maintaining becomings, or still more of arousing them, even within ourselves. How any group will turn out, how it will fall back into history, presents a constant 'concern.' There's no longer any image of proletarians around of which it's just a matter of becoming conscious. [...]

The difference between minorities and majorities isn't their size. A minority may be bigger than a majority. What defines the majority is a model you have to conform to: the average European adult male city-dweller, for example... A minority, on the other hand, has no model, it's a becoming, a process. One might say the majority is nobody. Everybody's caught, one way or another, in a minority becoming that would lead them into unknown paths if they opted to follow it through. When a minority creates models for itself, it's because it wants to become a majority, and probably has to, to survive or prosper (to have a state, be recognised, establish its rights, for example). But its power comes from what it's managed to create, which to some extent goes into the model, but doesn't depend on it. A people is always a creative minority, and remains one even when it acquires a majority: it can be both at once because the two things aren't lived out on the same plane. It's the greatest artists (rather than populist artists) who invoke a people, and find 'they lack a people': [Stéphane] Mallarmé, [Arthur] Rimbaud, [Paul] Klee, [Alban] Berg. The Straubs in cinema. Artists can only invoke a people, their need for one goes to the very heart of what they're doing, it's not their job to create one, and they can't.[1] Art is resistance: it resists death, slavery, infamy, shame. But a people can't worry about art. How is a people created, through what terrible suffering? When a people's created, it's through its own resources, but in a way that links up with something in art ([Philippe] Garrel says there's a mass of terrible suffering in the Louvre, too) or links up art to what it lacked. Utopia isn't the right concept: it's more a question of a 'fabulation' in which a people and art both share. We ought to take up Bergson's notion of fabulation and give it a political meaning. [...]

1   [Editors' note. Jean-Marie Straub and Danièle Huillet were French filmmakers who lived and worked primarily in Germany and Italy. Between 1963 and 2006 they made numerous films which combine radical politics and radical approaches to form.]

Gilles Deleuze, extracts from 'Conversation with Toni Negri' (1990), in *Negotiations, 1972–1990*, trans. Martin Joughin (New York: Columbia University Press, 1997) 172–174.

Nika Dubrovsky and David Graeber
Another Art World, Part 1: Art Communism and Artificial Scarcity & Part 3: Policing and Symbolic Order//2019, 2020

[...] We would like to offer some initial thoughts on exactly how the art world can operate simultaneously as a dream of liberation, and a structure of exclusion; how its guiding principle is both that everyone should really be an artist, and that this is absolutely and irrevocably not the case. The art world is still founded on Romantic principles; these have never gone away; but the Romantic legacy contains two notions, one, a kind of democratic notion of genius as an essential aspect of any human being, even if it can only be realised in some collective way, and another, that those things that really matter are always the product of some individual heroic genius. The art world, essentially, dangles the ghost of one so as to ultimately, aggressively, insist on the other. [...]

The art world, for all the importance of its museums, institutes, foundations, university departments, and the like, is still organised primarily around the art market. The art market in turn is driven by finance capital. Being the world's least regulated market among shady businesses, tax shelters, scams, money laundering, etc., the art world might be said to represent a kind of experimental ground for the hammering-out of a certain ideal of freedom appropriate to the current rule of finance capital.

A case can certainly be made that contemporary art is in effect an extension of global finance (which is itself, of course, closely tied to empire). Artsy neighbourhoods tend to cluster around the financial districts of major cities. Artistic investment follows the same logic as financial speculation. Still – if contemporary art were simply an extension of finance capital, works designed to look good in banks, or in bankers' homes, why should we even care? It's not as if cultural critics spend a lot of time debating the latest design trends in luxury yachts. Why should changing trends in decorative objects that the owners of such yachts like to place in their sitting rooms be considered relevant, in any way, to the lives or aspirations of bus drivers, maids, bauxite miners, telemarketers, or pretty much anyone outside the charmed circle of the 'art world' itself? [...]

The world's cities are full of young people who do see a life of expression as the ultimate form of freedom, and even those who dream of becoming soap opera stars or hip-hop video producers recognise that as things are currently organised, the 'art world' is the crowning height of that larger domain of 'arts', and as such, its regulatory principle, that which holds the elaborate ranks and hierarchies of genres and forms of art – so strangely reminiscent of earlier ranks and hierarchies of angels – in their proper place. This remains true even for those who have nothing but bemused contempt for the very idea of contemporary art, or are entirely unaware of it, insofar as they exist within a world where those who produce the forms of artistic expression they do appreciate, or their children, insofar as they aspire to move up in the world, will necessarily have to exist in a world where contemporary art is seen as the purest expression of human creativity – and creativity as the ultimate value.

The easiest way to measure the stubborn centrality of such structures, perhaps, is to consider how difficult it is to get rid of them. Attempts are always being made. There always seems to be someone in the art world trying to create participatory programs, explode the boundaries between high and low genres, include members of marginalised groups as producers or audiences or even patrons. Sometimes, they draw a lot of attention. Always in the end they fade away and die, leaving things more or less exactly as they were before. In the 1970s and 1980s, for example, there was a concerted effort in America to challenge the border between high art and popular music, even to the point where a few of the artists (Brian Eno, Talking Heads, Laurie Anderson, Jeffrey Lohn) actually did create work that hit the charts, and played to sold-out theatres full of young people who had never heard of Hugo Ball or Robert Rauschenberg. Critics declared that the very idea of high and low genres was quickly dissolving away. But it wasn't true. In a few years, it was all just another forgotten musical trend, an odd sidebar in the history of rock 'n' roll.

Hardly surprising perhaps, since the art market and the music industry always operated on entirely different economic principles: the one mainly financed by rich collectors and governments, the other by mass marketing to the general public. Still, if there was a real challenge to the logic of exclusion anywhere in the arts, during the twentieth century, it was precisely in the domain of music, where a defiant tradition from folk to rock and punk and hip-hop actually came closest to realising the old avant-garde dream that everyone could be an artist – though one can, of course, debate precisely how close this really came. At the very least, it established the idea that creativity is a product of small collectives as easily as individual auteurs. All this happened, significantly, at a certain distance from actual self-proclaimed artistic avant-gardes; and it is telling that the brief mutual flirtation with the art world in the 80s was a prelude to a backlash that left music far more corporatised, individualised, and with far fewer spaces for experimentation than it had since at least the 1950s.

Any market of course must necessarily operate on a principle of scarcity. In a way, the art market and the music industry face similar problems: materials are mostly cheap and talent is widespread; therefore, for profits to be made, scarcity has to be produced. Of course, in the art world, this is what the critical apparatus is largely about: the production of scarcity; which is, in turn, why even the most sincerely radical anti-capitalist critics, curators, and gallerists will tend to draw the line at the possibility that everyone really could be an artist, even in the most diffuse possible sense. The art world remains overwhelmingly a world of heroic individuals, even when it claims to echo the logic of movements and collectives – even when the ostensible aim of those collectives is to annihilate the distinction between art and life. Even the Dadaists and Surrealists are remembered today as a handful of romantic geniuses, whatever they might have claimed to be about.

It is also noteworthy that the only time a significant number of people believed that structures of exclusion really were dissolving, that a society in which everyone could become an artist was actually conceivable, occurred in the midst of social revolutions when it was genuinely believed that capitalism was in its death spirals, and markets themselves were about to become a thing of the past. Many of these trends, unsurprisingly, emerge directly from Russia, where the period from the revolution of 1905 to the avant-garde heyday of the 1920s saw an almost brutal efflorescence of new ideas of what artistic communism might be like.[...]

What Does This Have to Do with the Art World?
Our argument is that just as police ultimately operate to maintain poverty and white supremacy, what we call 'the art world' ultimately exists to maintain a structure of hierarchy. What happens inside the bubble makes little difference. The issue is the existence of the bubble itself. Or to put it slightly differently, 'the arts' are organised the way they are because 'art' sits on top of them. A poor child growing up in a shantytown in Brazil or Pakistan has likely never heard of any of the names featured at the latest Documenta, but whatever she might dream of becoming – a rapper, a movie star, a fashion designer, a comedian (basically

anything other than a tycoon, athlete, or politician) – it is already ranked on a scale in which 'artist' is the pinnacle. The fact that most people have little or no idea who contemporary artists are or what they do contributes to the mystery.

This may help to explain otherwise puzzling contradictions. In trying to explain why it would be a bad thing if our troublesome human species became extinct, 'art and culture' is often evoked as one of the few self-evident justifications for our existence. On the other hand, most people find artists rather useless. A recent *Sunday Times* poll challenged a thousand people to name the most essential and least essential professions. The five most important turned out to be doctor/nurses, cleaners, garbage collectors, vendors, and deliverymen. But the real headline news was that the least essential turned out to be artists (telemarketers came in second).

There's no reason to believe this reflects hostility towards artists, or a feeling that they would be better off collecting trash. Rather, it seems to reflect a feeling that 'artist' isn't really a job at all. Or perhaps that it shouldn't be. It should be a reward. It's as if artists are seen as people who insist that they, and they alone, already exist under communism. Put this way, it's not unreasonable to then ask: why should nurses and cleaners have to pay for artists? It's almost as if the contingencies of race, class, and national origin sort us all out into different historical epochs, wherein some of us toil away under capitalism, some are reduced to feudal retainers, others are even living under de facto slavery, while a chosen few are allowed to inhabit a communist future that might otherwise (perhaps) never come into being. Should we be surprised that nurses and cleaners look slightly annoyed as the artists wave from their communist starcruiser floating past?

Obviously, most artists don't see it that way. Some feel they are still blazing the trail to a utopian future in good avant-garde fashion. But by now it's just as obvious a pretext as someone telling himself his cushy job in brand management isn't really hurting anyone, since he doesn't actually do much more than spend his time updating his Facebook profile and playing computer games. Maybe this is true of his particular job, but then we also have to admit that the existence of brand management is clearly a disaster. The same goes for the art world, since to enter this communist tomorrow you need resources (and the art world's attempts to foreground more women, people of colour, and so forth does little to undercut this); to be recognised as an artist, you need to support a certain structure of recognition. To take an obvious example, you need to show in museums, those temples of our civilisation, where reigning symbolic codes are formed, assigned, and archived.

After all, the same is true of cops. 'All cops are bastards' is a structural statement; there have always been individual cops who have been well-meaning, even idealistic (Gene Roddenberry, the creator of Star Trek, spent seven years working for the LAPD). The point is that their personal character or even personal politics are mostly irrelevant; they are operating within an institutional structure that does inestimable harm, and whether any particular benevolent act does more harm by validating that structure, or good by mitigating it, is a secondary consideration.

Museums Are to the Art World as Prisons Are to the Police State
If we were to tell the history of the art world in the same way we just told the (very abbreviated) history of police, we would have to begin with the role of the museum. Of course, the French Revolution began with the storming of the Bastille (a prison), but it culminated in the seizure of the Louvre Palace, which became the first national museum, effectively initiating a new secular conception of the sacred to break the remaining power of the Church.

Of course, museums do not produce art; neither do they distribute art. They sacralise it. It's important to underline the connection between property and the sacred. To sacralise is to exclude; it's to set something apart from the world, whether because it is sacred to an individual ('private property') or sacred to something more abstract ('art' 'God', 'humanity', 'the nation'). Any revolutionary regime changes existing forms of property, and the organisation or reorganisation of museums plays a crucial role in this process, since the forms of property that exist within museums represent the summit of the pyramid. They are the ultimate wealth that police protect, and that the industrious poor can only see on weekends.

Virtually all museums today operate in a way that produces and maintains hierarchy. By archiving, cataloguing, and reorganising the museum's space, they draw a line between 'museum' quality and 'non-museum' quality objects. But there is no ultimate contradiction between commoditised art and art considered inalienable and not to be sold, because they are simply two variations of the sacred as radical exclusion. The fact that these objects are surrounded by armed security and high-tech surveillance simply serves to underline to any visitor how much their own creative acts (songs, jokes, hobbies, diary entries, care for loved ones, and precious mementos) are of no particular significance, and therefore, that visitor will need to return to their non-museum life and continue to carry on their 'non-inessential' job producing and maintaining the structure of relations that makes museums possible. Much like the cathedrals they were meant to replace, museums are there to teach one one's place.

In the same way, the art world – as the apparatus for the production of objects, performances, or ideas that might someday merit being sacralised –

is based on the artificial creation of scarcity. In the way that police guarantee material poverty, the existence of the art world – in its current form – could be said to guarantee spiritual poverty. What, then, would an abolitionist project directed at the art world actually look like? [...]

Nika Dubrovsky and David Graeber, extracts from 'Another Art World, Part 1: Art Communism and Artificial Scarcity', *e-flux journal*, no. 102, (September, 2019); 'Another Art World, Part 3: Policing and Symbolic Order', *e-flux journal*, no. 113, (November, 2020).

Not An Alternative
Institutional Liberation//2016

[...] Refusal and subtraction have been disastrous as left political tactics. They have surrendered the power aggregated in institutions to capital and the state. The tactics of institutional liberation treat institutions as tools, weapons and bases of political struggle. They take on and over the institution's radical premise: the collectivity and futurity that underpins any collection. The force that comes from organisation, collectivity and institutionality, the symbolic power that accompanies and exceeds aggregation, becomes a resource for the left, a resource that enables us to combine and scale.

Many can be more powerful than few, but only when they are organised. Contemporary capitalism relies on dispersing us into powerlessness. It celebrates individualism and uniqueness, as if one person alone could bring down the fossil fuel economy. This individualist dream entraps us in the nightmare of accelerating inequality and ecological devastation. Institutional liberation claims the power of collectivity, the necessity of alliance, combination, and commonality in struggle. This is why we see today the appearance and reappearance of common images, names, and tactics.

The various projects we see combining into an emergent movement for institutional liberation do not value critique qua critique. They turn the institution against itself, side with its better nature, and force others to take a side. They look for allies, 'double agents' already working within the institution, reinforce them, and in so doing activate the power that is already there. Institutional liberation is not reformist. It does not simply expose our complicities with state and capital. It directs its critical perspective in the service of a broader political movement, treating institutions as forms to be seized and connected into a counterpower infrastructure.

The liberation of institutions will not result from any singular procedure. It depends on sustained pressure, a commitment to long term struggle. More than a critique of institutions – because, face it, at this point the inequality, oppression, and violence of the capitalist state is not a mystery to be solved but a system to be abolished – institutional liberation affirms the productive and creative dimension of collective struggle. Our actions are not simply against. They are for: for emancipation, equality, collectivity, and the commons.

Institutional liberation is not a messianic event. It is the building of counterpower infrastructure. Once they take the side of the common, institutions liberate themselves from capitalist interests endeavouring to control and exploit them. So institutional liberation isn't about making institutions better, more inclusive, more participatory. It's about establishing politicised base camps from which ever more coordinated, elaborate, and effective campaigns against the capitalist state in all its racist, exploitative, extractivist and colonising dimensions can be carried out. This takeover will not happen overnight. But it is happening now at an international scale, accumulating force and momentum with every repetition of a common name and image, every iteration of associated acts: red lines, red squares, arrayed tents, money drops, blockades, occupations.

Not An Alternative, excerpts from 'Institutional Liberation', *e-flux journal*, no. 77 (November, 2016).

WE WILL NOT
ALLOW OUR
SONGS TO
BECOME ASHES,
OR OUR DREAMS
TO BECOME
NIGHTMARES.

Gulf Labour, 'Petition', 2011

Gulf Labor
Petition//2011

To: Richard Armstrong, Director
Solomon R. Guggenheim Foundation
1071 Fifth Avenue
New York, NY 10128

We, the undersigned, are writing to demand that the Guggenheim Foundation obtain contractual guarantees that will protect the rights of workers employed in the construction and maintenance of its new branch museum in Abu Dhabi.

Human rights violations are currently occurring on Saadiyat Island, the location of the new museum. In two extensive reports on the UAE, Human Rights Watch has documented a cycle of abuse that leaves migrant workers deeply indebted, poorly paid, and unable to defend their rights or even quit their jobs. The UAE authorities responsible for developing the island have failed to tackle the root causes of abuse: unlawful recruiting fees, broken promises of wages, and a sponsorship system that gives employers virtually unlimited power over workers.

These violations, which threaten to sully the Guggenheim's reputation, present a serious, moral challenge to those who may be asked to work with the museum. No one should be asked to exhibit or perform in a building that has been constructed and maintained on the backs of exploited employees.

Human Rights Watch has expressed its concerns to the Foundation on several occasions, but so far, adequate steps have not been taken to ensure that workers' rights will be respected at the Abu Dhabi site. While the Guggenheim is franchising its name and is not a direct party to the subcontractors who employ the migrant labour, it can and should assert responsibility for the well-being of these workers.

We urge the Foundation and its partners in Abu Dhabi, TDIC (The Abu Dhabi Tourism and Development Investment Company), to conform rigorously to the various commitments made in the TDIC's Employment Practices Policy (EPP), dated June 2010, the TDIC/Guggenheim Statement of Shared Values, published September 22, 2010, and the recent EPP update, amended 11 March, 2011. Moreover, we urge the Foundation and TDIC to address the current absence of independent monitoring of employers' compliance with international human rights and labour laws, and the lack of an effective enforcement mechanism.

A monitor must be empowered to make random visits to work sites and maintain a relationship independent of employer influence. It must also determine if its findings conform to international laws and standards, and it must issue public reports on these findings. In the absence of these conditions, violations will persist and continue to be underreported. Similarly, without explicit mechanisms for enforcing the terms of the contract or clearly enumerated remedies in the event of breaches, all efforts to protect workers will be in vain. TDIC has announced that it will appoint a 'reputable independent monitor' in May. We demand that the appointment be made as soon as possible and that the conditions outlined above be observed as part of the monitor's mandate.

Our cooperation with the Guggenheim in Abu Dhabi (and, for many of us, at other Guggenheim locations) will not be forthcoming if the Foundation fails to take steps to safeguard the rights of the workers who will be employed in the museum's operations on Saadiyat Island. Human Rights Watch will determine if and when adequate monitoring measures have been established and effectively implemented.

List of Original Signatories:

Hamra Abbas • Jumana Abboud • Adel Abidin • Dennis Adams • Shaina Anand • Yazid Anani • Ayreen Anastas • Doug Ashford • Haig Avazian • Kader Attia • Maja Bejevic • Khaled Barakeh • Yto Barrada • Regine Basha • Shumon Basar • Ute Meta Bauer • Anthea Behm • Zarina Bhimji • Doris Bittar • Monica Bonvicini • Gregg Bordowitz • Tania Bruguera • François Bucher • Ringo Bunoan • Janet Cardiff • Mario Caro • Mel Chin • Wendy Coburn • Pablo de Ocampo • T.J. Demos • Corinne Diserens • Willie Doherty • Sam Durant • Jimmie Durham • Koken Ergun • Annika Eriksson • Harun Farocki • Azin Feizabadi • Andrea Fraser • Rene Gabri • Emeren Garcia • Andrea Geyer • Leyla Gediz • Miriam Ghani • Paul Graham • Avery Gordon • Catherine Grout • Hans Haacke • Joana Hadjithomas • Khaled Hafez • Tone Hansen • Shuruq Harb • Mona Hatoum • Sharon Hayes • Sandi Hilal • Christine Hill • Thomas Hirschhorn • Vlatka Horvat • Alfredo Jaar • Emily Jacir • Luis Jacob • Jakob Jakobsen • Khalil Joriege • Lamia Joriege • Amar Kanwar • Thomas Keenan • Deborah Kelly • Laleh Khorramian • Marty Kirchner • Silvia Kolbowski • Barbara Kruger • Carin Kuoni • Laura Kurgan • Eileen Legaspi-Ramirez • Lani Maestro • Chus Martines • Angela Melitopoulos • John Menick • George Bures Miller • Naeem Mohaiemen • Rabih Mroué • Matt Mullican • Huma Mulji • Antonio Muntadas • Monica Narula • Issam Nassar • Yamini Nayar • Diana Nemiroff • Molly Nesbit • Shirin Neshat • Angel Nevarez • Tom Nicholson •

Marcel Odenbach • Gina Osterloh • Trevor Paglen • Cornelia Parker • Christine Peters • Nataša Petrešin-Bachelez • Alessandro Petti • Paul Pfeiffer • Walid Raad • Mike Rakowitz • Annie Ratti • Martha Rosler • Andrew Ross • Natascha Sadr Haghighian • Anjalika Sagar • Jayce Salloum • Rasha Salti • Katya Sander • Lina Saneh • Allan Sekula • Vivian Selbo • Stephen Sheehi • Adania Shibli • Gregory Sholette • Suha Shoman • Reid Shier • Katharina Sieverding • Ashok Sukumaran • Julia Scher • Carl Skelton • Hito Steyerl • Beth Stryker • Paolo W. Tamburella • Rirkrit Tiravanija • Valerie Tevere • Oraib Toukan • Tristan Tremeau • Gediminas Urbonas • Murtaza Vali • Fabienne Verstraeten • Krzysztof Wodiczko • Akram Zaatari • Florian Zeyfang

Gulf Labor, 'Petition', (16 March, 2011) (https://gulflabour.org/sign-the-petition/).

Liberate Tate
Disobedience as Performance//2012

Concerns

[...] Liberate Tate is an art activist collective exploring the role of creative intervention in social change. Our aim is to free art from the grips of the oil industry, primarily by focusing on Tate, the UK's leading art museum, and its sponsorship deal with BP [British Petroleum]. We believe that Tate is supporting BP more than BP is supporting Tate, and that through sponsorship Tate sustains BP's 'social licence to operate'.

'Social licence to operate' is a phrase coined by the PR industry.[1] It describes what BP needs in order to continue its operations irrespective of their impacts: by constructing a guise of social acceptability. No matter what harm it causes elsewhere, the company is able, through public perception, to retain its position within the UK cultural and political economy. The licence to operate is generated by building relationships with political elites, a process aided by some of the UK's largest cultural institutions, including Tate and the British Museum. Our perspective on this draws on our key collaborator Platform's concept of the Carbon Web, which they describe as the network of organisations that uphold international oil corporations such as Shell and BP.[2] The relationship with Tate is essential to BP's operations around the world; extracting social capital in London is a key part of extracting oil elsewhere, from Azerbaijan to Angola to Alberta (Canada).

History

Liberate Tate formed in 2010 when Tate tried to censor a workshop on art and activism for fear it might take issue with Tate's sponsors. Not only did Tate fail to inhibit discussion, Liberate Tate was catalysed by this act and the group formed in direct resistance to the attempt to limit freedom of expression.

We have been making performance work ever since. Sometimes durational, often reflective and full of melancholia, our work grieves the loss of life, habitats, forests, water sources, cultures and communities caused by this global corporation. At other times our performance work is short, shocking and full of anger, incensed by the irresponsible corporate destruction perpetrated by oil giants such as BP. Each performance intervention we create is different, but our ambition remains the same: for Tate to drop the sponsorship it currently accepts from BP. In our work we speak directly to Tate staff, directors, board, visitors, members and beyond to a wider public. We are 'a mild irritant, [that] is in danger of becoming an open wound', constantly reminding Tate of the social-ecological catastrophe brought upon us by their sponsor.[3] […]

Influences

Liberate Tate's interventions bring together performance art with civil disobedience and direct action techniques that have been used in political movements around the globe. Our initial choice to work in the medium of performance was born out of our desire to take oil back into the gallery and return the impacts of BP to the institution it supports, creating unsanctioned artworks in the gallery spaces that we select. Mostly silent, we speak through action and images; using our bodies in singularly direct and powerful ways to communicate our message.

We wear black clothing in our performances. Black clothing is formal, a kind of everyday clothing that most people own and which can bring performers together as a uniform group. Black veils theatricalise our performances, while covering our faces and making us anonymous. The veils operate in a similar way to the gorilla masks worn by The Guerrilla Girls, foregrounding the group over the individual performer, and enabling diverse bodies to function as a cohesive narrative whole. Through anonymity we not only represent ourselves as individuals but also represent others who are concerned with human rights violations, social and ecological injustice and the devastating effects of climate change.

Artworks

Collectively devised and carried out, performances sometimes have only a few days for preparation, while other works are developed more slowly over longer periods. Timing is important. *Licence to Spill* was planned as an intervention at the Tate Summer Party in June 2010. As BP was spilling oil in the Gulf of Mexico, Tate and BP were celebrating the twentieth anniversary of BP sponsorship. Our performance revealed the incongruity of the celebration while a disaster was playing out in the Gulf of Mexico.[4]

In *Licence to Spill*, Liberate Tate created a series of spills, both inside and outside Tate Britain. Wearing black, our faces veiled, we carried vats of molasses with BP's notorious sunflower logo stuck to them. Stealth-like, we appeared as if from nowhere spilling hundreds of gallons of molasses on the front steps of Tate Britain before disappearing as quickly as we arrived. Our message was a wake-up call and a shocking reminder of the devastating effects of BP's spill in the Gulf. Meanwhile, two members of Liberate Tate going by the names of Bobbi and Toni (named after Bob Dudley and Tony Hayward, respectively the current CEO of BP and his predecessor) had their own mini-spill inside the gallery. The two women had carried 10 litres of molasses into the Tate under the bouffant of their floral dresses to be inconveniently released amid champagne and canapés in the middle of the party itself. [...]

Questions

How our bodies operate in the gallery space is a subject of continued reflection and analysis. An organiser-participant in Platform's project *Shake! Young Voices in Arts, Media, Race, Power* made the challenge that Liberate Tate performances were possible because of the privileged position of white people and white bodies. Although not all Liberate Tate performers are white, a group with a majority of white performers might be less likely to be stopped by security staff than a group with a majority of black performers. This analysis raises questions around the position of social power and privilege to enter a gallery as a visitor, to feel democratic ownership over that institution and to seek to protest in a form that is relevant to the wider process of making an artist-led challenge to the public body that is Tate.

A further question that arises in consideration of how Liberate Tate relates to the space of the gallery or museum is around political strategy. To what extent does the site imbue the performances with the cultural value infused in the sacred space of the gallery, and thus give the work power? We believe it is precisely the sacredness and neutrality of the gallery that we are able concurrently to utilise and disrupt.

We also question to what extent Tate is able to absorb our work into its cultural political persona. Freedom of information requests to Tate have made us aware of the institutional response to our work, which has caused much discussion at board level. Tate has kept a detailed record of all our performances and their coverage in international media, doing the work of documenting our practice for us and also revealing the concerns held around the impact we have. In this way, Tate demonstrates that even if it is able to absorb the challenge to a certain degree, Liberate Tate has a significant impact.

Collaborations

Our artworks are not limited to performance. In 2011 we collaborated with oil industry campaign and arts group Platform on two projects: a limited-edition publication *Not if But When: Culture beyond oil* (available for purchase from Live Art Development Agency or to read online) and *Tate à Tate*, an audio tour from Tate Britain to Tate Modern via the Tate Boat. At www.tateatate.org, the public is invited to download, for free, audio files made by sound artists and to take the tour in the Tate themselves, creating a permanent installation inside the galleries that Tate cannot remove. *Tate à Tate* will continue to complicate the presence of BP in the gallery, as Liberate Tate performances have done previously, asking participants to enact a gently rebellious role by taking part in the tour and listening to stories of the impacts of the oil company. […]

Change

The choice for Tate, and all the other arts institutions that continue to accept BP's sponsorship, is how soon they will choose to get ahead of the game and commence the separation of oil from culture. Cultures are by definition constantly changing phenomena, bending to new influences and ideas. Curating works for a gallery or museum places and dates artworks in a process that fixes culture within a historically specific moment. Such selection processes hold sway over our understanding of an era, moment or culture, and questions have often been raised over whose telling of history reigns and whose voices have been left out.

As conservationists, cultural institutions may risk becoming conservative forces within cultures, preserving the status quo as they see it. Tate's relationship with BP nurtures the company's position within the British political establishment and runs in sharp contrast to the persona Tate creates for itself as the politically savvy home of creative enlightenment. The role and function of art and museums in culture is shown up as politically significant; there are no observers or neutral vessels for histories but, rather, powerful institutions whose decisions shape the future.

Through a shared history of performance, civil disobedience and direct action, Liberate Tate are dedicated to challenging and shaming Tate into dropping its big oil sponsor. This is disobedience as performance, the refusal of Tate's on-going sanctioning of oil giant BP.

1   Fishburn Hedges, 'IPRA Golden World Award win for Fishburn Hedges and Shell', (2 November, 2009) (www.fishburn-hedges.co.uk/news/articles/ipra-golden-world-award-winfishburn-hedges-and-shell)

2   Platform is a campaign group focused on the oil industry. The group brings together environmentalists, artists, human-rights campaigners, educationists and community activists to create innovative projects driven by the need for social and environmental justice. For more information visit www. platformlondon.org.

3   'Reverend Billy leads exorcism of BP's "evil spirit" from Tate Modern', *The Guardian*, (19 July 2011) (www.guardian.co.uk/environment/blog/2011/jul/19/reverend-billy-tate-modern-bp).

4   The BP Deepwater Horizon disaster involved an oil leak from the wellhead from 20 April until 15 July 2010. The ensuing spill and toxic clean-up has seen harmful impacts to human health and high rates of sea life fatalities that are ongoing.

Liberate Tate, extracts from 'Disobedience as Performance', *Performance Research*, vol. 17, no. 4 (2012) 135–138, 140.

Jessica A. Cooley and Ann M. Fox
Crip Curation as Care: *A Manifesto//2022*

Ours is a conversational manifesto of care that perhaps raises more questions than answers. […] What is crip curation and what's care got to do with it? How do we define care in an age where it can mean anything and everything? Finally, how might readers of this essay translate our practices into their own creative practice? […]

This manifesto and guide centres care for collaboration, care for intersectional analysis and care for access as central to our curatorial practice. This is a manifesto, a guide and a call for artists and curators to create crip art, performances and exhibitions that do not hinge on disability as a singular, siloed issue. This is a call to care for the ways in which identity is always already informed by all of who we are and how those intersecting identities become trapped under the weight of those oppressive values constructed by ableist, white supremacist, hetero-patriarchal society. This is our call to find liberation by insisting on our own indisposability.

'Indisposable: Structures of Support after the ADA' [Americans with Disabilities Act] emerged from a time of precarity.[1] While the original, prepandemic exhibition was conceived to reflect on the thirtieth anniversary of the ADA, COVID-19 made one fact all too visible: the pervasive ableism of society means that the scaffolding offered by the ADA is insufficient for too many people. Ours was a revelation of both what imperilled the support needed by so many and the structures put into place by crip communities to create survival, resistance and joy. But the pandemic realities meant that the execution and display of 'Indisposable' needed to be reimagined. Instead of curating a traditional in-person gallery exhibition, we reoriented our process toward a slow, multiphase (or multichapter) rollout. What emerged was a series of eight video commissions that we unveiled from mid 2020 through early 2022 (as of this writing, we anticipate an in-person gallery show in the fall of 2022). But what also emerged were care structures that established a significant way to think about curating disability art – in and beyond the finite space of the gallery. […]

Our emphasis on collaboration as a critical point of care began long before 'Indisposable'. Academic and art world hierarchies push for solo work: the monograph, the single-authored article, the solo exhibition, the dissertation. However, everyone who has embarked on any of these 'solo' endeavours knows there is nothing solitary about them. Our creative and intellectual work are inherently collaborative; most of us understand that our best ideas are created in that middle space between ourselves and others. Formally, we recognise this collaboration through the conventions of citations or an acknowledgment section. Yet while disability studies scholars have pointed to the mythology of individuality by prioritising collaboration, sharing agency and celebrating interdependence and mutual aid, the privileging of the solo performance within the academy – and, indeed, society itself – remains deeply ingrained. […]

Interdependent thinking is the crip alchemy that makes our collaborations a critical form of care and that makes our care work a critical crip practice. Interdependent thinking creates the care structures we use to care for each other and that make it possible to upend stale hierarchies that privilege the mythological solitary act and instead truly celebrate the collaborative project. […]

As we look back to our earliest projects, we understand that we often centred a white gaze – both in terms of artist and viewer – within the context of our curatorial work. But with 'Indisposable', the cultural moment and the precepts of disability justice demanded that our antiracist work be proactive rather than reactive.[2] With disability justice activists calling for cross-disability and cross-movement solidarity and with systemic ableism oppressing all those who do not 'fit' within the hegemony of normalcy, we knew prioritising intersectionality within our work was a powerful form of care. With the primacy of the disability justice movement, the murders of Breonna Taylor and George Floyd, the denial of resources and protection to those most imperilled by the pandemic and the global outcry for social justice in the summer of 2020, the ways we had already determined that our work needed realignment took on new urgency.

We are both white women who identify with disability in varying ways. We know that our whiteness has disproportionately provided us with educational, social and professional opportunities that so many BIPOC [Black, Indigenous and people of colour] people have been denied. We know, too, that the insidious nature of white supremacy is alive and that it is our responsibility to dismantle it as forcefully as possible. For this reason, we believe that a crip curatorial practice is one that centres people marginalised in multiple ways and that we as curators function as the support structures that build the platform for other voices, dreams, artworks and embodiments to shine. While our curatorial vision brought a group of artists together, as we discussed, we asked those artists to bring in other artists and thinkers they wanted to be in dialogue with. What we define as 'collaboration as care' is also a purposeful sharing of our platform so that others can amplify the work of their communities. This also allows us to be decentred as organising forces. We can instead act as the support structures ourselves, helping artists realise their visions, instead of artists helping us to realise our vision. In other words, this is not 'our' exhibition, but theirs. We aim not to speak for others but, rather, to create spaces to magnify their experiences so they will be known.

Intersectionality likewise becomes a critical point of care for dismantling a white supremacist assumption that disability somehow exists outside of race, gender, sexuality, class and nationality, or that ableism only has an impact on disabled people.[3] [...]

Over the course of meeting with artists about the quotidian details of 'Indisposable', the same somewhat startling thing kept happening: artists kept thanking us for the flexibility and support we had shown them; in some cases, they noted that this was one of the first times they had had such a chance to work expansively, as they were supported both by us and the gallery team. We were gratified but also somewhat distressed: no one should have to be grateful for being cared for.

Similarly, the performance of disability is not simply through the finished, highly polished representations with which an audience comes into contact. Rather, it begins from the moment the work is conceptualised, between collaborators at every step of the process and within the context of the complex ways in which disability is figured within the work and those beyond it in which disability justice has yet to be accomplished. We offer this manifesto and guide so that readers might reflect on how each of these principles of care is present – or has yet to be fully borne out – in their own artistic practice.

[W]e call on institutions to recognise the ways in which they might deconstruct conventional ways of valorising and making work, particularly those that prioritise individual virtuosity in a way that replicates bodily normalcy. We ask: have you made space for the crip time in which artists might need to make work? How can you support artists as they bring others into collaboration? In what ways have you incorporated disability into your diversity, inclusion and equity work? Have you thought expansively about access in a way that is proactive rather than reactive? Or, in other words, have you imagined what diverse artists and audiences might need rather than what you are required to do by law?

We call on practitioners to imagine how they can build access into the very act of creating work. Can you incorporate audio descriptions or captioning, for example, in ways that add to the aesthetic project of the work? If you are collaborating, how can you build space into your process for crip time, or a measured pace that allows for the variability and particularities of your partners? How can you repudiate the hackneyed trope of using disability as a metaphor for the damaging impacts of racism, sexism, homophobia and transphobia? Instead, how can you come to understand the ways in which ableism both snarls into and helps create those disabling forces? How can you understand that intersectionality in theatre is hollow without a rigorous understanding of disability as an identity, culture, aesthetic value and generative force?

We call on audiences to not mistake sentiment for care, particularly a kind of pathos that reinscribes contempt for the disabled body. Instead, we call on them to actively wrestle with what disability studies and theatre studies scholar Carrie Sandahl has called 'representational conundrums', neither dismissing complex, even contradictory portrayals of disability outright nor settling for sentimental, stereotypical, or sensationalistic images of disability that do damaging work in the world.[4]

Finally, we call on readers, regardless of field, to consider how they can curate care along the lines we describe above by transforming their discipline and creative practice. Only then can we create real, system-changing inclusivity. It is messy, difficult, contradictory work; it is also among the most humane that we, in our imperfect, impermanent, impeccable bodies, can undertake.

1   [Editors' note '"Indisposable: Structures of Support After the Americans with Disabilities Act" is a multi-module exhibition that will roll out as a series of online events over the course of 2020-2021 and will culminate in a physical exhibition to open in the gallery at a later date.' Ford Foundation Gallery, New York, 17 September 2020 – 24 February 2022, https://www.fordfoundation.org/about/ the-ford-foundation-center-for-social-justice/ford-foundation-gallery/exhibitions/indisposable-structures-of-support-after-the-ada/]

2   [Footnote 6 in source] We encourage readers to look at Leah Lakshmi Piepzna-Samarasinha's *Care Work: Dreaming Disability Justice* (Vancouver, BC: Arsenal Pulp, 2018), which traces the history of disability justice and activism in the work of disabled QTBIPOC communities.

3   [7] Talila A. Lewis, 'January 2021 Working Definition of Ableism', *Talila A. Lewis* (blog), 1 January, 2021, www.talilalewis.com/blog/january-2021-working-definition-of-ableism.

4   [18] Carrie Sandahl, 'Using Our Words: Exploring Representational Conundrums in Disability Drama and Performance', *Journal of Literary and Cultural Disability Studies*, vol. 12, no. 2 (2018): 129–44.

Jessica A. Cooley and Ann M. Fox, 'Crip Curation as Care: *A Manifesto*', *Theater*, vol. 52 no. 2 (2022), 5, 6, 8, 9, 11, 16–17.

Nan Goldin
I Survived the Opioid Crisis//2018

Leave the world a better place than when you entered it.
– Arthur Sackler to his children

I survived the opioid crisis. I narrowly escaped. I went from the darkness and ran full speed into The World. I was isolated, but I realised I wasn't alone. When I got out of treatment I became absorbed in reports of addicts dropping dead from my drug, OxyContin.

I learned that the Sackler family, whose name I knew from museums and galleries, were responsible for the epidemic. This family formulated, marketed, and distributed OxyContin. I decided to make the private public by calling them to task. My first action is to publish personal photographs from my own history. [...]

My life revolved entirely around getting and using Oxy. Counting and recounting, crushing and snorting was my full-time job. I rarely left the house. It was as if I was Locked-In. All work, all friendships, all news took place on my bed. When I ran out of money for Oxy I copped dope. I ended up snorting fentanyl and I overdosed.

[...] I was one of the fortunate ones who could afford an excellent hospital, which isn't an option for most people. [...] My endowment was cut off and I regret the money I wasted. I regret the time I lost, which is irretrievable. Now I find the world hard to navigate, but I have a sharpened clarity and a sense of purpose.

I believe I owe it to those affected by this epidemic to make the personal political. [...] I knew of no political movements on the ground like ACT UP. Most of my community was lost to AIDS. I can't stand by and watch another generation disappear.

The Sacklers made their fortune promoting addiction. OxyContin is one of the most addictive painkillers in the history of pharmacology. They advertised and distributed their medication knowing all the dangers. The Sackler family and their private company, Purdue Pharma, built their empire with the lives of hundreds of thousands. The bodies are piling up. In 2015, in the US alone, more than thirty-three thousand people died from opioid overdoses, half of them from prescription opioids; 80% of those who use heroin or buy fentanyl on the black market began with an opioid prescription. These statistics are growing exponentially.

I've started a group, PAIN (Prescription Addiction Intervention Now), to hold them accountable. To get their ear we will target their philanthropy. They have washed their blood money through the halls of museums and universities around the world. We demand that the Sacklers and Purdue Pharma use their fortune to fund addiction treatment and education. There is no time to waste.

We want to leave the world a better place than when we entered it.

Nan Goldin, extracts from *Artforum*, vol. 56, no. 5, (January 2018), 128.

MTL Collective
From Institutional Critique to Institutional Liberation? A Decolonial Perspective on the Crises of Contemporary Art//2018

The past decade has witnessed an intensive politicisation of the art system, one that goes beyond the ubiquity of political themes in the work of high-profile artists, critics and exhibitions. Rather, this politicisation has involved a far-reaching crisis of legitimacy for major cultural institutions among the publics they claim to serve, as well as the cultural workers upon whose labour they depend. Museums, galleries, biennials, nonprofits, universities, and public agencies have been targeted with protests, demands, and grievances concerning the ways they are governed, the agents who govern them, and the ends to which they are governed. Numerous initiatives have subjected art institutions to public scrutiny, highlighting their complicity in perpetuating, concealing, or neglecting unjust and oppressive practices within and beyond the institution in question. Frequently making creative use of the architectural spaces and brand identities of such institutions, these activities have involved a variety of tactics, including petitions, pickets, strikes, boycotts, disruptions, occupations, shutdowns, callouts, hacks and infiltrations. These initiatives have used the visibility of institutional platforms to hold institutional actors accountable to their own stated commitments, and have often involved demands for new commitments altogether.

Art institutions have thus been subjected to a double movement. On the one hand, their authority as gatekeepers and sanctifiers of cultural value has been significantly bypassed by cultural workers acting on their own accord without requiring institutional permission. On the other hand, the prestige of the institutions in question has proven valuable for leveraging visibility, publicity, and pressure relative to political aims and movements that straddle the artistic and extra-artistic realms. Even as their authority as guardians of artistic legitimacy decreases, such institutions find themselves subjected to increasing demands for accountability in light of, and often exceeding, their declared values and missions. This 'infrastructural turn' by artists and activists is informed, in part, by a classic principle of what is known in art history as institutional critique: that art is not autonomous from the economic systems, ideological apparatuses, and institutional spaces within which it is produced, presented, and circulated. [...]

What could 'institutional liberation' mean? Would it mean liberating the institutions in which many of us work – and if so, how, by whom, from what, and to what end? Would such a liberation itself be somehow institutional or institutionalised, or is it a liberation *from* institutions as they exist in favor of a new practice of anti- or counter-institutionality? As Samuel Weber once noted, 'institution' shares an etymological root with 'state', 'statue', and 'establishment'.[1] It implies the setting up, arranging, and consolidating of people and power in a fixed place with an enduring temporality. Although it may begin with an active event of positing, an institution typically tends toward the reproduction of a reified status quo through symbolic rites of authority, divisions of labour, distributions of resources, and normative forms of conduct. Liberation, on the other hand, implies the de-establishing of fixed arrangements of power. it suggests the unleashing of people and places from enduring structures and fixed boundaries that are unjust or oppressive.

It is precisely this tension between institution and liberation that makes 'institutional liberation' worth interrogating beyond the brisk manifesto published last year by the group Not an Alternative calling for 'liberating institutions from capitalism'. The group writes, 'The various projects we see combining into an emergent movement for institutional liberation do not value critique *qua* critique. They turn the institution against itself, side with its better nature, and force others to take a side.' This 'movement', as Not an Alternative calls it, sees 'institutions as forms to be seized and connected into a counterpower infrastructure. They activate the power that is already there. More than a critique of institutions, institutional liberation affirms the productive and creative dimension of collective struggle. Our actions are not simply against. They are for: for emancipation, equality, collectivity and the commons.' Not an Alternative understands institutional liberation as the 'commandeering' of institutions, and in the process they polemically define themselves *against* what they see as two other positions. First, they call the building of new institutions 'naive', and they resist 'overburdening ourselves with the overwhelming task of inventing entirely new political and social forms.' Second, they posit institutional liberation as a definitive surpassing of institutional critique, a plural and contested art-historical tradition that they reduce to a circular ethos of 'critique for its own sake'.

It is true that the imaginative charge of 'institutional liberation' comes from its alteration of the familiar term 'institutional critique.' it intimates a transition from a familiar operation to a newly dynamic one, and certainly the principle of liberation is an urgent one to reactivate in the present moment. However, any such reactivation must grapple with the legacies that the term brings with it, including those of national liberation, black liberation and women's liberation in the 1960s and beyond. These overlap with the resurgent discourse of decolonisation, especially in the case of Black Lives Matter, which has insisted, according to Keeanga-Yamahtta Taylor, that black liberation is the precondition of liberation for everyone.[2] Without such a perspective, appeals to 'liberation' are liable to result in the reproduction of settler futurity, entrenching rather than unsettling institutions that have been targeted for action in recent years. [...]

Whatever the ultimate fate of calls for decolonisation commissions at major museums, we are at a moment when the principles of institutional critique are being pushed to a breaking point and opening onto something radically new and radically old at the same time. As Decolonize This Place put it in a pamphlet distributed at the [Brooklyn M]useum, 'An innovative show here, a progressive event there . . . are not enough. The institution must be questioned in its very foundations, starting with the fact that it sits on occupied Lenape land and contains thousands of objects collected through imperial plunder. Why not make these starting points for a discussion, rather than the question of who curates what department? What would it mean to liberate this institution from the structures of oppression that are built into it from the beginning?'[3]

1   [Footnote 39 in source]. On the aporetic structure of institution as both positing event and enduring arrangement, status, and state, see Samuel Weber, *Institution and Interpretation* (Stanford: Stanford University Press, 1981).

2   [Footnote 44]. Keeanga-Yamahtta Taylor, *From #BlackLivesMatter to Black Liberation* (Chicago: Haymarket Books, 2016).

3   [Footnote 90 in original] *Decolonize This Museum* a pamphlet distributed at the Brooklyn Museum, 29 April, 2018.

MTL Collective, extracts from 'From Institutional Critique to Institutional Liberation? A Decolonial Perspective on the Crises of Contemporary Art', *October*, no. 165, (Summer, 2018) 193, 205–207, 227.

Françoise Vergès
Let's Decolonise the Arts! A Long, Difficult and Passionate Struggle//2020

Some years ago, just out of curiosity, I visited the Marine Museum in Paris. Its purpose was to 'make the sea and the adventure of the sea interesting to all French people' by telling 'stories of the sea and seafarers, both ancient and contemporary'. I saw the impressive and splendid figures from ships' prows (generally allegorical female figures), magnificent models of ships from all over the world, and evocations of the great French maritime companies and ocean liners from the early 20th century. Nowhere was mention made of the role of ships in the treatment of blacks in the history of colonialism, capitalism, or imperialism. One left the museum in total ignorance of the links between progress in shipping and navigation and the slave trade, between maritime history and colonial conquests, between maritime history and colonial wars. Nonetheless, without boats there would have been no slaves and thus no tobacco, no sugar, no coffee, no cotton. One finds the same phenomenon in other museums, where nothing is totally false, but the story is riddled with blind spots, resulting in mutilated history and cartography. This is how things get erased. Erasure works not by being noisy, but through a pedagogical discourse that tells a story which is not inexact per se, but which rests on certain things being covered up and thus forever forgotten. One does not see any more because has taught oneself not to. To decolonise means to learn to see again – transversally and intersectionally. To de-naturalise the world where we evolve, created by human beings and by economic and political regimes. It means to learn to place all the pieces into the puzzle and to study relationships, circulation and intermingling. Thus new cartographies emerge, questioning the European narrative and making evident regionalisations and globalisations that do not exclusively obey the logic of North and South. It means understanding the world around us while neglecting neither the large nor the small, exploring the faults, the conflicts, the betrayals, and all the forms of complicity, solidarity, solitude and resistance. To decolonise means to inevitably begin with colonial exploitation and slavery, both constructed like something as natural as the day and the night. The church, the state, culture and law justify them. The slaves were the first to tear the curtain of lies, of this naturalisation which served to cover the rejection of their humanity, the most brutal exploitation, the greediness of the European powers and the fiction of universal human rights. The slaves accepted any risk when they wanted to make known their humanity.

Their strategies for surviving, living, and creating preserved, reinterpreted, invented and transmitted art and culture which expresses resistance to being wiped out. Anti-slavery and anti-colonial revolts and insurrections proposed to decolonise images and narratives, putting forth new histories and new forms of expression. Maroon communities – places of liberty in the midst of a world which denied that the principal of liberty was universal – created languages, art, and culture. [...] All fields – art, literature, poetry, photography, dance, cinema, music, theatre, museums, design, crafts – were re-explored, and a vast library of works, images, sounds, and archives was built up all around the world. This history and this vast archive of the decolonisation of the arts are accessible, and knowledge of this corpus is indispensable. Not everything begins with Europe or revolves around Europe. The processes of wiping history out have not ceased, however. They find new forms or use old ones like censorship, lack of funding, denial of visas, theft and appropriation. For many years now, without changing their structure, organisations have gradually taken it upon themselves to organise conferences, debates, and expositions about the notions of diversity, hybridisation, creolisation and decolonisation. Should we not be happy about this? Some progress has certainly been made. Africa has become a fascinating new space for 'discovery' in the art market, which means that some artists have seen their works acquire value and have been able to obtain substantial financial support. But to admit that these things have happened does not mean, as far as we are concerned, that there has been a decolonisation. On one hand, there is often a bowdlerisation of the works, emptying some of all radical content; on the other hand, the structural organisation of those institutions and the economy of production and distribution of works have not been transformed.

Decolonisation of the arts starts with understanding the phenomena and processes being used to wipe people out. As we have mentioned, these can often advance in disguise. Decolonisation demands a huge effort, because one must first unlearn in order to learn. One must develop a form of curiosity which always asks how, who, why and for whom. Education teaches us not to be curious but to disconnect ourselves from our world and the world in general. This reminds me of an anecdote told by Rabindranath Tagore, where he tells the following story: at a school, one of his young friends climbs a tree during recess and goes out on a branch to read. The schoolmaster scolds him and makes him come down from the tree, but this same schoolmaster encourages him to learn botany. Tagore remarks that the schoolmaster 'believed in impersonal knowledge of the tree, but not personal experience'.[1] Who does not remember how, as a child, one was asked to stop asking so many questions because they tire out the adults? This is even more pronounced for non-white children. Everything that constitutes their world is excluded from being represented, not a single street name carries the name of a hero or heroine that looks like them, and the world as presented to them conveys a deformed image of their origins, religions, memories and history. And it is not only their curiosity which is presented as a defect; no, they must be integrated 'without having chosen, into Western values'.[2] It is thus only at a great cost that lost traditions can be recovered. 'To make oneself autonomous and construct for oneself a niche of resistance, then, as best one can, to connect it with other niches of resistance.… and to free oneself from the yoke of the great national, official narrative so as to re-appropriate and write one's own narrative, to exhibit one's own vision of things',[3] says Kader Attia. One must unlearn in order to learn anew, to re-educate all of one's senses – sight, hearing, touch, smell – which have been damaged, but one must also re-learn silence. […]

Racialised persons are, meanwhile, asked every day to explain that racism and discrimination exist. They are required to prove at all times their allegiance to an abstract discourse about rights – abstract because it takes no account of differences of class or gender, inherited from a patriarchal, misogynist and colonial history – while their right to equality is regularly denied. Their freedom to create is denied. At DLA (Décoloniser les arts, in English 'Let's decolonise the arts'), we defend this right.[4] But we are also in favour of liberation, that collective action which concerns not just individual creativity but the liberation of creative energy in society at large. While inequality between men and women in the artistic world is now recognised, and official declarations are made in order to reduce it, there is still indifference or condescension towards the accumulation of inequality when the victims are racialised persons. This phenomenon is described by the notion of intersectionality, which insists on the fact that people can simultaneously suffer multiple forms of domination or discrimination. At an institutional level, greater value is put on male/female equality precisely because it permits one to ignore demands for equality based on an intersectional analysis, and white bourgeois feminism – a feminism which refuses to analyse the links between the formation of the 'white woman' (innocent, beautiful, maternal, gentle, needing protection) and the invention of the 'black woman' (Jezebel, lacking femininity or a maternal instinct, indifferent to pain) – thus becomes a formidable ally in the fight against equality for all. […]

In France, society has learned to neglect the personal experiences of racialised women, to demean them, to reject them by putting them into categories such as 'victimisation' or 'communitarianism', often without taking the time to see or read the works inspired by those experiences. These experiences are – a priori – illegitimate, denied validity, or assigned validity in pre-determined narratives such as victim, terrorist, drug-dealer. Let us not kid ourselves: if these works ever find a place in our artistic world, it is thanks to individual favours or because of mass protests. One undeniable fact is that for years now, racialised artists have been taking control of their personal experiences, digging in archives, rediscovering forgotten narratives and figures, exhuming memories, returning to objects the story of their wanderings and transformations. For these artists, this is not about responding face to face to Europe and its obsession with the west, but rather about liberating themselves from Europe's grip and exploring other image banks, timeframes, spaces and spiritualities. It is not about writing history, strictly speaking, but about inspiring, revising, or reinterpreting narratives, images, sounds; it is about investigation [of] the victim but also the executioner. [...]

At DLA, we do not separate the decolonisation of the arts from the scandal of unpunished crimes by the police, from the criminalisation of solidarity, from laws that weaken social protections, or from injustice, inequality, racism and environmental destruction in France and across the seas. Since racism is indistinguishable in our eyes from sexism, misogyny, or ethno-nationalism (in fact they act in symbiosis), as militant anti-racists we are particularly concerned now. We observe the ravages of neoliberalism and individualism, which lead to attacks on movements involving decolonisers, women, trans people, queers, or indigenous people. We are aware that it is necessary to distinguish between worry and malignant attacks, between a request for explanation and an accusation.

[...] Accept that you are troubled and disturbed, and take the time to reflect. We are the first to admit that nothing is ever final as far as knowledge is concerned, and that we too can have prejudices, that decolonisation is nothing to be acquired, but rather a process. To our allies and friends, we say that we know how difficult it is to construct a collective path, but nevertheless it is important to construct it. Listening, attention, and solidarity are fundamental, just as is working on our disagreements so that common ground can be found anew each time. Let's decolonise the arts will be a painful and tedious movement, joyful and happy, because it affects me as an individual and also the collective. You do not have to be afraid of our anger, because just as Audre Lorde wrote,

> to exteriorise anger, to transform it into action in the service of our vision and our future, is an act of clarification that liberates us and gives us strength, because it is via this painful process of putting theory into practice that we find out who are our allies, with whom we may have serious differences, and who are our real enemies.

To the others, who defend at all cost their little square of terrain, all the while pretending to defend the universal: your universalism hides your particularism, the transformation of your singular culture into universal culture, and your refusal to analyse the current forms of racism. Your antiracism is moral, which means that it does not seek to detect how racism has insinuated itself into the practices and institutions of the state. When shown concrete examples of racism, you counter with grand abstract principles. [...] Those of you who refuse a true humanism which cannot but take the form of a concrete, political antiracism, know that our determination is real. It is not your job to tell us which past is important, and your injunctions are but minor obstacles to our producing more complex and jarring narratives. Our adversaries should get used to our cumbersome presence, joyful and bothersome. And to ourselves, to those of us involved in decolonising the arts, know that our path will be long, difficult, and exciting. We will have to decolonise our own spirits, overcome divisions inside ourselves, interrogate our own prejudices, and to make a constant effort to go beyond the fragmentation caused the patriarchy, sexism, racism and capitalism. But let us feel free to choose the forms that we want to develop. Let us refuse to be assigned to certain topics, problems, or forms. Let us deliver ourselves from the politics of respectability, from the desire to be accepted at the cost of compromises that would destroy us. In a world made of obstacles, uncertainty, and arbitrariness, let us develop a methodological and epistemological critique of colonialism and let us decolonise the arts in order to overcome the dehumanisation which has always been at the heart of the modernity which now has hegemony. We do not prohibit ourselves from tackling any topic, and we will have our opinion on the restitution of stolen African objects in French museums just like we will have an opinion on the intellectual cannibalism that absorbs our ideas and content while preserving the dominance of certain institutions and their programming. We engage ourselves to combat racism, because as we see it the decolonisation of the arts contributes to the decolonisation of French society. We believe that our voices, our narrations, our stories, our forms of expression and representation deserve to be recognised as well as to be criticised. We will not be fooled by token attempts at recuperation. We reserve the right to disturb and overturn, as well as the right to make mistakes. [...]

1   [Footnote 8 in source] Rabindranath Tagore, 'My school', lecture delivered in America and published in *Personality*, London (1933). Available at: http://schoolofeducators.com/wp-content/ uploads/2011/12/03.pdf [link updated].

2   [9] Maryse Condé, *La vie sans fards*, (Paris: JC Lattès, 2012) 101–102.

3   [10] Available at: http://www.lofficiel.com/ art/kader-attia-macval-palais-de-tokyo.

4   [Editors' note Décoloniser les arts (DLA) is a cultural association created in 2015.

Francoise Vergès, 'Let's Decolonise the Arts! A Long, Difficult and Passionate Struggle', trans. Adriano Hundhausen, *Artalk Revue*, Winter (2020) 1–9.

Achille Mbembe
African Contemporary Art: Negotiating the Terms of Recognition, In Conversation with Vivian Paulissen//2009

Vivian Paulissen [...]   What is your experience with private and/or public funding?

Achille Mbembe When I was the Executive Director of the Council for the Development of Social Science Research in Africa (CODESRIA), I had to engage with public donors in France, Japan, the Netherlands, with UN agencies, and more importantly with Nordic countries. A lot depended on the intellectual and political calibre of the individuals and policy-makers I had to face. The most creative encounters were with those who believed that Africa's fate was inextricably bound to the fate of the rest of the world. They agreed that to intervene creatively and efficiently in the Continent required a demanding, prolonged, meticulous exploration, analysis and critical thinking. With such interlocutors, we usually came up with inventive, cutting-edge programs.

Otherwise, the overall scene was quite depressing. One constantly had to deal with cynical bureaucrats, people who profoundly hated the Continent but had become addicted to it and to some of its perverse pleasures. They could hardly let go the addiction. They interacted with the Continent the way some people do when they are trapped in an abusive relationship. They did not believe in the catechism of 'development' they were nevertheless preaching. Going through some of those meetings was like visiting for the first time an *asile de fous* – people who had failed everywhere else and who could never make an honourable career elsewhere except in Africa. They needed not think because for them, Africa is simple. In fact, there were very hostile to anything that looked like an idea.

Even more unsettling was the implicit assumption, especially in Nordic countries, that Africans could only speak as 'victims'. In the course of expressing their solidarity with Africa's past struggles, many Nordic countries have unfortunately encouraged the sense of victimhood some Africans intellectuals and politicians have been peddling all along – which they try to mask under the guise of anti-imperialism. They have tolerated mediocrity and encouraged lethal forms of populism and lumpen-radicalism to prevail in African social science discourse for instance. They poured – and I guess they still do – millions of dollars each year into sustaining hugely bureaucratic and inefficient organisations that should have been closed long ago and where countless middlemen enjoy diplomatic immunity and earn salaries equivalent to those in UN structures. This form of benevolent paternalism, of course, has deep unconscious racist undertones. [...] But I hear that in these neoliberal times, even these progressive and somewhat avant-garde organisations are under tremendous pressure. Indeed, they have to justify their activities to bureaucrats and tax payers. Some have adopted a strong anti-intellectual bias and bought into romanticised but uncritical and debilitating forms of grassroots activism and populism. To a certain extent, they are all forced to pay lip service to the fiction of 'development'.

This is all the more regrettable because what we need right now is a critical cultural politics that confronts the rhetoric of 'development' and reveals the deeply reactionary nature of this project. [...]

Most Western donor agencies have a simplistic notion of what 'Africa' is and of what 'development' is. They are unaware of – or pretend to be ignorant about – what recent critique of 'development' (as an ideology and as a practice) has revealed. They want to operate as if such a critique had not been done.

The fact of the matter is that on the ground, where many of us live and work, the paradigm of 'development' is functionally dead. This we can see in ordinary people's everyday experiences and actions. But the 'development machine' itself is still alive. It keeps disbursing fat salaries to experts, middlemen and consultants, good per diems to its native clients, auxiliaries and courtiers, and it keeps delivering untold tragedies to the poor and their communities. The 'development machine' keeps running on. But it is running on empty. This emptiness is what worries me because it is productive of tremendous waste.

The other fact, nowadays, is that most Western donors consider Africa to be a zone of emergency, a fertile ground for humanitarian interventions. The future is not part of their theory of Africa – in the very rare cases such a theory exists. For them, Africa is not only a land of empiricism. It is also the land of a never-ending present, a serial accumulation of 'instants' that never achieve the density and weight of human, historical time. It is the place where today and 'now' matters more than 'tomorrow', let alone the distant time of the future and of hope.

This is what the temporality of 'development' has done to us – the fragmentation of time, the erasure of history-as-future and our mental incarceration in a never ending form of presentism and nihilism. This nihilistic impulse worries me too.

Under these circumstances, it seems to me, the function of art in Africa is precisely to free us from the shackles of development both as an ideology and as a practice. It is to subsume and transcend the instant; to open the vast horizons of the not-yet – what my friend Arjun Appadurai calls 'the capacity to aspire'.

Such too is, at least to me, the function of cultural criticism and of critical theory because art cannot thrive in the absence of a strong critical theory tradition.

In circumstances under which millions of poor people indeed struggle to make it from today to tomorrow, the work of theory and the work of art and the work of culture is to pave the way for a qualitative practice of the imagination – a practice without which we will have no name, no face and no voice in history. This struggle to write our name in history and to inscribe our voice and our face in a structure of time that is future-oriented – for me this is a profoundly human struggle. It is a struggle of a different kind than the struggle for mere livelihood, physical sustenance and biological reproduction.

I hate the idea that African life is simple bare life – the life of an empty stomach and a sick and naked body waiting to be fed, clothed, healed or housed. It is a conception that is structurally embedded in 'development' ideology and practice. This kind of base materialism radically goes against people's own daily experience with the immaterial world of the spirit, especially as this spirit manifests itself under conditions of extreme precariousness and radical uncertainty. This kind of metaphysical and ontological violence has long been a fundamental aspect of the fiction of development the West seeks to impose on those it has colonised. We must oppose it and resist such surreptitious forms of dehumanisation. [...]

Achille Mbembe, extracts from 'Interview with Vivian Paulissen, African Contemporary Art: Negotiating the Terms of Recognition', *Africultures* (1 December, 2009), (https://africultures.com/african-contemporary-art-negotiating-the-termsof-recognition-9030/).

Nora Al-Badri and Jan Nikolai Nelles
In Conversation with Aude Launay//2018

While the European press shouts itself hoarse about the French President's recent declarations to do with his promise to return African art objects to their countries of origin, as if this symbolic gesture might act like a meaningful political withdrawal, one question – among many others – is in fact raised: what constitutes the memory of history? Is it the carefully lit ancient artefact on view in its protective display case that is best able to transmit this memory, or, alternatively, is it an on-site experience in the field? And what if this question were no longer really relevant, both with regard to the wholesale destruction of cultural assets and historic sites perpetrated in recent years by ISIS and to the imminent destruction in the wake of the climatic disorder we are all aware of? And what if objects became fluid, re-appropriated their own history, and became capable of sharing it with everyone? This last question lies at the heart of the work of Nora Al-Badri and Jan Nikolai Nelles. In 2015, when they disclosed the data required for the 3D printing of the bust of Nefertiti held captive in the Neues Museum in Berlin, they opened the way to a whole series of remixes, but also, and above all, to a new way of seeing the work of art based on the yardstick of the common good: accessible to as many people as possible and no longer hidden away behind the thick stone walls of a frozen history. [...]

Aude Launay Your latest bodies of works, *The Other Nefertiti* and *Not a Single Bone*, challenge the traditional concept of the museum as a closed place for conservation and a safe space for the remnants of extinct civilisations, and attempt to conceive an alternative framework to it that I would summarise as such: the museum as an open data centre. Can you expand on your views on this issue?

Nora Al-Badri and Jan Nikolai Nelles Our main observation is that we prefer to see the museum as a process, as a place of constant negotiation. Yet, the reality in the Global North is rather different: we are dealing with 19th century museums, imperial museums, which are conservative and slow-moving public structures. Those institutions cling to their role as gatekeepers towards cultural objects and their data. It seems that the change of conditions induced by the digital technologies has rather increased an institutional angst of losing control and relevance. Thus, these institutions are committing a so-called copyfraud, because most of their collections are actually cultural commons and in the public domain. And we truly believe that this institutional angst is unjustified: if they change their mindset, the museums won't be empty (which seems to be their biggest concern, to be forced to restitute everything).

We truly believe in museums as having a potential to be relevant spaces for a society and for its discursive space, but in order to achieve that, museums have to move on and reinvent themselves. And change doesn't necessarily come from the inside: the artists and the public actively need to reclaim the museums as a public space – and especially the public ones. This is one part of the negotiation mentioned earlier. Another part is, for example, dealing with the questionable practice of collecting, the sharing of finds, which was totally accepted in the past, but not anymore…

In our practice, we look at technology to try to figure out its emancipatory potential, other canons and the perspective of 'the digital' as a social practice and cultural technique.

So far, all around the Western world, we see plenty of small scale 'digitisation experiments' coming and going where museums really don't risk much. Actually, on the contrary, when we talk about digital repatriation for example (where objects are returned as data), it becomes clear that those actions actually reaffirm the present framework. Because the objects stay put. In addition, just a few of these experiments articulate or deal with the biases of technology, which we regard as crucial. The majority of people and museum experts are not aware that technology is not neutral but socially shaped! Yet, especially when we look at colonial contexts, this needs to be addressed, reflected and articulated.

Museums as we know them are dead, they host dead objects for a passive, consuming, entertained audience. This museum practice seems fairly anachronistic to us. But how to invoke change? For Frantz Fanon, struggles for decolonisation are first and foremost about self-ownership. They are struggles to repossess, to take back, if necessary by force that which is ours unconditionally and, as such, belongs to us. The museum could potentially be an open data centre, but we would prefer a re-centring of the data, following Ngũgĩ Wa Thiong'o,[1] which happens automatically if data is open and in the public domain.

We would go as far as to imagine possible non-anthropocentric futures as an experience to contribute to a collective imaginary through what we call 'data as technoheritage'. Thus, what we try to promote in our practice is the creation of new and meaningful platforms of (re)presentation of the subaltern instead of an echo of the 'conventional' – borrowing the term from Ciraj Rassool – yet vicious museum and to admit that objects in museums are deeply political objects.

Launay And what if museums restituted every item to the places where they come from, could the flows of people travelling to see them be substantial enough to modify some geopolitical situations or would it solely reinforce the idea of nation-states which seems to be no longer the paradigm under which it is relevant to think our globalised-post-digital turn world? Isn't this whole idea of 'restitution' here again the fruit of a Western-centric viewpoint, such as exemplifies the anecdote narrated by the historian Adrienne Mayor in one of the interviews that you chose to present in your latest exhibition in Berlin,[2] when she tells about some Native Americans refusing the repatriation of fossils that was offered to them by a museum as they wouldn't understand them, not knowing which powers their ancestors imbued them with?

Al-Badri and Nelles In our pieces, we don't talk explicitly about restitution because this idea is based on the concept of nation-states, as you mention it, although there is also restitution within countries such as the USA or New Zealand with their indigenous groups. More important than the actual flow of objects (and their data) or of actual people travelling to see the objects is the recognition of ownership and everything that comes with it, such as the decision if objects should be exhibited at all, should be digitised, how they are named and labelled, etc. That is something that should be at the centre of this debate, but the power ownership (not location) is exactly what institutions and researchers are not willing to give up because they believe they can take better care (e.g. in terms of preservation and exhibition) of the objects. Thus one could say it is also somehow a symbolic struggle. And this is also where the structural racism begins or continues to exist – situation that proves colonial continuity.

Launay By disclosing the data of the Nefertiti bust (which, as you often mention, existed for already eight years in the Neues Museum) and calling for its appropriation, as well as by putting a neural network at work on images of dinosaur bones to produce new ones, you bring back to light the fact that history is largely based on speculation, especially for scarcely documented periods, just as much as natural sciences are. So the part of fiction and interpretation which has always been embedded in the discovery and then in the display of historical objects finds here its reflection in the way a neural network processes information to produce its output. This way, you raise this highly metaphysical question: is an object more defined by its data or by the embodiment of it?

Al-Badri and Nelles How an AI Imagines a Dinosaur comes from our interest in the results of a machine looking at the evolution of a long gone species versus the usual human-centred gaze. The machine produced thousands of possible evolutions, which is in stark contrast to the (human) natural science approach seeking for the 'truth' and facts.

As for the appropriation of the data of Nefertiti, it becomes clear that the data embodies different information than the actual object – you can see more layers, you can explore the object from the inside – and thus changes the perception of the object itself. The relevant aspect in this piece is the emancipatory potential of data, which by being intangible and diasporic itself dissolves the questions of ownership.

Launay You even look further into the emancipation of objects with your *NefertitiBot*. Here again, it's easy to draw a parallel between the criticisms directed at museums and at AI programs regarding the Western biases they generally embed. Can you tell me more about this new iteration of the Nefertiti project?

Al-Badri and Nelles NefertitiBot is a chatbot which seeks to take over the power of interpretational sovereignty from administrative and curatorial museum structures. A bot through which material objects of other cultures in museums of the Global North will start speaking for themselves, shaking off the violent and ugly colonial patina by deconstructing the fiction inherent in institutional narratives and challenging the politics of representation.

With the development of the Nefertiti AI and avatar, we aim at asking questions about the state of humanity and at discussing the agency of inanimate things, challenging the human-centric way of seeing the world. When machines will not only be super-intelligent but more human towards the world and all its inhabitants, it will be a transition from a failing human towards a new species. At the very moment this future arrives, their avatars will already be present, their voices will sound familiar to us. […]

1   [Footnote 2 in source] Ngũgĩ Wa Thiong'o, *Moving the Centre: the Struggle for Cultural Freedoms*, (London: James Currey, 1993).

2   [4] 'Not a Single Bone' at Nome, Berlin, 9 September to 11 November, 2017.

Nora Al-Badri and Jan Nikolai Nelles, extracts from 'Interview with Aude Launay', *ZéroDeux*, no. 84, (Winter 2017/2018).

The strike

will be an exercise in radical imagination informed by dreams of beloved community and histories of militant resistance

OCCUPY AESTHETICS

Lina Khatib
Image Politics in the Middle East//2013

Politics in the Middle East is now *seen*. The image has claimed a central place in the processes through which political dynamics are communicated and experienced in the region. States, non-state actors, oppositional groups and ordinary people are engaging in political struggle through the image, and the media, especially the visual media, are not only mediators in this context, they are also political actors, deliberately using images to exert political influence. The image is at the heart of political struggle, which has become an endless process of images battling, reversing, erasing and replacing other images. [...] Political struggle, then, is an inherently visually productive process. It is also itself visual to a large degree: It is a struggle over presence, over visibility. For authoritarian states, political power means having control over visual production and consumption. For political oppositions, democratic representation merges with visual representation. For people, possessing political agency means possessing the ability to be seen, not only heard.

The visual manifests itself in several forms in processes of political struggle: as a mass media image; a digital image; a cartoon; a piece of art; a physical space or object; an ephemeral image on paper, a wall or another physical medium; and as a human embodiment. It can also be a conceptual image, a visual idea. All those forms merge and interact, so that it is no longer possible to look at an image in any one form in isolation from the others. [...]

The Visual Rush of the Arab Spring
[...] The January 25 Revolution is an example of this dynamic, producing new forms of visual expression in public space in Egypt: community art, graffiti and murals. Those forms of visual expression can be understood as a way through which citizens have reclaimed public space, and have freely expressed sentiments that before could only be expressed obliquely or fleetingly.

The revolution saw the rise of the Revolution Artists Union, a collection of artists who roped off an area of Tahrir Square to be used as an open-air space where people could create and display art. This democratisation of art space challenges the traditional authority of the curator and opens up artistic practice as an equal right. In this space, pencil drawings on notebook paper hung side by side next to watercolours, satire was displayed next to documentary and the secular and the religious shared equal representational potential. On one day, the simple line drawing of a snake above the slogan 'No to ideology' was displayed just beneath that of a Muslim sheikh and a Christian priest holding their hands together and raising them as the former carried a Quran and the latter a cross. [Joel F.] Handler argues that '[l]anguage is an act of power, a form of social action. "To acquire and exercise a language is to engage in the most profound of political acts . . .". It is through democratic dialogue that the powerless become engaged. Democratic dialogue denies closure.'[1] The image is also an act of power. The visual art created and displayed in Tahrir Square acted as a means of democratic dialogue as well as of the expression of power: Everybody could participate, everybody was empowered. The square became a new creative space that dissolved the barrier between the viewer and the art and united diverse communities in art.

Another art form produced by the revolution that also created 'a more immediate, direct form of engagement with the viewer' is graffiti.[2] Before the 25 January Revolution, graffiti and murals were virtually non-existent in the public areas of Cairo, as control over visual representation in public space was firmly in the hands of the government, which had erased any such visual expressions almost as soon as they appeared. The revolution saw a rapid rise in graffiti that ranged from the simple to the elaborate. At first, simple stencils depicting light bulbs appeared, symbolising the shining light of the revolution, as were those of a clenched fist, the symbol of the 6 April movement (in turn symbolising the power of the people). The stencils quickly grew into the more elaborate form of murals.

The graffiti artist Banksy says that graffiti is a form of 'answering back.' During and after the 25 January Revolution, graffiti and murals were another way for Egyptian citizens to answer back through reclaiming space as well as sending messages countering those of the regime. It is this duality of roles that Neil Jarman highlights in his argument that murals should be understood as both art and artifacts. Murals are art because of their symbolic content, and they are artifacts because of their fixed location in space.[3]

[...] Graffiti and murals as works of art performed two key roles. First, they were used to reclaim the notion of agency for citizens. Stencils of revolution martyrs started appearing early on, depicting the faces of martyrs along with slogans such as 'Glory to the martyr' and 'Glory to freedom'. Martyr depictions then evolved into large murals giving an individual identity to each martyr through depicting his or her image along with the person's name, age and profession. The murals later evolved beyond individualisation. A graffiti image that has been repeated in Cairo shows the stencil of a young man, with an aura around his head, along with the slogan 'I am the people'. The use of the aura is an appropriation of its visual use by authoritarian rulers in the Middle East like Khomeini, Qaddafi and Hafez al-Assad, which relies on its connotation with eternity. In doing so, the image is presenting a new discourse for the Egyptian nation, based on the endurance of the people, not the leader, which in turn responds to Mubarak's appropriation of pharaonic symbols associated with eternity.

Second, they were used to reclaim the notion of community-based nationalism. This was shown through depicting the people as diverse while erasing the previous chaperoning of this diversity by a ruler or a ruling party (as in the Mubarak and NDP billboards of Egyptians from different walks of life [...]). An example is a drawing on a wall that showed a woman and a child standing under the protective arm of a man carrying the Egyptian flag. Community-based nationalism was also connected with alluding to the people's defiance of the regime. One graffito had two panels: on the right panel, the drawing of a traditional Egyptian man wearing a turban on his head, an indication of being a peasant, is shown above the word 'subjected'. The man is outlined in black and white, but is shown to be crying red blood. The panel on the left simply depicts the word 'No' written in red, signalling the defiance of the disenfranchised individual as written in blood.

Graffiti and murals as artifacts performed a political role that went beyond symbolism. This role was produced by their interaction with the space in which they existed. As Jarman argues, location infuses murals with meaning, while murals' presence in a location also lends meaning to that particular site. In other words, murals interact with their social and physical environment, and can act as boundary markers or identity definers. Murals were used as such boundary markers in Tahrir Square. [...] The revolution saw a manifestation of this after the government's violent attacks on protesters resulted in the death of several martyrs. The northern entrance of Tahrir Square became an experiential space. It displayed a large painting with the words 'Martyrs' Square' on it, in acknowledgement of the role of those who died during the revolution. The government was no longer the power in charge of directing the perception of public space; the people possessed this power.

Graffiti and murals also became a relatively established way of sending direct political messages, with a number of artist activists becoming known as they continued to create murals to comment on political developments after Mubarak's departure. Ganzeer is one such artist whose work is an attempt at overt intervention in the political trajectory in post-Mubarak Egypt. In particular, he achieved acclaim for his work against the rule of Egypt's Supreme Council of the Armed Forces (SCAF) in the summer of 2011, as the SCAF sought to retain its political power. Ganzeer created a graffito showing the pillars of the SCAF who were still in power, under the slogan 'The people want the fall of those loved by the regime'. Another huge graffito he created showed, on the right, a traditional bread vendor, peddling the streets on his bike, standing off against a tank on the left, a sharp departure from the rosy picture of the military that protesters in Tahrir Square had painted through handing the Egyptian army roses and proclaiming that the army and the people were one; with the SCAF holding on to power, the military was no longer seen as being on the side of the people. The importance of location for Ganzeer's work is that it appears in the same space where protesters succeeded in overthrowing Mubarak, thereby calling attention to the need for sustaining protest in this space. [...]

Graffiti was also used as a call to action. An example is the embrace of the floating image of Khaled Said. On the first anniversary of the killing of Khaled Said, in June 2011, stencils of his face were painted all over the exterior of the Ministry of Interior after protesters stormed the military line surrounding the building. The stencils bore the writing: 'Will my blood become water, in your eyes? Will you forget my clothes that are stained with blood?' The floating image of Khaled Said, then, became both a 'physical' political weapon (due to its being painted on the wall of the Ministry of Interior) as well as a symbolic one.

This stencil of Khaled Said was part of a larger set of anti-SCAF graffiti. Some of this graffiti was created to announce planned anti-SCAF demonstrations. [...] Just before the protest itself, a large mural of a man throwing a gas canister back in the direction of where the police line had been during the revolution appeared in Tahrir Square, not only referencing real photographs of protesters who had engaged in this act during the revolution, but also symbolically indicating the people's refusal of a police state, as well as warning of a repeat of revolutionary tactics. Another graffito sending this message had the words 'The People' under the computer icon for 'Standby', indicating that the people are in a state of temporary stillness, prepared to reactivate popular protest at any moment. This use of a computer world reference is part of a larger symbiosis between graffiti and computer iconography, which includes social media. Street art frequently referenced the role that the social media played in the revolution, extending the media's experience into physical space. An example is a mural in Zamalek that showed the head of a screaming young man, his neck emerging from a broken chain as three arms extend to him carrying a mobile phone, the Facebook logo and a crescent. The power of the digital media was thus presented as a pillar on par with religious belief, and the interaction between street art, physical space and the social media lent all those communication tropes further power.

In addition to graffiti's derivation of power from interacting with physical space and referencing the social media, this art form has also claimed further clout from its remediation through the mass media and the social media. The online graffiti map of Cairo set up by Ganzeer, Cairo Street Art, is an example of this process put into practice. The map documents new pieces of graffiti and murals appearing in Cairo through adding their images to their precise locations on a Google map. Clicking on the map's place markers opens windows showing photos of the street art pieces with the dates the photos were taken. The photo entries are updated if a piece of art is defaced. 'The lovers of the regime' mural by Ganzeer, for example, had such a fate, which led to the uploading of a new photo of it after its defacing that was added to the original entry, with an explanation by Ganzeer that the new photo showed the mural 'after it was defaced by stupid people'. In this way, the social media reverse the ephemeral nature of graffiti and murals, granting them a 'permanent' place in (virtual) space. In doing so, not only do they extend the experience of those murals, they also create a digital visual archive of the revolution and its aftermath. The notable political role of graffiti and murals is that they transform space from mundane to politicised, extending the message of resistance into an everyday experience. Moreover, different graffiti spaces 'interact with one another . . . and with the social actors inhabiting these spaces in creating complex networks of meaning, or "semiotic aggregates".'[4] The remediation of street art aids both processes: It allows this art form to send its messages to a wider public while also addressing the local one, and it in turn extends the scope of semiotic aggregates, as remediation is itself based on the virtual presence of images that become part of people's networks of meaning.

[...] The Arab Spring was a process very firmly grounded in geographical location; the fact that the domino effect of uprisings was limited to the *Arab world* is important. It illustrates the rise of a *regional* (not global) civil society that is also grounded in time and space. But the notion of 'regional' itself has been challenged by the Arab Spring, for it now not only refers to those present in a neighbouring location, but also those in the diaspora in physically far-away places. The Syrian and Libyan diasporas, for example, played a key role in circulating factual information, photographs and videos as well as lobbying during the Arab Spring. This expanded notion of the 'regional' entails an expansion and redefinition of political space: It is at once local, national, regional and global. Tahrir Square becomes the symbolic locus of this much wider, fluid 'terrain of resistance.'[5] Its boundaries go beyond its physical dimensions. The uprisings' domino effect is an indicator of the presence of an Arab imagined community and unity of cause that is nevertheless *rooted in particular national contexts.*[6] The images may be similar but the underlying challenges in each country are articulated and dealt with according to the particularities of each location. [...]

Protest is where hard politics and soft politics meet, and images are one way in which this conjuncture is articulated. The image is one of 'the often unstated processes by which struggles over power occur in everyday life.'[7] Paying attention to the image, then, is one way of acknowledging the importance of the diffused politics of the everyday.

1   [Footnotes 114 in source] Joel F. Handler, 'Postmodernism, Protest, and the New Social Movements', *Law and Society Review,* vol. 26 no. 4, (2002) 697–732, 723.

2   [115] Adam Jaworski and Crispin Thurlow, 'Introducing semiotic landscapes,' in *Semiotic Landscapes: Language, Image, Space* (London and New York: Bloomsbury, 2010) 9.

3   [117] Neil Jarman, 'Painting Landscapes: The Place of Murals in the Symbolic Construction of Urban Space', in *National Symbols, Fractured Identities: Contesting the National Narrative,* ed. Michael Geisler (Lebanon, NH: Middlebury College Press) 172–92.

4   [120] 'Introducing semiotic landscapes', op. cit., 8.

5   [113] Paul Routledge, *Terrains of Resistance: Nonviolent Social Movements and the Contestation of Place in India* (Westport, CT: Praeger, 1993).

6   [134] Benedict Anderson, *Imagined Communities: Reflections on the Origin and Spread of Nationalism* (London: Verso, 1983).

7   [145] Sonia Livingstone, extracts from 'On the Mediation of Everything', *Journal of Communication* 59 (2009) 9.

Lina Khatib, extracts from *Image Politics in the Middle East: The Role of the Visual in Political Struggle* (London: I.B. Tauris, 2013) 1, 153–159, 161–162, 165.

Judith Butler
Bodies in Alliance and the Politics of the Street//2012

[...] Many of the massive demonstrations and modes of resistance we have seen in the last months not only produce a space of appearance, they seize upon an already established space permeated by existing power, seeking to sever the relations between the public space, the public square, and the existing regime. So the limits of the political are exposed and the link between the theatre of legitimacy and public space is severed; that theatre is no longer unproblematically housed in public space, since public space now occurs in the midst of another action, one that displaces the power that claims legitimacy precisely by taking over the field of its effects. Simply put, the bodies on the street redeploy the space of appearance in order to contest and negate the existing forms of political legitimacy – and just as they sometimes fill or take over public space, the material history of those structures also works on them, becoming part of their very action, remaking a history in the midst of its most concrete and sedimented artifices. These are subjugated and empowered actors who seek to wrest legitimacy from an existing state apparatus that depends upon the regulation of the public space of appearance for its theatrical self-constitution. In wresting that power, new space is created, a new 'between' of bodies, as it were, that lays claim to existing space through the action of a new alliance, and those bodies are seized and animated by those existing spaces in the very acts by which they reclaim and resignify their meanings.

Such a struggle intervenes in the spatial organisation of power, which includes the allocation and restriction of spatial locations in which and by which any population may appear, which implies a spatial regulation of when and how the 'popular will' may appear. This view of the spatial restriction and allocation of who may appear – in effect, of who may become a subject of appearance – suggests an operation of power that works through both foreclosure and differential allocation.

What, then, does it mean to appear within contemporary politics, and can we consider this question at all without some recourse to the media? If we consider what it is to appear, it follows that we appear to someone and that our appearance has to be registered by the senses, not only our own, but someone else's. If we appear, we must be seen, which means that our bodies must be viewed and their vocalised sounds must be heard: the body must enter the visual and audible field. [...]

Of course, there are many reasons to be suspicious of idealised moments, but there are also reasons to be wary of any analysis that is fully guarded against idealisation. There are two aspects of the revolutionary demonstrations in Tahrir Square that I would like to underscore. The first has to do with the way a certain sociability was established within the square, a division of labour that broke down gender difference, that involved rotating who would speak and who would clean the areas where people slept and ate, developing a work schedule for everyone to maintain the environment and to clean the toilets. In short, what some would call 'horizontal relations' among the protestors formed easily and methodically, alliances struggling to embody equality, which included an equal division of labour between the sexes – these became part of the very resistance to the Mubarak regime and its entrenched hierarchies, including the extraordinary differentials of wealth between the military and corporate sponsors of the regime and the working people. So the social form of the resistance began to incorporate principles of equality that governed not only how and when people spoke and acted for the media and against the regime, but how people cared for their various quarters within the square, the beds on the pavement, the makeshift medical stations and bathrooms, the places where people ate, and the places where people were exposed to violence from the outside. We are not just talking about heroic actions that took enormous physical strength and the exercise of compelling political rhetoric. Sometimes the simple act of sleeping there, on the square, was the most eloquent political statement – and even must count as an action. These actions were all political in the simple sense that they were breaking down a conventional distinction between public and private in order to establish new relations of equality; in this sense, they were incorporating into the very social form of resistance the principles they were struggling to realise in broader political forms.

Second, when up against violent attack or extreme threats, many people chanted the word *silmiyya*, which comes from the root verb *salima*, which means 'to be safe and sound', 'unharmed', 'unimpaired', 'intact', and 'secure'; but also 'to be unobjectionable', 'blameless', 'faultless'; and yet also 'to be certain', 'established', 'clearly proven'.[1] The term comes from the noun *silm*, which means 'peace', but also, interchangeably and significantly, 'the religion of Islam'. One variant of the term is *hubb as-silm*, which is Arabic for 'pacifism'. Most usually, the chanting of *silmiyya* comes across as a gentle exhortation: 'peaceful, peaceful'. Although the revolution was for the most part nonviolent, it was not necessarily led by a principled opposition to violence. Rather, the collective chant was a way of encouraging people to resist the mimetic pull of military aggression – and the aggression of the gangs – by keeping in mind the larger goal: radical democratic change. To be swept into a violent exchange of the moment was to lose the patience needed to realise the revolution. What interests me here is the chant, the way in which language worked not to incite an action, but to restrain one: a restraint in the name of an emerging community of equals whose primary way of doing politics would not be violence.

Finally, then, to what extent was the revolution a media revolution, and how does that make actual bodies less central to the political action? How important was the locatedness of bodies to the events that took place? Of course, Tahrir Square is a place, and we can locate it quite precisely on the map of Cairo. At the same time, we find questions posed throughout the media: will the Palestinians. have their Tahrir Square? Where is the Tahrir Square in India? That's to name but a few. So it is located, and it is transposable; indeed, it seemed to be transposable from the start, though never completely. And of course, we cannot think the transposability of those bodies in the square without the media. In some ways, the media images from Tunisia prepared the way for the media events in Tahrir, then those that followed in Yemen, Bahrain, Syria, and Libya, all of which took different trajectories and take them still. As you know, many of the public demonstrations of these last months have not been against military dictatorships or tyrannical regimes. They have also been against the monopoly capitalism, neoliberalism and the suppression of political rights, and in the name of those who are abandoned by neoliberal reforms that seek to dismantle forms of social democracy and socialism, that eradicate jobs, expose populations to poverty, and undermine the basic right to a public education [through the US, Europe and elsewhere].

The street scenes become politically potent only when and if we have a visual and audible version of the scene communicated in live or proximate time, so that the media does not merely report the scene, but is part of the scene and the action; indeed, the media is the scene or the space in its extended and replicable visual and audible dimensions. One way of stating this is simply that the media extend the scene visually and audibly and participate in the delimitation and transposability of the scene. Put differently, the media constitute the scene in a time and place that includes and exceeds its local instantiation. [...]

Of course, the dominant media are corporately owned, exercising their own kinds of censorship and incitement. And yet, it still seems important to affirm that the freedom of the media to broadcast from these sites is itself an exercise of freedom and so a mode of exercising rights, especially when they are rogue media, from the street, evading the censor, where the activation of the instrument is part of the bodily action itself. This is doubtless why both Hosni Mubarak and David Cameron, eight months apart, both argued for the censorship of social media networks. At least in some instances, the media not only report on social and political movements that are laying claim to freedom and justice in various ways; the media also are exercising one of those freedoms for which the social movement struggles. I do not mean by this claim to suggest that all media are involved in the struggle for political freedom and social justice (we know, of course, that they are not). Of course, it matters which global media do the reporting and how. My point is that sometimes private media devices become global precisely at the moment in which they overcome modes of censorship to report protests and in that way become part of the protest itself.

What bodies are doing on the street when they are demonstrating is linked fundamentally to what communication devices and technologies are doing when they 'report' on what is happening in the street. These are different actions, but they both require the body. The one exercise of freedom is linked to the other, which means that both are ways of exercising rights and that, jointly, they bring a space of appearance into being and secure its transposability. Although some may wager that the exercise of rights now takes place quite at the expense of bodies on the street, that Twitter and other virtual technologies have led to a disembodiment of the public sphere, I disagree. The media requires those bodies on the street to have an event, even as those bodies on the street require the media to exist in a global arena. But under conditions when those with cameras or Internet capacities are imprisoned or tortured or deported, the use of the technology effectively implicates the body. Not only must someone's hand tap and send, but someone's body is on the line if that tapping and sending gets traced. In other words, localisation is hardly overcome through the use of media that potentially transmit globally. And if this conjuncture of street and media constitutes a very contemporary version of the public sphere, then bodies on the line have to be thought as both there and here, now and then, transported and stationary, with very different political consequences following from those two modalities of space and time. [...]

1   [Footnote 5 in source] Hans Wehr, *Dictionary of Modern Written Arabic*, ed. J. Milton Cowan (Ithaca: Spoken Language Services, 1994) s.v. 'salima'.

Judith Butler, extracts from 'Bodies in Alliance and the Politics of the Street', in *Sensible Politics: The Visual Culture of Nongovernmental Activism*, eds. Meg McLagan and Yates McKee (New York: Zone Books, 2012) 125–126, 128–131.

Basel Abbas and Ruanne Abou-Rahme
The Archival Multitude: In Conversation with Tom Holert//2013

Tom Holert [...] How did the media practices of the Arab uprisings inform your notion of the archive and ultimately your own archival practice?

Basel Abbas and Ruanne Abou-Rahme Critically for us, a fundamental change in our understanding of the archive solidified when the revolutions began to take place in the Arab world. We experienced and engaged with these movements through the real time material that was being uploaded on such sites as YouTube and Twitter. Living in Palestine,[1] a place that culturally and geographically is close to the Arab world but, subjected to a colonial regime, is cut off from it and the rest of the world for that matter. The sudden ability to be connected at any moment to a continual stream coming from people involved in the revolution was phenomenal. Through streams and live feeds of people's textual and visual accounts, the distance between here and there was suspended for that period. We woke and slept in Tunisia and then Egypt. This was an electric moment for us. Suddenly the potential of the people to subvert the representations of the state was palpable. We came face to face with a living archive, and it felt precisely as just that when the people in Tahrir were bearing witness in real time and uploading their testimonials onto servers to be simultaneously heard, read, watched and experienced by us – there was no mediator between us and them apart from the platforms where the material appeared unfiltered. [...] For us the vitality that turns the archive into something living is fundamentally connected to a moment of political becoming, when the individual through a subjective gesture or act becomes part of a common moment and articulates the potential of the multitude. Here the very act of producing and sharing subjective, horizontal archives is precisely about the instance on and the fight for a living common archive, from the ground up. These subjective archives, as expression of the new archival multitude and as (part of) common archives have a liberatory potential, they are full of a creative vitality that expresses the desire for an outside of the hegemony of power.

For us the most illuminating moment of this was during the revolutions in the Arab world, although it is significant to note that this liberatory potential is articulated in multiple ways and moments and not just in the moment of revolt (this being the more obvious). Its first expression is in the very possibility of creating horizontal archives. When experiencing the 2011 revolution we saw how every minute people were recording the event and producing a politically radical and unofficial archive of the moment. The archival activity of this insurgency was an integral part of people reclaiming the right to speak, assuming agency over their political lives and future. Amazingly the regime, while narrating the event and producing the archive, had been challenged in the very moment of its production and on a mass scale. […]

What worries us most is the possibility that the radical potential of the moment will be lost, in the sense that our initial interest in the surge of archival activity online is directly connected to the surge in people's political activity on the ground. For us the potential for archival activity, or the 'archival multitude' to produce subversive discourses, in terms of both content and form, is only one current that is shaping the field of possibilities for the archives to come. Another current is in many ways connected to the logic of contemporary capital, the speed of the feed as we have mentioned creates an incomprehensible overflow at points. Significantly it re-produces contemporary capitalism's obsession with the 'now', the immediate, producing a vast amount of material only to render it obsolete the very next moment in a continuous stream of information. As you indicated, many of the platforms or social media sites that open the possibility for anyone and everyone to publicly bear witness to their lives are now owned by or have ballooned into mega companies. We can clearly see how in an information economy these archival activities, the radical potential of these forms are instrumentalised by capital. Maybe we should give a clearer sense of what we mean by these new forms. They are not just a matter of 'poor images' [a term coined by artist and theorist Hito Steyerl], i.e. images that are small in size, malleable and able to travel quickly such as a lo-fi video that by the time it reaches you has been uploaded, downloaded and re-uploaded several times. They are also comments on and re-contextualisations of these videos through other video responses, through the stream of tweets, re-tweets, memes, not to mention the endless blog sites. An event on the ground, once it is documented, uploaded and shared online is able to trigger a series of ephemeral streams of responses and articulations through these various different forms. […]

Of course, the malleability and speed of information are also very much on a par with neo-liberal globalisation. What's even more, the very site of open exchange is also a site of surveillance, tracking and profiling. Our lives are documented like never before and turned against us in case of any dissidence. Facebook posts, shares and even 'likes', tweets, videos are used as evidence against political agitators, dissidents and 'security threats'. There is a decisive struggle being waged over the future of these archives: over the future of these very forms. After all the culture and politics of publicly sharing information, texts, images, films, music, the very possibility for people's uses of the digital/

virtual to subvert capital's insistence on the production of knowledge as commodity is under persistent threat and pressure. There are intensifying struggles over legislation that is trying to control the flows of information and exchanges between people. By that same logic, anything can be removed, erased not only for infringing copyright but also for simply being dissonant. It is this struggle that will be decisive in shaping what is archivable.

Perhaps much of this clarifies where we hope the archival multitude will go. Ultimately, we are engaged in this struggle. Most of all we are invested in the archival multitude in the sense that it is at times constitutive of a heterogeneous political body that calls for and performs various forms of daily and small resistances. [...]

If we return to the Arab world, and to the moment of revolution, it is evident that people's archival activity, their bearing witness to the moment on the ground and the possibility of sharing this testimony *en masse* was a critical means of destabilising power. Not only were insurgent citizens shaping the event on the ground, they were at the same moment producing and circulating counter-narratives through images, videos, sound and text. In one video from the period when protesters are leaving Tahrir Square someone tellingly reminds them: 'Don't forget to upload online everything you filmed before you sleep, before you sleep – so we can wake up to a new Egypt without Hosni Mubarak'. In a highly palpable way this dynamic archive-of-the-moment ruptured the symbolic power of the state, 'the very control of appearances – so central to the state's edifice of symbolic power in the age of Spectacle – was fatally jeopardized'.[2]

Holert What happened in this moment of the collective re-appropriation of the image of the people? How did the availability of an uncensored and post-spectacular representation of the events change the power relations?

Abbas and Ruanne Abou-Rahme The dispersed 'public' of the Arab world – at least those not aligned with the regime – experienced in *that* moment through *that* archival activity the electric pulse of people's will for change: the not-yet-imaginable was becoming the-not-yet-material. Having spent decades under a repressive weight of fear and control (something felt across the Arab world), unable to speak publicly against the abuse of power, there was great difficulty in imagining or projecting the moment of such a regime's collapse, let alone a collapse brought on by the political actions and insurgency of ordinary citizens. There can be no doubt that the moment where the un-imaginable almost miraculously materialised has profoundly impacted the political and cultural imaginary in the Arab world. Fundamentally, it began to thaw out the crisis of the imaginary that we have felt for a very long time. For our ability to even imagine a different political horizon, a different way of being politically, culturally and socially is what has been at stake for so long. A feeling that we could take hold of our political lives and realise the not-yet-material will towards social justice was palpable even if not entirely sustainable. [...]

For us the activist-archivists certainly demanded a reconfiguration of our own archival practice, they illuminated something that we had somehow failed to see. We felt strongly that we were in the midst of a new becoming for the archives. The position that the artist as archivist used to occupy is now being taken up by the activist as archivist, and not only the activist but also all the individuals who are amassing and uploading records of their daily life, the mundane and the everyday. Such archival ambitions are everywhere; they are proliferating, and wittingly or unwittingly producing a living archive. The interrogation of the archive that artists and writers had been dedicated to, through counter-narratives and images, is now coming alive through the practices of this new archival multitude. We read the artist as archivist as a precursor for this moment. Now that we have arrived here it has meant a shift in our gaze beyond ourselves as artist–archivists and towards the possibilities of this overwhelming archival activity. [...] Perhaps what we feel now is that we are one small part of this immense archival multitude.

1   [Footnote 2 in source] Here we are speaking of the experience of Palestinians living in the West Bank and Gaza under Israeli military rule and inside Israel 'proper', in Jerusalem, Haifa and Nazareth for example, areas that fall under direct Israeli jurisdiction.

2   [5] Nasser Abourahme and May Jayyusi, 'The Will to Revolt and the Spectre of the Real: Reflections on the Arab Moment', in *City*, vol. 15, no. 6 (December 2011), 627.

Basel Abbas and Ruanne Abou-Rahme (in conversation with Tom Holert), extracts from 'The Archival Multitude', in *Journal of Visual Culture*, vol. 12, no. 3 (December, 2013), 352–353, 355–357, 361.

David Harvey

Rebel Cities: From the Right to the City to the Urban Revolution//2012

The history of urban-based class struggles is stunning. The successive revolutionary movements in Paris from 1789 through 1830 and 1848 to the Commune of 1871 constitute the most obvious nineteenth century example. Later events included the Petrograd Soviet, the Shanghai Communes of 1927 and 1967, the Seattle General Strike of 1919, the role of Barcelona in the Spanish Civil War, the uprising in Cordoba [Argentina] in 1969, and the more general urban uprisings in the United States in the 1960s, the urban-based movements of 1968 (Paris, Chicago, Mexico City, Bangkok, and others including the so-called 'Prague Spring', and the rise of neighbourhood associations in Madrid that fronted the anti-Franco movement in Spain around the same time). And in more recent times we have witnessed echoes of these older struggles in the Seattle anti-globalisation protests of 1999 (followed by similar protests in Quebec City, Genoa, and many other cities as part of a widespread alternative globalisation movement). Most recently we have seen mass protests in Tahrir Square in Cairo, in Madison, Wisconsin, in the Plazas del Sol in Madrid and Catalunya in Barcelona, and in Syntagma Square in Athens, as well as revolutionary movements and rebellions in Oaxaca in Mexico, in Cochabamba (2000 and 2007) and El Alto (2003 and 2005) in Bolivia, along with very different but equally important political eruptions in Buenos Aires in 2001-02, and in Santiago in Chile (2006 and 2011).

And it is not, this history demonstrates, only singular urban centres that are involved. On several occasions the spirit of protest and revolt has spread contagiously through urban networks in remarkable ways. The revolutionary movement of 1848 may have started in Paris, but the spirit of revolt spread to Vienna, Berlin, Milan, Budapest, Frankfurt, and many other European cities. The Bolshevik Revolution in Russia was accompanied by the formation of worker's councils and 'soviets' in Berlin, Vienna, Warsaw, Riga, Munich and Turin, just as in 1968 it was Paris, Berlin, London, Mexico City, Bangkok, Chicago, and innumerable other cities that experienced 'days of rage', and in some instances violent repressions. The unfolding urban crisis of the 1960s in the United States affected many cities simultaneously. And in an astonishing but much underestimated moment in world history, on February 15, 2003, several million people simultaneously appeared on the streets of Rome (with around 3 million, considered the largest anti-war rally ever in human history), Madrid, London,

Barcelona, Berlin, and Athens, with lesser but still substantial numbers (though impossible to count because of police repression) in New York and Melbourne, and thousands more in nearly 200 cities in Asia (except China), Africa, and Latin America in a world wide demonstration against the threat of war with Iraq. Described at the time as perhaps one of the first expressions of global public opinion, the movement quickly faded, but leaves behind the sense that the global urban network is replete with political possibilities that remain untapped by progressive movements. The current wave of youth-led movements throughout the world, from Cairo to Madrid to Santiago – to say nothing of a street revolt in London, followed by an 'Occupy Wall Street' movement that began in New York City before spreading to innumerable cities in the US and now around the world - suggests there is something political in the city air struggling to be expressed.[1] [...]

The Party of Wall Street has ruled unchallenged in the United States for far too long. It has totally dominated the policies of presidents over at least four decades, if not longer, no matter whether individual presidents have been its willing agents or not. It has legally corrupted Congress via the craven dependency of politicians in both political parties upon its raw money power and upon access to the mainstream media that it controls. Thanks to the appointments made and approved by presidents and Congress, the Party of Wall Street dominates much of the state apparatus as well as the judiciary – in particular the Supreme Court, whose partisan judgments increasingly favour venal money interests, in spheres as diverse as electoral, labour, environmental, and contract law.

The Party of Wall Street has one universal principle of rule: that there shall be no serious challenge to the absolute power of money to rule absolutely. That power must be exercised with one objective: those possessed of money power shall not only be privileged to accumulate wealth endlessly at will, but they shall have the right to inherit the earth, not only taking either direct or indirect dominion of the land and all the resources and productive capacities that reside therein, but also assuming absolute command, directly or indirectly, over the labour and creative potentialities of all those others it needs. The rest of humanity shall be deemed disposable. [...]

But now, for the first time, there is an explicit movement to confront the Party of Wall Street and its unalloyed money power. The 'street' in Wall Street is being occupied – oh horror upon horrors – by others! Spreading from city to city, the tactics of Occupy Wall Street are to take a central public space, a park or a square, close to where many of the levers of power are centred, and, by putting human bodies in that place, to convert public space into a political commons – a place for open discussion and debate over what that power is doing and how best to oppose its reach. This tactic, most conspicuously re-animated in the noble and ongoing struggles centred on Tahrir Square in Cairo, has spread across the world (Puerta del Sol in Madrid, Syntagma Square in Athens, and now the steps of St Paul's Cathedral in London and Wall Street itself). It shows us that the collective power of bodies in public space is still the most effective instrument of opposition when all other means of access are blocked. What Tahrir Square showed to the world was an obvious truth: that it is bodies on the street and in the squares, not the babble of sentiments on Twitter or Facebook, that really matter. [...] To succeed, the movement has to reach out to the 99%. This it can do and is doing, step by step. First there are all those being plunged into immiseration by unemployment, and all those who have been or are now being dispossessed of their houses and their assets by the Wall Street phalanx. The movement must forge broad coalitions between students, immigrants, the underemployed, and all those threatened by the totally unnecessary and draconian austerity politics being inflicted upon the nation and the world at the behest of the Party of Wall Street. It must focus on the astonishing levels of exploitation in workplaces – from the immigrant domestic workers who the rich so ruthlessly exploit in their homes to the restaurant workers who slave for almost nothing in the kitchens of the establishments in which the rich so grandly eat. It must bring together the creative workers and artists whose talents are so often turned into commercial products under the control of big-money power.

The movement must above all reach out to all the alienated, the dissatisfied, and the discontented – all those who recognise and feel in their gut that there is something profoundly wrong, that the system the Party of Wall Street has devised is not only barbaric, unethical, and morally wrong, but also broken.

All this has to be democratically assembled into a coherent opposition, which must also freely contemplate the future outlines of an alternative city, an alternative political system, and, ultimately, an alternative way of organising production, distribution, and consumption for the benefit of the people. Otherwise, a future for the young that points to spiralling private indebtedness and deepening public austerity, all for the benefit of the 1 percent, is no future at all. [...] In the face of the organised power of the Party of Wall Street to divide and rule, the movement that is emerging must also take as one of its founding principles that it will be neither divided nor diverted until the Party of Wall Street is brought either to its senses – to see that the common good must prevail over narrow venal interests – or to its knees. Corporate privileges that confer the rights of individuals without the responsibilities of true citizens must be rolled back. Public goods such as education and health care must be publicly provided and made freely available. The monopoly powers in the media must be broken. The buying of elections must be ruled unconstitutional. The privatisation of knowledge and culture must be prohibited. The freedom to exploit and dispossess others must be severely curbed, and ultimately outlawed.

[…] The struggle is global as well as local in nature. It brings together students who are locked in a life-and-death struggle with political power in Chile to create a free and quality education system for all, and so begin the dismantling of the neoliberal model that Pinochet so brutally imposed. It embraces the agitators in Tahrir Square, who recognise that the fall of Mubarak (like the end of Pinochet's dictatorship) was but the first step in an emancipatory struggle to break free from money power. It includes the indignados in Spain, the striking workers in Greece, the militant opposition emerging all around the world, from London to Durban, Buenos Aires, Shenzhen, and Mumbai. The brutal dominions of big capital and sheer money power are everywhere on the defensive.

Whose side will each of us, as individuals, come down on? Which street will we occupy? Only time will tell. But what we do know is that the time is now. The system is not only broken and exposed, but incapable of any response other than repression. So we, the people, have no option but to struggle for the collective right to decide how that system shall be reconstructed, and in whose image. The Party of Wall Street has had its day, and has failed miserably. The construction of an alternative on its ruins is both an opportunity and an inescapable obligation that none of us can or would ever want to avoid.

1   The saying 'city air makes one free' comes from medieval times, when incorporated towns with charters could function as 'non-feudal islands in a feudal sea': The classic account is Henri Pirenne, *Medieval Cities*, (Princeton: Princeton University Press, 1925).

David Harvey, extracts from *Rebel Cities: From the Right to the City to the Urban Revolution*, (London and New York: Verso, 2012) 115–117, 159, 161–164.

Arts Strike

[…] The arts will be crucial to our collective economic noncompliance on May Day 2012. The arts are embedded in the broader cultural and media sectors of the neoliberal urban economy. People who work in these sectors, including musicians and writers, performers and architects, dancers and designers, photographers and filmmakers, typically work numerous other jobs to make ends meet. We work as students, educators, bartenders, proofreaders, interns, tour guides, caretakers, art handlers, administrative assistants, street vendors and more. Though some of us belong to unions, cultural workers are largely precarious and unorganised. Many of us do not have jobs at all. And cultural workers are debtors – we share this 'negative commons' with the rest of the 99%.

Cultural workers are variously striated by class background, race, gender, age, immigration status, education, institutional affiliation and cultural prestige, with the most elite often serving as the avant-garde of gentrification. Building a strike-alliance involving cultural workers will thus be complicated. Matters of privilege and hierarchy will need to be deeply examined. But it will also be quite powerful, given that the cultural workers of the 99% create the cultural commonwealth from which the 1% in the entertainment, tourism, and real estate industries draw their astronomical profits.

As cultural workers, we can contribute our various skillsets to the build-up for May Day through creative media, research, and direct action. At the same time, we can do formal and informal outreach in our workplaces, institutions, communities and social networks.

May Day will be beautifully disruptive. As we shut down the privatised city of capital, we will open new public spaces that are empowering and inspiring. The strike will be an exercise in radical imagination informed by dreams of beloved community and histories of militant resistance. It will draw upon and reinvent the creative tactics of earlier struggles for freedom, equality, and justice from across the world. We will continuously add and multiply our collective creativity so that every act of defiance also demonstrates the possibility of another world beyond neoliberalism.

When we withdraw from work, let's not just stay home or go shopping. Imagine May Day and its build-up as a Spring celebration of the arts, a people's jubilee of the cultural commons. Everyone will be invited to the party: the kids and the elders, the singers and the dancers, the clowns and the monsters.

Let's go out into to the streets, parks, and lots to reclaim our city. Let's march, converge, and assemble with our friends and families, communities and allies. Let's make some art, pitch some tents, plant some seeds... and see what grows for the Summer and beyond.

With contributions from: Suzahn Ebrahimian, Thomas Hintze, Yates McKee, Team Tidal, and conversations within different working groups and assemblies [of Occupy Wall Street].

Tidal Magazine, extract from 'Getting Ready for May Day 2012', *Tidal Magazine: Occupy Theory, Occupy Strategy*, no. 2 (March 2012) 19.

Andrea Fraser
There's No Place Like Home//2012

[...] As I begin working on this text, the Occupy Wall Street movement is spreading across the United States and beyond. Along with many of what is most certainly an overwhelming majority of artists, curators, art critics, and historians who profess a progressive if not radically left political orientation, I have been looking for ways to support and participate in this movement and believe it represents a long overdue expression of collective revulsion over the excesses of the financial industry, the corruption of our political process and the economic policies that have produced levels of inequality in the United States not seen since the 1920s. Indeed, the Occupy movement seems to be taking the art world by storm, especially in New York, with dozens of symposia, lectures, and teach-ins as well as Occupy-themed or inspired artists groups and protests at art-related sites. Who knows where this movement will be four months from now when this essay is published. I find myself asking, however, where was it four months ago? Why did it take an art world that prides itself on criticality and vanguardism so long to confront its direct complicity in economic conditions that have been evident for more than a decade now? [...]

It is widely known that private equity managers and other financial industry executives emerged as major collectors of contemporary art early in the last decade and now make up a large percentage of the top collectors worldwide. They also emerged as a major presence on museum boards. Many of these collectors and trustees from the financial world were directly involved in the [2007/8] sub-prime mortgage crisis – a few are now under federal investigation. Many others have been vocal opponents of financial reform as well as any increase in taxation or public spending in response to the recession they precipitated and have pursued these positions through contributions to politicians and political groups, with some giving generously to both parties.[1]

More broadly, it is clear that the contemporary art world has been a direct beneficiary of the inequality of which the outsized rewards of Wall Street are only the most visible example. A quick look at the Gini Index, which tracks inequality worldwide, reveals that the locations of the biggest art booms of the last decade have also seen the steepest rise in inequality: the United States, Britain, China, and, most recently, India. Recent economic research has linked the steep increase in art prices over the past decades directly to this growing inequality, indicating that 'a one percentage point increase in the share of total income earned by the top 0.1% triggers an increase in art prices of about 14 percent.'[2] And we can assume that this hyperinflation in art prices, typical of how luxury goods and services respond to increases in concentrations of wealth, has also catapulted an unprecedented number of art dealers, consultants and artists themselves into the ranks of the top 1, .1, and even .01 percent of earners, with the reported prices of many artworks well above $344,000, the 2009 threshold for 1 percent status.[3]

Indeed, the art world itself has developed into a prime example of a winner-take-all market, one of the economic models that emerged to describe the extremes of compensation that have become endemic in the financial and corporate worlds and now also extend to major museums and other large non-profit organisations in the United States, where compensation ratios can rival those of the for-profit sector.[4] At all levels of the art world, one finds extreme wealth breezing past grinding poverty, from the archetypal struggling artist to the often temporary and benefitless studio and gallery assistants to the low-wage staffers at nonprofit organisations. Museums plead poverty in negotiations with workers and leave curators to scramble for exhibition budgets and often-meagre artist and author fees, while raising hundreds of millions for big-name acquisitions and expansions, which proceed in many institutions despite the continuing recession.[5]

[...] However, it has been during this same period of inequality-fuelled art world expansion that we have also seen a growing number of artists, curators, and critics take up the cause of social justice – often within organisations funded by corporate sponsorship and private wealth. We have seen a proliferation of degree programmes focusing on social, political, critical, and community-based art practices – based mostly in private nonprofit and even for-profit art schools that charge among the highest tuitions of any masters-level degree programmes. We have seen art magazines take up apparently radical political theory and even a critique of the art market – while weighted down with advertising for commercial galleries, art fairs, auction houses, and luxury goods. We have seen museums embrace the discourse and even functions of public service – while the charitable deduction from which they benefit reduces public coffers, while they attract private donors away from social-service charities,[6] and while many of their patrons actively lobby for a shrinking public sector. We have seen artworks identified with social and even economic critique sell for hundreds of thousands and even millions of dollars. And we have seen critical, social, and political claims for what art is and does proliferate, becoming central to art's dominant legitimising discourse.

[...] While I believe that we still can speak of 'the art world' as a singular field, this expansion has led to the growth and coalescence of increasingly distinct artistic subfields, each defined by particular economies as well as configurations of practices, institutions, and values. There are the art worlds that revolve around commercial art galleries, art fairs, and auctions; the art worlds that revolve around curated exhibitions and projects in public and nonprofit organisations; the art worlds that revolve around academic institutions and discourses; and there are the community-based, activist and DIY art worlds that aspire to exist outside of all these organised sites of activity, and, in some cases, even outside of the art world itself. At their extremes, participants in these subfields may indeed escape some of the art world's contradictions, although certainly not those of the world at large: there are those who feel at home with wealth and privilege, for whom art is a luxury business or an investment opportunity and perhaps not much more, as well as those who see art as a purely aesthetic domain in which the political and economic should play no part. And there are those who see art as social activism and who have nothing to do with commercial galleries and art fairs, society openings, gala benefits, and privately funded museums. Most of us, however, and most of the art world, exist uncomfortably and often painfully in between these extremes, embodying and performing the contradictions between them and the economic and political conflicts those contradictions reflect, unable to resolve them within our work or within ourselves, much less within our field.

Art discourse – which includes not only what critics, curators, artists and art historians write about art, but what we say about what we do in the art field, in all its forms – seems to play a double role in this expanded and increasingly fragmented art world. As a critical discourse, it often proposes to describe these conditions and contradictions, account for them, and even to provide the tools to resolve them. At the same time, however, it remains largely and broadly shared, often traversing the most diverse art institutions, economies, and communities without any significant alteration in artistic, critical and political claims or theoretical frame of reference. In this way, art discourse serves to maintain links among artistic subfields and to create a continuum between practices that may be completely incommensurable in terms of their economic conditions and social as well as artistic values. This may make art discourse one of the most consequential – and problematic – institutions in the art world today, along with mega-museums that aim to be all things to all people and survey exhibitions (like the Whitney Biennial) that offer up incomparable practices for comparison.

It is not only the immaterial character of art discourse that predisposes it to this function and mode of operation. Rather, it is the consistent tendency of art discourse to segregate the social and economic conditions of art from what it articulates as constitutive of the meaning, significance, and experience of artworks, as well as what it articulates as the motivations of artists, curators, and critics, even when it asserts that art is acting on these very conditions. While this is not surprising in the perspectives of those who view art as a purely aesthetic domain – and who even may make political arguments for art's autonomy as such – it seems increasingly symptomatic in an art world ever more intently focused on producing effects in the 'real world' and on seeing art as an agent of social critique, if not of social change. The result has been an ever-widening gap between the material conditions of art and its symbolic systems: between what the vast majority of artworks are today (socially and economically) and what artists, curators, critics, and historians say that artworks – especially their own work or work they support – do and mean. [...]

As much as art discourse may reveal structures and relationships to us, it also serves to conceal, with direction and sometimes misdirection; with affirmations accompanied by implicit or explicit negations of other ways of seeing, experiencing, and understanding; with abstraction and formalisation that distance and neutralise; or simply through a pervasive silence about aspects of art, our experience of it, and the relationships it performs that, once internalised, may even cause them effectively to disappear for us. Through these operations of art discourse, we not only banish entire regions of our own activities and experiences, investments and motivations to insignificance, irrelevance, and unspeakability, we also consistently misrepresent what art is and what we do when we engage with art and participate in the art field. [...]

Indeed, it may be that the way out of the seemingly irresolvable contradictions of the art world lies directly within our grasp, not in the next artistic innovation – not, first of all, in what we do – but in what we say about what we do: in art discourse. While a transformation in art discourse would not, of course, resolve any of the enormous conflicts in the social world or even within ourselves, it might at least allow us to engage them more honestly and effectively.

1   This information is readily available at websites such as CampaignMoney.com. For a brief survey of some of the financial and political activities of top collectors, see my essay 'L'1% C'est Moi.'

2   William N. Goetzmann, Luc Renneboog, and Christophe Spaenjers, 'Art and Money', Yale School of Management Working Paper nos. 09-26, Yale School of Management, April 28, 2010.

3   Damien Hirst, reported by London's *Sunday Times* to be worth £215 million in 2010, may top the list of wealthy artists. The *Wall Street Journal* has reported estimates that international art dealer Larry Gagosian sells more than $1 billion in art annually, making it very likely that most if not all of the seventy-seven artists he represents have incomes well above the $1.4 million threshold for .1 percent status. See Kelly Crow, 'The Gagosian Effect', *Wall Street Journal*, 1 April, 2011.

4   According to *Newsweek*, the highest paid CEOs in the non-profit sector in 2010 were leaders of cultural organisations, with Zarin Mehta of the New York Philharmonic (at $2.6 million in total annual compensation) and Glenn Lowry of the Museum of Modern Art (at $2.5 million) topping the list. Greg Bocquet, '15 Highest-Paid Charity CEOs', *Newsweek*, (26 October, 2010). According to the Economic Policy Institute, the ratio of average CEO total direct compensation to average production worker compensation in the United States was 185 to 1 in 2009. http://www.stateofwork-ingamerica.org/charts/view/17

5   The Whitney Museum recently broke ground on a new building in Manhattan's Meatpacking District that is estimated to cost $680 million to complete. The Museum of Modern Art is beginning a fundraising campaign to expand into the former site of the American Folk Art Museum, which it purchased in August 2011 for $31.2 million. MoMA sought major concessions from unions while raising $858 million for its last expansion, completed in 2004, resulting in a prolonged strike.

6   [Footnote 7 in source] According to Charity Navigator, donations to cultural charities increased 5.6 percent in 2010, while donations to health charities went up only 1.3 percent and donations to human service charities did not increase at all. See, http://www.charitynavigator.org/index.cfm?bay=content.view&cpid=42.

Andrea Fraser, extracts from 'There's No Place Like Home', in *Whitney Biennial 2012*, (New York and New Haven: Whitney Museum of Art and Yale University Press, 2012) 28–30, 32–33.

Süreyyya Evren
Gezi Resistance in Istanbul//2013

It started with a small group of activists trying to defend a public park against government's plans to build a huge shopping mall. In few days, as police used increasing violence against that tiny cluster of protestors, more and more people came to show their support. On 31 May [2013], the whole country woke up at 3am to find that a small protest had turned into a huge revolutionary moment. Taksim Square and Gezi Park (in central Istanbul) were 'captured' on 1 June and remained government-free zones for two weeks.... It was a bit ethereal for everyone: a stateless mega city-centre! The Taksim Commune! And anarchists were clearly not the only people who enjoyed the temporary autonomous zone.[1] The heterogeneous movement was politicised through a common process. Different political stances converged for the first time. There was clearly a 'multitude' on the streets during the uprising and this multitude is still active in different forms. What happened, how did it develop? I believe that the events deserve discussion.

There are aspects of Gezi resistance that are truly local and you need to understand the Turkish political and social background to be able to connect fully to the events. On the other hand there are so many similarities, even links with other international uprisings and movements, that the protest seems very familiar. I would like to suggest placing the Gezi resistance in the context of the 2011–2013 uprisings, that is, the new wave of resistance that has emerged in the aftermath of the anti-globalisation movement (whatever we call it). Many aspects of 2011–2013 events resonate with the Zapatistas in 1990s. The *encuentros* [encounters/assembly meetings] in Chiapas and the writings of Marcos make sense of what is happening in Turkey. For me, this is a new web of radicalism and the main outcome is not overtly 'political'; rather, it is about the empowerment of people. Gezi has transformed Turkish people.

As to the details: the festival-like atmosphere of Taksim after the police withdrew was very interesting. The square was full of revolutionary groups and parties. But none were able to control the festival, so to speak. In a typical May Day celebration in Turkey, for example the one I witnessed on 1 May 2012, (which was also held in the Taksim Square), there was one main programme, one focus; it was a very good plan and it involved a lot of security. Huge flags, huge placards, all displaying the glory of the revolutionary parties. It was a grandiose show. The 31 May uprising and the June TAZ in Taksim was instead based on 'affect' rather than flamboyance. There was room for everyone's creativity. People made jokes everywhere: on the walls, on upturned police vehicles, on signs; there were performances in every corner of the square, not all by artists but some by activists, even some by passers-by. Some helped to design a park library. People used a police car to make a wish tree, like Yoko Ono's Wish Trees.[2] There were live concerts in various parts of the square, different types of music. Some groups marched and chanted, others worked on an indie radio station, organised painting workshops for children, or just shouted against the government…. The Gezi Resistance included apolitical youth, precarious employees, workers, activists, anarchists, Marxists, Kemalists, teachers, lawyers, doctors and most importantly many artists. This movement was initiated by a new generation of young activists but their mothers supported them too, conquering bread: giving food, helping youngsters to protect themselves against police brutality. For many it was the first political action they had taken part in. After the government inflicted a series of oppressive actions designed to transform Turkey into an Islamic authoritarian regime, people reacted.

The Gezi Resistance was an internet-based uprising, a Twitter revolution if you like. Facebook, Twitter and other internet environments were *de facto* places of the resistance. The anarchistic organisational principles of the original activists in Gezi Park subordinated ideology to practical action and attracted thousands of people who have never been involved in a demonstration before and who wanted to help the activists. The internet helped many people from all walks to step out.

Gezi Resistance resulted in clashes with police in several areas of Istanbul. In most cases, protestors didn't even throw stones. Usually, their 'crime' was to return stubbornly having been attacked with pepper, gas and water cannons, to face down the police once more. People regrouped after all kinds of attacks and those chased by police found themselves in narrow streets, without places to hide. Twitter campaigns started asking residents in areas of police pursuit to open their doors and give the protesters access to the internet to upload images of police violence. Keys and passwords, things we associated with private protection created collective bonds, bonds that didn't exist before. One piece of graffiti, written under heavy police attack, illustrated this perfectly: 'THAT'S ENOUGH, IF YOU CONTINUE LIKE THIS I'M GOING TO CALL THE POLICE!'

One question preoccupied the Turkish Prime Minister Tayyip Erdoğan: How should my citizens live? Erdoğan's troubling answer was to interfere with the daily lives of citizens – repeatedly in favour of an Islamic way of life. Bans on drinking alcohol were followed by advice not to eat white bread and for women to have at least three children. He came out against abortion. The Minister of Health talked about banning abortion even in cases of rape. The threats encouraged a campaign of civil disobedience by Turkish women. The slogan 'My Body My Decision' appeared on women's bodies, photographed and published online. Women played a huge role in the resistance: on the barricades, behind the barricades, in Gezi Park, banging pots and pans in Istanbul and in other cities, in Twitter campaigns. This was a response to the oppressions experienced in their daily lives. 'My body my decision' evolved into 'my park my decision' and even: 'my country my decision'.

Gezi Resistance fits Emma Goldman's description of a revolution that you can dance to. There was always someone dancing in Taksim and Gezi. It was also the first completely grassroots Turkish social movement. There are no leaders, no parties dominating the movement. No initiators. This distinguished it from all previous revolutionary moments. It was a surprise for everyone involved: we never saw ourselves like this, rioting without a plan, without a programme, without a leader, and trying to create a new life afterwards; testing our limits from a small park. Anarchistic movements have always included numerous encounters and flows of ideas and people. And because there is no one centre, these connections play an important role for all participants in shaping a common politics. There is no single starting-point, no point of origin for the Gezi Resistance. It has no birth certificate, no figuration. It has no end. Always in the middle. Always on the network. And that creates a very fruitful platform for all kinds of creativity.

The 'Turkish Summer' began on 27 May 2013 when attempts to bulldoze the Gezi Park were stopped by few activists in the middle of the night. Those environmentalists wanted to stop a shopping mall being put up in the place of this nice, small park in Taksim. In few days the number of protestors grew in parallel with the escalation of police brutality against environmentalists. On 31 May, the police kicked the activists out of the park. That sparked an unforeseen public reaction. People organised through social media platforms. Protests began immediately. Protests attracted tens of thousands of people to the streets. And despite harsh policing, people refused to go back home. Demonstrations continued all night, in both the Asian and the Anatolian side of Istanbul. The next day, on 1 June 2013, the number of protestors grew and protests were seen in other cities as well. At some point in the afternoon, police left the area to the protestors. People immediately built barricades on main roads. As a result, for the first time in its history, Gezi Park, Taksim Square and Istiklal Avenue became state-free locations governed by the people and the people only. There were of course plainclothes officers but nobody in uniforms. Soon it was possible to get free food and clothes, thanks to donations and more than a thousand volunteers. Infirmaries, a new garden, workshops and a library also appeared. Different political groups occupied different parts of the park; also lots of young students without any political affiliation occupied the space. It was such a shock for the citizens of Istanbul. In the night time, Gezi Park and Taksim Square became festival areas with various concerts and shows.

A direct reference to the flow of the system could again be found in art, in an earlier performance of the Turkish artistic group HaZaVuZu. Their performance *Cut the Flow* (2007) was a parody of how police forces regulate human flows on Istiklal Avenue in Istanbul, one of the main pedestrian streets in the city. As a group, they were first unnoticed as a part of the human flow on the street, but suddenly they created a 'human barrage', a gesture of cutting the flow. Reclaim the Streets, one of the well-known groups of the anti-globalisation movement, has also been known for stopping flows. Interventions in flows do not aim to stop the flow right away, but to show its ideological rhythm. And of course, also to make us feel that we can 'reclaim' our control over it. HaZaVuZu's performance was a pioneering work in this sense, because all Gezi resistance demonstrations were about reclaiming our control over the flow: over the flow of people, ourselves in our cities and our parks, over the flow of money that motivates the state to exchange a park with a shopping mall, and over the flow of information, which is heavily monitored by the government.

1   [Editors' note: the Temporary Autonomous Zone (TAZ) is a concept devised by Hakim Bey in 1985, to designate emancipatory moments of anarchist practice and creative commonality that do not conform to the typical delimitation of the public sphere under capitalism. See Hakim Bey, *T.A.Z.: The Temporary Autonomous Zone, Ontological Anarchy, Poetic Terrorism* (Brooklyn, NY: Autonomedia, 1991]

2   See http://imaginepeacetower.com/yoko-onos-wish-trees.

Süreyyya Evren, 'Gezi Resistance in Istanbul: Something in Between Tahrir, Occupy and a Late Turkish 1968', *Anarchist Studies*, vol. 21, no. 2 (Lawrence Wishart, 2013) 7–10.

Dave Beech
To Boycott or Not to Boycott//2014

Boycott the Sydney Biennial! Boycott Manifesta 10! Withdraw from the Whitney Biennial! Protest against the corporate sponsorship of Tate by BP! Protest against the Dia Art Foundation's retrospective of Carl Andre in honour of the late Ana Mendieta! Boycott all art materials suppliers in the name of art's 'dark matter'! Boycott the Creative Time exhibition! Campaign against unpaid internships in art's institutions! Boycott! Withdraw! Protest!

Thirty years of conspicuous apathy and professional cynicism in the art world appear to have come to a glorious end. Political protest has reasserted itself in public acts of dissent, direct action and speaking truth to power. Although art's funding, management and links to business and the state have been subject to scrutiny by artists on and off since the formation of institutional critique in the 1970s, the current mode of art's political critique has become more general and more activist. Individual artists and isolated art groups have withdrawn from exhibitions for various reasons in the past (Art in Ruins had a reputation for pulling out of exhibitions as a matter of principle), but the current spate of art boycotts is rooted in a genuine political turn.

In its announcement to withdraw from Manifesta 10, Russian art collective Chto Delat? (What is to be done?) said: 'Manifesta has shown that it can respond with little more than bureaucratic injunctions to respect law and order in a situation where any and all law has gone to the wind. For that reason, any participation in the Manifesta 10 exhibition loses its initial meaning.' Meanwhile, under the slogan 'Don't Add Value to Detention', 92 artists boycotted the 19th Sydney Biennale, which resulted in the Biennale severing links with its chief corporate sponsor, Transfield, which operates refugee detention centres off the Australian mainland. [...]

The art boycott has established itself as a political device for calling institutions, corporations and the state to account. We don't imagine museum directors, CEOs and heads of government retreating to their underground bunkers, but for them the art boycott is certainly unwelcome. The art boycott is a political act. If the laundering of corporate brands through art sponsorship entails the repression of a damaging corporate narrative – and its substitution by a fantasy narrative – then the boycott holds the threat of the unconscious. Or, if art institutions are the perfect medium for ideology, in which material practices are displaced with high ideals, the art boycott confronts ideology with the social reality that it misrepresents.

All boycotts have political or ethical agendas, but what exactly is the political anatomy of the art boycott? The art boycott combines qualities of the consumer boycott with the industrial strike and it puts anti-art in the proximity of the refusal of work. Undeniably, the art boycott fuses the politics of art with political activism generally, not only in its technique, which is used by both, or its content insofar as the art boycott tends to respond to the political circumstances surrounding an exhibition, but primarily in their shared historical constellation.

Despite the fact that boycotts withdraw from sites rather than take them over, the art boycott derives its political character – and its momentum – from the Occupy movement. It belongs to a political landscape that was redrawn by the Arab spring of 2011, which ushered in new modes of political organisation across Europe and the US, especially through the implementation of new techniques for political activism. The Spanish 'indignant' protests, also known as 15M, were the first of the new movements. They inaugurated a new mode of mass political protest based on occupations that reached decisions with consensus-based procedures, and they initiated a new icon for protest by wearing the Guy Fawkes masks now associated with Anonymous.

Occupy Wall Street, and the global Occupy movement that followed, was consciously modelled on this Spanish prototype, spreading its techniques and norms back across the world from whence it came. Occupy describes itself as 'consensual, non-hierarchical, and participatory self-governance', not merely asking the state to be more democratic but 'literally laying the framework for a new world by building it here and now'.[1] The theory of Occupy was already split by 2012 between hyperbole and disappointment. Noam Chomsky observed that the movement no longer occupied small tent camps but 'now occupies the global conscience' in the form of a 'message spread from street protests to op-ed pages to the highest seats of power'. Peter Osborne deflated the utopianism of this quick transition of Occupy from political activism to a 'symbolic' event by characterising Occupy as the protest of 'powerlessness and refusal' which, he argued, 'places it in a social space related to, yet institutionally distinct from, art'.[2]

If Occupy and the boycott are alike in being largely symbolic, then artists will tend to feel that these forms of protest speak their language. However, in some instances Occupy has exceeded the symbolic and overshot its horizon of powerlessness and refusal. In June 2011, for instance, a group of 80 actors, artists, workers and citizens occupied the Teatro Valle in Rome to protest against the threat of privatisation from Rome's city council. Three years later, the occupiers have successfully run the theatre while experimenting with new models of cultural management based on the notion of the *bene comune* (common good), and the occupation has spread to other theatres.

[...] [T]he art boycott, which often speaks up for the disempowered and despairing, is the province of privilege. If consumer boycotts hand over more political agency to the wealthy, art boycotts hand over political agency to a minority of successful artists.

Nevertheless, artists who boycott large survey exhibitions represent the first serious challenge to the rise of the curator and the corporate sponsor that has shaped the neoliberal art institution. Putting aside the content of each boycott, therefore, we can say that the art boycott generally is a method for renegotiating the balance of power within art. The art strike was too general to threaten specific institutions and specific curators whereas the Yams Collective, for instance, which withdrew from the Whitney Biennial in protest against the alleged racism of the curatorial selection of artwork, points fingers, names names and calls for actual reforms . [...]

Pushing in the opposite direction of the art boycott, power occasionally withdraws from political confrontation. One example of what we might call the inverted boycott took place when the organisers of the 13th Istanbul Biennial cancelled the public programme out of fear that these events would become targets of the popular protest that had gripped the city. In another variant, institutional critique reverses the ethical charge of the boycott, using it as a rationale for participation rather than withdrawal. [...] Following the example of institutional critique rather than the art boycott, Liberate Tate stages protest events actually within Tate, dissensually participating in, rather than withdrawing from, the institution. Justifying its entry into the museum by the fact that it is normatively opposed to Tate's objective economic entanglement with BP, Liberate Tate is more fleeting than Occupy and more embroiled in the institution than the art boycott.

Occupy takes over a place through ethical self-organisation; institutional critique participates in an institution through ethical practices of critique; and the art boycott is ethically obliged to withdraw from institutions. The art world has a highly attuned sense of art's complicity with social forces, and a poorly attuned sense of art's role in the broad political struggle. The art boycott satisfies both of these conditions by conducting its site-specific activism by absenting itself. Paradoxically, the boycott takes a stand by standing off, which raises the question of whether it is an example of activism or inertia. Is the boycott an instance of 'nothing happening' or is participating in controversial exhibitions better understood as nothing but business as usual? Indisputably, if the boycott is a political act, then this is a formalist politics to which the artwork's content or specific properties cannot contribute. And if participating in exhibitions is necessarily to comply with its objective institutional form, then this too amounts to a formalist politics that condemns the work regardless of its actual material and semiotic qualities. And this is why the art boycott obtains its highest justification when the content of the artwork appears to be nullified by the political circumstances of its institutional display. […]

The art boycott can be politically aligned to the cultural occupation, but they are tactically distinct. Akin to worker takeovers, in which unprofitable facilities under threat of closure become worker- and community-owned firms that flourish under worker management, the occupied theatres go further than the art boycott's ethically charged abstinence. The point is not that the boycott is negative and the occupation is positive but that the illegal occupation is a strong negation of the status quo. The difference in principle is that the boycott is limited by the horizon of protest while the occupation can be engaged directly in the process of political transformation. In politics, however, principles can be outflanked by events.

Prior to its announcement to boycott Manifesta 10, Chto Delat? had explained that it was opposed to the art boycott, especially in Russia where 'a cultural blockade will only strengthen the position of reactionary forces'. Instead of boycotting Manifesta, Chto Delat? hoped, as a local collective, to occupy the role of 'alternative hosts and representatives of the city'. As the Manifesta curator, Kasper König, sought increasingly to marginalise any political disruptions emanating either from the state and its discontents or from participating artists, Chto Delat? decided that its original hopes would be thwarted by the circumstances under which they would be staged. Remaining in principle against the boycott, the group boycotted Manifesta under duress. Despite its limitations, therefore, the art boycott is a technique for reinstating political dissent at the heart of hegemonic complacency.

1   [Editors' note. Noam Chomsky, *Occupy*, (London: Penguin Books, 2012) back cover.]

2   [Editors' note. Peter Osborne, 'Disguised as a Dog: Cynical Occupy?', *Radical Philosophy*, no. 174, (Jul/Aug 2012) 20.]

Dave Beech, extracts from 'To Boycott or not to Boycott', *Art Monthly*, no. 380 (October, 2014) 380–382.

Global Ultra Luxury Faction (G.U.L.F.)
On Direct Action: An Address to Cultural Workers//2015

What time is it on the clock of the world?
– Grace Lee Boggs

We amplify a cry reverberating across the globe. From Istanbul and Sydney to New York and São Paulo, the proliferation of direct actions is disrupting business as usual at elite cultural institutions: Black Lives Matter at the Museum of Natural History, climate protests at Tate Modern and the Metropolitan Museum of Art, collective pressure for boycott at Haifa's Technion, and worker solidarity disruptions at the Guggenheim Museum NYC, to name only a few.

We see that actions are employing a diversity of tactics. At times, uninvited assemblies inside museums are announced. At other times the unexpected occurs, unheralded. Actions take aim at a range of targets: labour exploitation, white supremacy, the capture of public space, climate injustice, gentrification, police violence, Israeli apartheid, rape and sexual assault, and more. They are beautifully disruptive within their own arenas of concern. But these concerns are also connected.

We know that by hacking the media machine our actions can have deeply transformative potential or they can reinforce existing norms and power relations. They can accept the limits of a given context – and implicitly affirm them – or they can change the nature of that context altogether. Let our actions be an opportunity to test, to unlearn, and to train in the practice of freedom.

We are the Global Ultra Luxury Faction (G.U.L.F.). Our name aggressively reflects back to the actually existing artworld its true nature: a spectacular subsystem of global capitalism revolving around the display, consumption, and financialisation of cultural objects for the benefit of a tiny fraction of humanity – the 1%. But we believe that a shift is beginning to occur. We strike the global ultra luxury economy in the interest of making a new space of imagination, one that builds power with people and facilitates the rearrangement of our own desires in the struggle for justice and freedom.

We are cultural workers. We are students, teachers, thinkers, makers, painters, writers, musicians, and more. We recognise and use our privilege to speak out but must always be wary of reproducing the privilege of our location. We work with the imagination and the senses, with hearts and minds, with bodies and voices. We recognise that our work, our creativity, and our potential are channelled into the operations and legitimisation of the system. We work

– often precariously – as both exploiters and exploited, but we do not cynically resign ourselves to this morbid *status quo*. We will not allow our songs to become ashes, or our dreams to become nightmares. We see our proximity to the system as an opportunity to strike it with precision, recognising that the stakes in general far exceed the discourses and institutions of art as we know them.

We are living, working, and creating in an expanded field of empire. This field is marked by mortal crises – crises of finance resulting in gaping inequality, of climate, of dispossession and displacement, of poverty and neocolonialism, of state violence and creeping fascism, and always of patriarchy. But this field is also traversed by freedom struggles, from striking workers in Abu Dhabi and Dubai to insurgents in Palestine, Ferguson, Athens, and beyond. G.U.L.F. itself emerged, in part, from the occupation of Wall Street. There, inspired by uprisings in Tunisia, Egypt, Greece, and Spain, we bypassed the institutions of a corrupted representative democracy. We put our bodies directly on the line at the symbolic doorstep of global capital. Wall Street is an abstract space, everywhere and nowhere at once. By de-occupying it, we created space for collective powers to surge forth and for struggles to connect. Walking together, we have asked questions. How do we live? What is freedom? What does solidarity look like? What role can art play?

We target global systems and local conditions at once. G.U.L.F. names an overarching system, but it also evokes a specific location that exemplifies that system in its most spectacular form: the oil sheikdoms of the Persian Gulf. These states aspire to be a prime recreational playground for the global 1 percent. Artistic and educational institutions from New York to Paris have eagerly contributed their brands to the development of the *de luxe* cityscapes of the Emirates. We see monuments to 'culture' woven into a monstrous assemblage of fossil fuels, financial power, and imperial geopolitics. Holding up the pyramid – bearing the weight of the entire edifice – are the legions of workers from Bangladesh, India, Pakistan, Nepal, Philippines, Sri Lanka, and, most recently, Cameroon, Uganda, and Nigeria, who seek dignity and a better future for their families. They are drawn to the Gulf by economic precarity in their home countries, and typically end up bonded to their work through debt. Many of these workers have been at the forefront of struggles for wages and labour reforms that challenge the very terms of Gulf petro-capitalism, which is itself embedded in flows of capital and labour. The global cultural brands setting up in Abu Dhabi – Guggenheim, Louvre, British Museum, NYU – claim zero responsibility. They insist that the problems of the workers should be addressed to the government, to the subcontractors, to the middlemen, to the 'sending country', but never to the disinterested heights of art institutions themselves who possess a leverage they refuse to acknowledge.

We combine analysis, art, and action. What can be done? Our partners in the Gulf Labor Coalition first brought these conditions of life, work, and debt to public attention. They called for an artists boycott of the Guggenheim Abu Dhabi in particular, demanding that certain conditions on the Island of Happiness be met. Trips have been taken to labour camps and construction zones in Abu Dhabi and Dubai. Reports have been written. Extensive meetings have been convened. G.U.L.F. brought a new element to this arsenal: artistic direct actions targeting the flagship museum in New York, and its Venice branch, designed to incite solidarity, rather than benevolence. We have made unsolicited alterations to the building, to the spectator environment, and to the internal protocols of the museum itself, making it into a temporary zone of the marvellous while drawing connections between the speculative real estate booms and busts from Manhattan to Abu Dhabi. Banners were dropped, propaganda flung like confetti from the heights of the famous spiral, dissenting voices thundered and echoed throughout the rotunda. Police were called in to secure the museum as it shut down. We have disfigured its corporate brand and magnified the pressure on the museum's trustees to accept responsibility for the human suffering at the bottom of the subcontracting chain.

We realise solidarity is a verb. When we act in New York – the capital of the global artworld and global media alike – we perform on an outsize stage, and can amplify many voices, especially those that go unheard on Saadiyat Island. How do we understand that the struggles of the UAE's migrant workers are connected to our own, and are a precondition to our own liberation? We do this not by imagining the worker as a victim to be saved, but rather as a fellow human whose freedom is bound up with our own. We have connected with their plight because our own dignity depends on it. Our liberation is either collective or it is nonexistent, and so we assail the Guggenheim in New York because it is our gateway into a larger struggle. When we proclaim solidarity, we do not ignore very real differentials of condition, temporality, experience, power, and privilege. We hold on to the specificities of struggle because we understand that history is more awesome than good will. We will not be solidarity tourists. Spectacular actions are necessary yet insufficient on their own, but how do we sustain solidarity?

We imagine escalation – at the Guggenheim and beyond. The Guggenheim has been for us an urgent target in its own right. But it has also been a testing ground, a laboratory of learning, a training in the practice of freedom with ramifications far beyond the museum itself. Even if the Guggenheim Foundation trustees accede to the demands of the Gulf Labor Coalition and take independent action to protect the rights of workers and abolish their debts, our work will not be over. Saadiyat Island will still be there as a challenge and a target, along with every other cultural stockpile designed to embellish the lives of ultra-luxury elite at the expense of the lives of a great majority – especially the lives of black and brown people who are systemically devalued and rendered disposable under carceral neoliberalism. The workings of the artworld have long been bound up in the fine art of gentrification – the by-now formulaic intertwining of culture-driven development, realty speculation, and enclave policing that disciplines and displaces poor peoples from urban neighbourhoods. On Saadiyat Island, we see these components in a slightly different, but fundamentally related, combination – brown and black bodies in accommodations that resemble detention camps, toiling under debt bondage and brutal law enforcement to build a real estate paradise for a light-skinned overclass.

We who believe in freedom cannot rest. The ultra-luxury economy is deeply racialised, locally and globally. In the Gulf, Americans and Europeans doing business are called 'expats', whereas people constructing and maintaining these surreal cities in the desert are 'bachelor migrant workers'. Actions within and against this economy must make the struggle against racism and white supremacy an essential part of their drive. This extends to the occupation, exploitation, and ethnic cleansing characteristic of Israeli policy – indeed, a global cultural boycott of institutions connected to Israeli Apartheid is well within our sights. Boycotts, strikes, pickets, die-ins, occupations, web-hacks, media hijacks.... Whatever the combination of tactics, our actions are at once oppositional and abundantly creative. As we disrupt and refuse the role that art is now playing in the normal functioning of this global system that propagates racism and inequality in its shadows, we make space for something new to come into the world that would have otherwise seemed impossible. The heart of this new culture is solidarity and human dignity. We who believe in freedom cannot rest... until it is won.

Global Ultra Luxury Faction (G.U.L.F.), 'On Direct Action: An Address to Cultural Workers', in *The Gulf: High Culture/Hard Labor*, ed. Andrew Ross, (New York and London: OR Books, 2015) 133–136.

Yates McKee
Strike Art: Contemporary Art and the Post-Occupy Condition//2016

[…] Far from two separate entities, Occupy and contemporary art were in fact immanent to one another, involving a dual dynamic in which artists who engaged with Occupy undertook an exodus or desertion from the art system, on the one hand, while taking that system itself as a target of action and leveraging on the other.

A little known fact about Occupy is that, beginning with the inception of the camp itself in September 2011 and subsequently throughout its various phases, artists were core actors in the movement, often dissolving their specialised identities and articulating their skills within an expanded field of movement work. With Occupy, artists were not just decorative adjuncts to the real business of organising for a movement that would otherwise exist without them. Rather, in the words of Amin Husain and Nitasha Dhillon of MTL […] Occupy involved the emergence of 'the artist as organizer'. The phrase alludes to Walter Benjamin's famous figure of the 'author as producer', wherein he argues that the political significance of an artist's work lies not simply in expressing a radical tendency within the established institutions of the art system — as suggested above, contemporary art is suffuse with radical tendencies and content — but rather when it takes on an "organizing function" in the creation of a new collective assemblage of authorship, audience, and distribution networks embedded in political struggle.[1]

During Occupy and beyond, artists engaged in every facet of movement work, including facilitating massive assemblies; designing direct actions; choreographing trainings; preparing and serving food; developing messaging, slogans, chants, and songs; producing concerts; writing communiqués; publishing pamphlets and magazines; and making puppets, costumes, screen-prints, props, banners, signs, posters, stickers, memes, and every other conceivable media form. To be sure, artists were not the only participants in Occupy engaged in such activities, nor did they play a privileged role *qua* artists – a professional identity that was of secondary importance even while specific artistic skills and resources proved highly valuable. Reciprocally, as theorised by the Beautiful Trouble training network, organisers and participants in Occupy with no professional training in art per se found their own work inflected by aesthetic concerns with visuality, performance, and poetics.[2]

It might be objected that just because artists are involved in a particular kind of activity – say, facilitating an assembly, dropping a banner, or setting up a Facebook page – does not mean that this activity is worthy of consideration from the vantage of contemporary art. This is a fruitful line of questioning that goes to the heart of both the discourse of contemporary art as well as Occupy as a cultural and political phenomenon. Two major points can be made in response to this concern. The first is to emphasise that questions about the boundary between – or merging of – 'art' and 'non-art' are themselves recurrent and essential in the history of modern art. The second point is that Occupy as a totality – rather than just this or that phenomena within it – can itself arguably be considered an artistic project in its own right, assuming we reimagine our sense of what art is or can be.

[...] [A]t one end of the spectrum, there is the looming question among critics about what separates art from entertainment, tourism, or speculative investment. In this scenario, art is threatened with dissolution into the capitalist culture industry, a condition to be lamented and, in principle, resisted. At the other end of the spectrum, the boundary separating art from other kinds of social activity, such as education, academic research, urban planning and environmental engineering, is increasingly porous. This 'de-disciplining' of art, as Silvia Kolbowski has put it, often emphasises the virtues of collaborative processes over finite works and rhetorically distances itself from art and its institutions even while being dependent thereon. We are then presented with the question: how and why, if at all, does art survive as specific form of making, experiencing, and perceiving?[3]

The tendency in the contemporary art system to strive for the dissolution of art into other fields of social practice is informed, however faintly, by the dream of the historical avant-garde to liquidate the bourgeois institution of art itself, understood as a specialised, individualised realm of aesthetic appreciation whose aura of autonomy served to cut it off from collectivity with struggle.[4] This aspiration animated the late work of William Morris, who was influenced by the visions of 'communal luxury' enacted by the radical art workers of the Paris Commune.[5] Dada and Surrealism aspired to renew art outside of both bourgeois institutions as well as the world of waged labour in favour of new forms of collective existence, while the Russian Constructivists momentarily became officially sanctioned artistic engineers of the Soviet Union.[6]

Following World War II, this avant-garde impulse would live on in various ways in the United States. For several generations, art historians focused on a narrow 'neo-avant-garde' milieu of the contemporary art system, including happenings, pop art, minimalism, and conceptualism, all defined by agonised meditations on how art might grapple with the conditions of everyday life under the dominance of consumerism and mass media spectacle.[7] More recently, however, historians have begun to rediscover artistic groupings in the 1960s that deserted the institutions and economies of the art system in favour of direct participation in the cultural-political world of the antiauthoritarian Left as activists and organisers in their own right. The ur-example of course comes from the Situationist International in France, which aimed to reactivate the memory of the Paris Commune and redeem the incipient revolutionary desires of Dada and Surrealism. During the late fifties and early sixties they developed a set of analyses and concepts – spectacle, detournement, psychogeography – that would feed directly into the events of May '68, which for them exemplified the simultaneous liquidation and fulfilment of art as such.[8]

In the United States, several examples of what Gavin Grindon has called 'the communization of the avant-garde' are pertinent to thinking about the stakes of Occupy.[9] These would include the counter-spectacular interventions of the Yippies, the DIY movement media of Guerilla Television and Third World Newsreel, the militant direct actions of Black Mask, the creative 'zaps' of women's liberation groups like New York Radical Women and WITCH, and the revolutionary cultural apparatus of the Black Panthers.[10] All such work was embedded in an expanded sense of movement culture of the New Left and the creation of new forms of collective life beyond not only the art system but the wage system as well. [...]

[T]he second major point regarding the dialectic of art and non-art in thinking about the expanded realm of activity undertaken by artists during Occupy: namely, the possibility that *Occupy itself could be considered a kind of artistic project.* Of course, this suggestion requires many caveats, and it is but one of many analytical lenses one could bring to Occupy.

To begin with, this provocation should be read alongside well-established analyses of the transformative role of art and culture in social movements. For example, in his classic study *The Art of Protest*, cultural studies scholar T.V. Reed cites the Freedom Songs of the Civil Rights Movement, the poetics of feminist consciousness-raising circles, and the theatrical actions and agitational graphics of ACT UP as essential forces in the work of these movements.[11] In a similar vein, Robin D.G. Kelley has called for activists to rediscover the poetic powers of the 'black radical imagination' coursing through the 'freedom dreams' of twentieth century liberation movements.[12] Challenging the long-standing left aversion to 'spectacle' understood unilaterally in terms of the mystificatory delusions of the culture industry, Stephen Duncombe (a former ACT UP and alterglobalisation activist himself) has called for progressive forces to highjack the imaginative powers of mass media spectacle – now diffused and hybridised in expanded social networks – in the construction of new dream-images of anticapitalist resistance under conditions of seemingly ironclad capitalist realism.[13] With filmmaker Meg McLagan, I myself have contributed to a growing body of literature concerning the aesthetic dimension of activism that emphasises the importance of the sensuous, embodied experiences of sight, sound, and touch in the staging of nongovernmental political claims and the forging of movement imaginaries relative to the media assemblages within which political action is inscribed.[14] [...]

Occupy took the avant-garde dialectic of 'art and life' to a new level of intensity, whose immediate predecessors since the 1960s would be [...] ACT UP in the late 1980s and the New Anarchism of the 2000s. Like ACT UP, Occupy involved an expansive sense of art and life, one touching on the biopolitical reality of collective survival and sustenance. And yet, also like ACT UP, art in the more limited sense of the word was woven throughout the practices, cultures, and actions of Occupy in a variety of ways. From the prominent presence of precarious, indebted cultural workers in the overall demographic profile of the movement, to the deployment of imagery and tactics inherited from art history, to the targeting of artistic institutions as sites of injustice, to the leveraging of artistic spaces as organising platforms and resource pools, Occupy and its afterlives would be unthinkable without a certain proximity to and entwinement with the art system and its attendant tensions and contradictions.

1   [Footnote 59 in source] MTL, 'Occupy Wall Street: A Possible History', in Nicholas Mirzoeff, ed., *The Militant Research Handbook* (New York: New York University Press, 2013) 16–18. The paraphrase is Walter Benjamin, 'The Author as Producer', in Peter Demetz, ed., Edmund Jophcott, trans. Harry Zohn, ed., *Reflections: Essays, Aphorisms, and Autobiographical Writings* (New York: Schocken, 1986) 220–238.

2   [60] See Andrew Boyd and Dave Oswald Mitchell et al., *Beautiful Trouble: A Toolbox for Revolution* (New York: O/R Books, 2012).

3   [62] See Silvia Kolbowski, David Joselit, and Matthew Friday, 'The Social Artwork', *October* no. 142, (2013), 74–85. This rich discussion is framed in part as an exploration of the ramifications of Occupy for contemporary art.

4   [63] See Peter Bürger, *Theory of the Avant-Garde*, trans. Michael Shaw, (Minneapolis: Minnesota University Press, 1984).

5   [64] Kristin Ross, *Communal Luxury: The Political Imaginary of the Paris Commune* (London and New York: Verso, 2015), and *The Emergence of Social Space: Rimbaud and the Paris Commune*, (Minneapolis: Minnesota University Press, 1988).

6   [65] Gavin Grindon, 'Surrealism, Dada, and the Refusal of Work: Autonomy, Activism, and Social Participation in the Radical Avant-Garde', in *Oxford Art Journal*, vol. 34, no. 1, (2011) 79–96.

7   [66] Benjamin Buchloh, *Neo-Avantgarde and Culture Industry* (Cambridge: MIT Press, 2000).

8   [67] See Thomas McDonaugh, ed., *Guy Debord and the Situationist International: Texts and Documents* (Cambridge: MIT Press, 2002). Also see McKenzie Wark, *The Beach Beneath the Street: The Everyday Life and Glorious Times of the Situationist International* (London and New York: Verso, 2011);

and Kristin Ross, *May '68 and Its Afterlives* (Chicago: University of Chicago Press, 2002).

9   [68] Gavin Grindon, 'Poetry Written in Gasoline: Black Mask and Up Against the Wall Motherfucker', in *Art History,* vol. 38, no. 1, (Autumn, 2014), 170–209.

10   [69] For a reading of the Yippies and Guerilla TV set off against both the contemporary art system and the media landscape of the 1960s, see David Joselit, *Feedback: Television Against Democracy,* (Cambridge: MIT Press, 2007). For primary documents on the performative actions of New York Radical Women and WITCH, see Robin Morgan, ed., *Sisterhood Is Powerful* (New York: Vintage, 1970).

11   [74] T.V. Reed, *The Arts of Protest: Culture and Activism from the Civil Rights Movement to the Streets of Seattle* (Minneapolis: University of Minnesota Press, 2005).

12   [75] Robin D.G. Kelley, *Freedom Dreams: The Black Radical Imagination,* (Boston: Beacon, 2003).

13   [76] Stephen Duncombe, *Dream: Re-Imagining Progressive Politics in an Age of Fantasy* (New York: New Press, 2007). See also Duncombe's entry on 'ethical spectacle' in eds. Andrew Boyd and David Oliver Mitchell, *Beautiful Trouble,* op. cit. With Steve Lambert, Duncombe is the co-director for the Center for Artistic Activism, which has developed a training program for activists informed by these insights. See artisticactivism.org.

14   [77] Yates McKee and Meg McLagan, eds., *Sensible Politics: The Visual Cultures of Nongovernmental Activism,* (London and New York: Zone Books, 2012).

Yates McKee, extracts from *Strike Art: Contemporary Art and the Post-Occupy Condition* (London and New York: Verso, 2016) 25–28, 30, 32.

Occupy [...] can itself arguably be considered an artistic project in its own right, assuming we reimagine our sense of what art is or can be.

Yates McKee, *Strike Art: Contemporary Art and the Post-Occupy Condition*, 2016

HOW CAN WE CREATE A PUBLIC MEMORY FOR A MANY-CULTURED MANY-CULTURED SOCIETY?

ECOLOGY AND THE COMMONS

Félix Guattari
The Three Ecologies//1989

[...] The Earth is undergoing a period of intense techno-scientific transformations. If no remedy is found, the ecological disequilibrium this has generated will ultimately threaten the continuation of life on the planet's surface. Alongside these upheavals, human modes of life, both individual and collective, are progressively deteriorating. Kinship networks tend to be reduced to a bare minimum; domestic life is being poisoned by the gangrene of mass-media consumption; family and married life are frequently 'ossified' by a sort of standardisation of behaviour; and neighbourhood relations are generally reduced to their meanest expression . . . It is the relationship between subjectivity and its exteriority – be it social, animal, vegetable or Cosmic – that is compromised in this way, in a sort of general movement of implosion and regressive infantalisation. Otherness (*l'altérité*) tends to lose all its asperity. Tourism, for example, usually amounts to no more than a journey on the spot, with the same redundancies of images and behaviour.

Political groupings and executive authorities appear to be totally incapable of understanding the full implications of these issues. Despite having recently initiated a partial realisation of the most obvious dangers that threaten the natural environment of our societies, they are generally content to simply tackle industrial pollution and then from a purely technocratic perspective, whereas only an ethico-political articulation which I call ecosophy – between the three ecological registers (the environment, social relations and human subjectivity) would be likely to clarify these questions.

Henceforth it is the ways of living on this planet that are in question, in the context of the acceleration of techno-scientific mutations and of considerable demographic growth. [...] The only true response to the ecological crisis is on a global scale, provided that it brings about an authentic political, social and cultural revolution, reshaping the objectives of the production of both material and immaterial assets. Therefore this revolution must not be exclusively concerned with visible relations of force on a grand scale, but will also take into account molecular domains of sensibility, intelligence and desire. A finalisation of social labour, regulated in a univocal way by a profit economy and by power relations, would only lead, at present, to dramatic dead-ends. [...]

As for young people, although they are crushed by the dominant economic relations which make their position increasingly precarious, and although they are mentally manipulated through the production of a collective, mass-media subjectivity, they are nevertheless developing their own methods of distancing themselves from normalised subjectivity through singularisation. In this respect, the transnational character of rock-music is extremely significant; it plays the role of a sort of initiatory cult, which confers a cultural pseudo-identity on a considerable mass of young people and allows them to obtain for themselves a bare minimum of existential Territories. [...]

The same ethico-political aim runs through the questions of racism, of phallocentrism, of the disastrous legacy of a self-congratulatory 'modern' town planning, of an artistic creation liberated from the market system, of an education system able to appoint its own social mediators, etc. the ecosophic problematic is that of the production of human existence itself in new historical contexts. [...]

I know that it remains difficult to get people to listen to such arguments, especially in those contexts where there is still a suspicion – or even an automatic rejection – of any specific reference to subjectivity. In the name of the primacy of infrastructures, of structures or systems, subjectivity still gets a bad press, and those who deal with it, in practice or theory, will generally only approach it at arm's length, with infinite precautions, taking care never to move too far away from pseudo-scientific paradigms, preferably borrowed from the hard sciences: thermodynamics, topology, information theory, systems theory, linguistics, etc. It is as though a scientistic superego demands that psychic entities are reified and insists that they are only understood by means of extrinsic coordinates. Under such conditions, it is no surprise that the human and social sciences have condemned themselves to missing the intrinsically progressive, creative and auto-positioning dimensions of processes of subjectification. In this context, it appears crucial to me that we rid ourselves of all scientistic references and metaphors in order to forge new paradigms that are instead ethico-aesthetic in inspiration. Besides, are not the best cartographies of the psyche, or, if you like, the best psychoanalyses, those of [Johann Wolfgang von] Goethe, [Marcel] Proust, [James] Joyce, [Antonin] Artaud and [Samuel] Beckett, rather than [Sigmund] Freud, [Carl] Jung and [Jacques] Lacan? In fact, it is the literary component in the works of the latter that best survives (for example, Freud's *The Interpretation of Dreams* can perhaps be regarded as an extraordinary modern novel!). [...]

I have stressed these aesthetic paradigms because I want to emphasise that everything, particularly in the field of practical psychiatry, has to be continually reinvented, started again from scratch, otherwise the processes become trapped in a cycle of deathly repetition (*répétition mortifère*). The precondition for any revival of analysis – through schizoanalysis, for example – consists in accepting that as a general rule, and however little one works on them, individual and collective subjective assemblages are capable, potentially, of developing and proliferating well beyond their ordinary equilibrium. [...]

Félix Guattari, extracts from *The Three Ecologies* (1989), trans. Ian Pindar and Paul Sutton, (London: Athlone Press, 2000) 27–28, 33, 34, 36–37, 39.

Christoph Brunner, Roberto Nigro and Gerald Raunig
Post-Media Activism, Social Ecology and Eco-Art//2013

In his essay *The Three Ecologies* published in 1989 Félix Guattari invents an 'eco'-art (*art de 'l'éco'*).[1] This concept can be misunderstood in several ways. First, one might think of eco-art as 'green art', as art of the Green movement or a Green party. Conceiving of such art simply as an effect of a new ideology constitutes a problematic and instrumentally restricted relation between art and (environmental) politics – be it green politics as a single-issue case or as holistic mythologies of nature. Second, another possible problem resides in a specific form of *oiko*-logy, connoting the domestication, the domestic capture of artistic praxis. And, third, there is the danger of an art-life cliché following on from the bumpy genealogy from Richard Wagner to Joseph Beuys. Inherent to all these misinterpretations of the Guattarian eco-art is an identitarian or moralistic projection of a full, complete and uniform community.

By contrast, Guattari's concept of ecology aims at an opening towards a very broad ethico-political plane of immanence. According to the threefold scheme (or metamodel) of *The Three Ecologies*, Guattari points out three (ecological) fields leading towards an expanded definition of subjectivity: the emergence of subjective factors at the heart of the major political and social transformations of the 1980s, the increasing development of machinic forms of subjectivation, and finally the growing amplification of relevant ethico-aesthetic perspectives throughout the 1980s. Guattari addresses these three tendencies as mental ('nascent subjectivity'), social ('a constantly mutating socius') and environmental ecology ('an environment in the process of being reinvented').[2] The emergence of ecological issues goes hand in hand with the development of mechanisms of decentralisation, de-multiplication of forms of antagonisms, and processes of singularisation. Ecosophy is the name indicating new ways of imagining and analysing production; the mode of thinking, living, experimenting and struggling in another way. In other words, it concerns not the attempt to unify dispersed forms of antagonisms but the invention of new modes of being, new ways of living in the molecular space of existence, within urban spaces, family, relationships, work, etc. What is at stake here is a functional multicentrism going against universal projects of society and abstract syntheses. From a molecular point of view each attempt at ideological unification is a reactionary operation.

Eco-art avoids unifying the three ecological perspectives. It rather implies the possibility of 'opening up processually from a praxis that enables it to be made "habitable" by a human project. It is this praxic opening-out which constitutes the essence of "eco"-art.'[3] Guattari attempts to expose intrinsic antagonisms between the three ecological perspectives. This leads to a chaosmotic mode of recomposition, as Guattari affirms in his last collaboration with Gilles Deleuze: 'Art is not chaos, but a composition of chaos that yields the vision or sensation, so that it constitutes, as Joyce says, a chaosmos, a composed chaos – neither foreseen nor preconceived.'[4]

Art constituting a chaosmos becomes an ecological practice, not in the simple manner of connecting many things, but by itself being of an intrinsic ecological and cosmological quality. As ecological process it resonates with a milieu or habitat (*oikos*).[5] As cosmological event, it ties in 'incorporeal Universes of value' and folds potential becomings into its own processual unfolding.[6] In that respect the eco-aspect does not define domestication but allows for 'giving existential consistency to new pragmatic fields'.[7] Guattari also uses the term existential territory pointing at the complex (if not chaosmic) relational process of a production of subjectivity interlacing milieu, socius and incorporeal ecological dimensions.[8] He underlines throughout his writings that a pragmatics of existence lies at the heart of his politics, where pragmatic means not a generalised utilitarian method but an internal and 'local' operation according to what happens. Accordingly, therefore, the main concern resides less in hermeneutic closure (domestication) through the deterministic use of concepts than in foregrounding the potential 'mutation of environment for praxis'. Each praxis moves in resonances with its milieu, pragmatically figuring out what is happening and what belongs to the process.

How do such ecologies evolve, mutate and activate their potential for relation? For Guattari these processes have to move through ecological registers of existence, always investigating the production of subjectivity as the main territory for constitutions of power-relations and the resistance thereof. A crucial aspect in this processual outline of subjectivity is the need for operations of co-composition and concrete expression (enunciation). As a consequence relational concepts such as transversality take on a central role. Each singularity is given by objectives which are not only local but which themselves expand steadily until they define points of trans-sectoral contact at transnational levels. The processual nature of the production of subjectivity problematises how things might become (as we do not know yet what they can do) instead of just defining their being.

[…] Within this context, and also in relation to his conception of the machine, Guattari develops an understanding of the relation between social ecology and media that thwarts the dichotomy between techno-euphoria and culturally pessimistic demonisation of new media. The matter of concern is based rather on overlapping social and media developments, leading us away from mass media capture and towards completely different machinic ecologies of relation. What does it then mean to talk about a *post-media age*? In a first step, Guattari's claim for a post-media era addresses the anaesthetising effect of mass media in contrast to a renewed democratisation of media technologies for creative purposes. Already in the late 1980s Guattari outlines four crucial points against the ubiquitous fatalism of mass media:

(1) sudden mass consciousness-raising, which always remains possible;
(2)... room for [new] transformative assemblages of social struggle;
(3) the technological evolution of the media and its possible use for non-capitalist goals, in particular through a reduction in costs and through miniaturization;
(4) the reconstitution of labour processes on the rubble of early twentieth-century systems of industrial production, based upon the increased production – as much on an individual basis as on a collective one – of a 'creationist' subjectivity (achieved through continuous training, skill transfer and the re-tooling of the labour force, etc.).[9]

Considering that these four points still sound surprisingly contemporary, how would an actualisation of them look twenty three years later? We propose to investigate this question through the scope of the Occupy movement, following two major lines of post-media activism: the mediality of social organisation and the social ecology of new media. What comes to be termed post-media describes a general transformation away from media as mere technological entities. Opposed to mass-media technologies of the twentieth century, post-media emphasise the modular and open process of the production of subjectivity at the heart of each media-inflected process [...]

The social ecology of the human microphone actualises media not as 'conservative reterritorialization', not as a container or entity. It performs a leap into the gestural realm. In a similar way recent media works around the Occupy movement have adopted a gestural 'style' of making expression felt not through signs, signifiers and languages but through varying camera angles, live video streams and giant projections on public buildings. The seeming flat- and hollowness of the most pertinent phrases such as 'We are the ninety-nine per cent' or 'We are unstoppable, another world is possible' are not a unification of opinions or the general label of a new all-encompassing social movement. They function as expression of collective assemblages of enunciation. The question raised by Guattari concerning eco-art as ecological affair receives a potential extension or modulation through new media technologies. Hence, the terms social media or media of sociality require a careful reconsideration. As much as the human microphone is neither human nor a mere technological device, social media are neither social nor media in the conventional sense of the terms. Guattari's concept of the machine gets closer to the open relaying of relations moving through social, technical, material and abstract layers of existence.[10]

Post-media outlines techniques much more than it defines a technology. As a technique, post-media praxes engage with the potential of technological advancement without disregarding the technology's own mode of existence. A medium here is a relational platform interlinked in transversal processes of creation. The use of hand-cameras capturing actions on the ground of the Occupy movement, which are relayed through live video streaming around the globe, is one way of interlacing struggles at the same time singular and collective. What becomes shareable is not only valid information for another politics of representation (i.e. the violent acts of the police at UC Davis) but also a multiplicity of sensations, through voices, sound and movement.[11] [...]

1   Félix Guattari, *The Three Ecologies*, trans. Ian Pinder and Paul Sutton, (London: Continuum, 2008) 35, 36.

2   Ibid., 19, 20, 38, 45.

3   Ibid., 35.

4   Gilles Deleuze and Félix Guattari, *What is Philosophy?*, trans. Hugh Tomlinson and Graham Burchell, (New York: Columbia University Press, 1994) 204.

5   *The Three Ecologies*, op. cit., 95 fn52.

6   Félix Guattari, *Chaosmosis: An Ethico-aesthetic Paradigm*, trans. Paul Bains and Julian Pefanis, (Indianapolis: Indiana University Press, 1995) 9.

7   Félix Guattari, *Soft Subversions: Texts and Interviews 1977–1985*, ed. Sylvère Lothringer, (Los Angeles: Semiotext(e), 2009), 304.

8   *Chaosmosis*, op. cit., 6.

9   [Footnote 11 in source] Guattari consciously uses quotation marks for the word 'creationist' in the French original. Guattari seemed to have been aware of other uses of the term, pertaining to Christian discourse on evolution. In contrast, his use of the term aims at a different production of subjectivity as a processual and open mode of existence and becoming.

10   [14] *Chaosmosis*, op cit, 34.

11   [15] Félix Guattari, 'On Contemporary Art, Interview with Olivier Zahm', in *The Guattari Effect*, eds. Eric Alliez and Andrew Goffey, (London and New York: Continuum, 2011) 47.

Christoph Brunner, Roberto Nigro and Gerald Raunig, extract from 'Post-Media Activism, Social Ecology and Eco-Art', *Third Text*, vol. 21, no. 1, (January 2013) 10–16.

Mark Fisher and Franco 'Bifo' Berardi
In Conversation: Give Me Shelter//2003

Mark Fisher [...] The idea of the 'slow cancellation of the future' captures very well the sense of the ebbing away of a certain conception of cultural time. We live in what we might call a 'post-progressive' era, where the kind of retrospective time prophesied by Jean Baudrillard and Fredric Jameson is so taken for granted that it is hard to perceive. In *After the Future*, you wrote that you'll never be able to adjust to this new mode of time – a feeling that I certainly share. We also agree on the explanation for the end of the future: the arrival of neoliberalism and post-Fordist capitalism at the end of the 1970s. Since then, the end of the future has been intensified by the kinds of technology which have become dominant in the 21st century: smartphones and cyberspace don't speed up culture so much as overload the human nervous system with unmanageable quantities of stimuli.

But we disagree on the way out of this impasse. You've argued that, in a world where parliamentary politics and mainstream media are pawns of corporations, the best we can hope for is a withdrawal into technologically connected enclaves. In an important recent essay titled 'Strategies of Radical Politics and Aesthetic Resistance', the Belgian political theorist Chantal Mouffe contrasts this strategy with her own approach, which emphasises the struggle for terrain. The role of radical politics and art, Mouffe argues, is to disarticulate the series of connections made by the currently dominant form of power, and to instead create a new set of connections. I must say that I agree. Never in my lifetime has capitalist ideology been weaker; neoliberalism is now played out as a force which has forward momentum (though that isn't to say that it can't continue in perpetuity as a zombie). Now isn't the time to further withdraw from institutions but to reoccupy them. In fact, part of the reason that neoliberalism became so dominant is that we did withdraw, persuaded that mainstream media was dead and that parliamentary politics was a waste of time. But the very success of neoliberalism indicates that these things are far from dead. [...] if we want to recover the future, now is the time to re-engage with such institutions.

Franco 'Bifo' Berardi It isn't easy for me to answer, because you've put your finger on a painful wound – that is, our present theoretical impotence in the face of the de-humanising process provoked by finance capitalism. This feels like a sort of personal defeat. But I can't deny reality, which seems to me to be this: the last wave of the movement – say 2010 to 2011 – was an attempt to revitalise a massive subjectivity. This attempt failed: we have been unable to stop the financial aggression. The movement has now disappeared, only emerging in the form of fragmentary explosions of despair. I use the term 'the movement' to refer to any form of mass action which is able to change the prevailing culture and perception. […] We should be able to produce a theoretical model which assumes that the form of subjectivation that we used to know is now over. The mutation that has infested the post-alphabetical generation – that is, the first generation to learn more words from the machine than from the mother – has deeply eroded the ability to solidarise. A process of social recomposition of precarious labour seems impossible, at least in the form of collective action, political solidarity and class consciousness. I really don't know if that means that my generation is unable to see the new process of social composition that will one day give the new generation the opportunity to free themselves from fear and loneliness. Mouffe writes that 'various modes of artivist intervention influenced by the Situationist strategy of détournement like The Yes Men are very effective in disrupting the smooth image that corporate capitalism is trying to impose, bringing to the fore its repressive character'. This may be true, but the unveiling of the repressive character of power is not going to bring about rebellion. On the contrary, it only reinforces a sense of impotence. The techniques of subversion have been quite efficient in 'revealing' the true nature of financial capitalism, but consciousness of what is real is not class consciousness. It isn't enough to only see the danger – you also need to be able to escape it or to dispel it. The majority of people hate finance capitalism but, as far as I can see, this hatred is turning into depression rather than into autonomy. […] In the last 15 years, however, activism has been totally unable to stop the systematic offensive of corporations and financial agencies. Look at the last wave of struggles against the financial dictatorship, from UK Uncut to the Spanish acampada to Occupy Wall Street. This wave of movements has produced an effect of widespread awareness among the majority of the population, but it hasn't slowed the dismantling of social life. Not only is political activism unable to change the reality of finance capitalism, but the mainstream political parties cannot do anything if they do not follow the automatisms of power. […] I think that autonomy is only possible when people become able to change their daily lives – by breaking the links of dependence on consumerism and exploitation, for instance. In the last two or three years, however, I've started to believe that this precarious generation is unable to start a process of autonomisation. This is because of a sort of psychic frailty produced by precariousness, competition and loneliness.

Fisher That is a very moving and honest answer, but I actually think you highlight the strengths of Mouffe's position. Those strengths have, I think, to do with political strategies, rather than aesthetic ones. Mouffe's examples of subversive or counter-hegemonic art were very unconvincing – the strategies of détournement she referred to have long since been incorporated by capital. Nothing sells better than anti-capitalism – look at the way corporations are depicted in Hollywood films such as *Wall E* (2008) and *Avatar* (2009). It's asking too much of art or culture to expect it to provide resources for overcoming the decomposition of solidarity that you so acutely describe. Art and culture are themselves the victims of this decomposition. Under post-Fordist working practices, neoliberal ideology and communicative capitalism, social imagination struggles to find the time to grow. The current austerity programme in the UK – with its attacks on social housing, welfare benefits, squatting and higher-education funding – will make the unpressured time in which social imagination could develop even scarcer.

It's not that the rise of finance capital is unstoppable, it's that the strategies that the movement has deployed against it are not the right ones – it is easy for capital to route around them. Which is not to say that important things have not happened in the last decade or so: the wave of insurrection in the Middle East in 2011, for instance, showed that the so-called end of history is now over. But an intelligent system needs to learn from its failures, not keep repeating them. As David Harvey has said, we shouldn't fetishise particular organisational forms. Rather, we need to do what neoliberalism has done, and use an ensemble of different strategies. [...] That means fighting for terrain in the dominant media ecologies, as well as in parliamentary politics. [...] We need to reclaim the future whose disappearance you mourn, and that means recovering a *prospective* time, where we are not endlessly protesting against or obstructing capital, but thinking ahead of it. Here is the space for art to reinvent itself – as the site for a multiplicity of visions of a post-capitalist future.

Berardi I don't mean that we should be opposing an aesthetic action to the power of capital. I'm not so naïve. I'm looking for (but not finding) an effective way to destroy the oppressing and depressing and impoverishing power of finance capitalism, which is essentially based on the submission of society. Why has society submitted so easily? This is the question that has to be explained and understood. [...]

Mark Fisher and Franco 'Bifo' Berardi, extracts from 'Give Me Shelter', *Frieze*, no. 152, (2003) 150–152.

Elias Canetti
The Open and the Closed Crowd//1960

The crowd, suddenly there where there was nothing before, is a mysterious and universal phenomenon. A few people may have been standing together – five, ten or twelve, not more; nothing has been announced, nothing is expected. Suddenly everywhere is black with people and more come streaming from all sides as though streets had only one direction. Most of them do not know what has happened and, if questioned, have no answer; but they hurry to be there where most other people are. There is a determination in their movement which is quite different from the expression of ordinary curiosity. It seems as though the movement of some of them transmits itself to the others. But that is not all; they have a goal which is there before they can find words for it. This goal is the blackest spot where most people are gathered.

This is the extreme form of the spontaneous crowd [...] In its innermost core it is not quite as spontaneous as it appears, but, except for these 5, 10 or 12 people with whom actually it originates, it is everywhere spontaneous. As soon as it exists at all, it wants to consist of *more* people: the urge to grow is the first and supreme attribute of the crowd. It wants to seize everyone within reach; anything shaped like a human being can join it. The natural crowd is the *open* crowd; there are no limits whatever to its growth; it does not recognise houses, doors or locks and those who shut themselves in are suspect. 'Open' is to be understood here in the fullest sense of the word; it means open everywhere and in any direction. The open crowd exists so long as it grows; it disintegrates as soon as it stops growing.

For just as suddenly as it originates, the crowd disintegrates. In its spontaneous form it is a sensitive thing. The openness which enables it to grow is, at the same time, its danger. A foreboding of threatening disintegration is always alive in the crowd. It seeks, through rapid increase, to avoid this for as long as it can; it absorbs everyone, and, because it does, must ultimately fall to pieces.

In contrast to the open crowd which can grow indefinitely and which is of universal interest because it may spring up anywhere, there is the *closed* crowd.

The closed crowd renounces growth and puts the stress on permanence. The first thing to be noticed about it is that it has a boundary. It establishes itself by accepting its limitation. It creates a space for itself which it will fill. This space can be compared to a vessel into which liquid is being poured and whose capacity is known. The entrances to this space are limited in number, and only these entrances can be used; the boundary is respected whether it consists of stone, of solid wall, or of some special act of acceptance, or entrance fee. Once the space is completely filled, no one else is allowed in. Even if there is an overflow, the important thing is always the dense crowd in the closed room; those standing outside do not really belong.

The boundary prevents disorderly increase, but it also makes it more difficult for the crowd to disperse and so postpones its dissolution. In this way the crowd sacrifices its chance of growth, but gains staying power. It is protected from outside influences which could become hostile and dangerous and it sets its hope on *repetition*. It is the expectation of reassembly which enables its members to accept each dispersal. The building is waiting for them; it exists for their sake and, so long as it is there, they will be able to meet in the same manner. The space is theirs, even during the ebb, and in its emptiness it reminds them of the flood.

The Discharge

The most important occurrence within the crowd is the *discharge*. Before this the crowd does not actually exist; it is the discharge which creates it. This is the moment when all who belong to the crowd get rid of their differences and feel equal.

These differences are mainly imposed from outside; they are distinctions of rank, status and property. Men as individuals are always conscious of these distinctions; they weigh heavily on them and keep them firmly apart from one another. [...]

Only together can men free themselves from their burdens of distance; and this, precisely, is what happens in a crowd. During the discharge distinctions are thrown off and all feel *equal*. In that density, where there is scarcely any space between, and body presses against body, each man is as near the other as he is to himself; and an immense feeling of relief ensues. It is for the sake of this blessed moment, when no-one is greater or better than another, that people become a crowd.

But the moment of discharge, so desired and so happy, contains its own danger. It is based on an illusion; the people who suddenly feel equal have not really become equal; nor will they *feel* equal for ever. They return to their separate houses, they lie down on their own beds, they keep their possessions and their names. They do not cast out their relations nor run away from their families. Only true conversion leads men to give up their old associations and form new ones. Such associations, which by their very nature are only able to accept a limited number of members, have to secure their continuance by rigid rules. [...]

But the crowd, as such, disintegrates. It has a presentiment of this and fears it. It can only go on existing if the process of discharge is continued with new people who join it. Only the growth of the crowd prevents those who belong to it creeping back under their private burdens. [...]

The Eruption

The open crowd is the true crowd, the crowd abandoning itself freely to its natural urge for growth. An open crowd has no clear feeling or idea of the size it may attain; it does not depend on a known building which it has to fill; its size is not determined; it wants to grow indefinitely and what it needs for this is more and more people. In this naked state, the crowd is at its most conspicuous, but, because it always disintegrates, it seems something outside the ordinary course of life and so is never taken quite seriously. Men might have gone on disregarding it if the enormous increase of population in modern times, and the rapid growth of cities, had not more and more often given rise to its formation.

The closed crowds of the past [...] had turned into familiar institutions. The peculiar state of mind characteristic of their members seemed something natural. They always met for a special purpose of a religious, festal or martial kind; and this purpose seemed to sanctify their state. A man attending a sermon honestly believed that it was the sermon which mattered to him, and he would have felt astonished or even indignant had it been explained to him that the large number of listeners present gave him more satisfaction than the sermon itself. All ceremonies and rules pertaining to such institutions are basically intent on capturing the crowd; they prefer a church-full secure to the whole world insecure. The regularity of church-going and the precise and familiar repetition of certain rites safeguard for the crowd something like a domesticated experience of itself. These performances and their recurrence at fixed times supplant needs for something harsher and more violent.

Such institutions might have proved adequate if the number of human beings had remained the same, but more and more people filled the towns and the accelerating increase in the growth of populations during the last few centuries continually provided fresh incitements to the formation of new and larger crowds. And nothing, not even the most experienced and subtle leadership, could have prevented them forming in such conditions.

[...] I designate as *eruption* the sudden transition from a closed into an open crowd. This is a frequent occurrence, and one should not understand it as something referring only to space. A crowd quite often seems to overflow from some well-guarded space into the squares and streets of a town where it can move about freely, exposed to everything and attracting everyone. But more important than this external event is the corresponding inner movement: the dissatisfaction with the limitation of the number of participants, the sudden will to attract, the passionate determination to reach *all* men.

Since the French Revolution these eruptions have taken on a form which we feel to be modern. To an impressive degree the crowd has freed itself from the substance of traditional religion and this has perhaps made it easier for us to see it in its nakedness, in what one might call its biological state, without the transcendental theories and goals which used to be inculcated in it. The history of the last 150 years has culminated in a spate of such eruptions; they have engulfed even wars, for all wars are now mass wars. The crowd is no longer content with pious promises and conditionals. It wants to experience for itself the strongest possible feeling of its own animal force and passion and, as means to this end, it will use whatever social pretexts and demands offer themselves.

The first point to emphasise is that the crowd never feels saturated. It remains hungry as long as there is one human being it has not reached. One cannot be certain whether this hunger would persist once it had really absorbed all men, but it seems likely. Its efforts to endure, however, are somewhat impotent. Its only hope lies in the formation of double crowds, the one measuring itself against the other. The closer in power and intensity the rivals are, the longer both of them will stay alive. [...]

Elias Canetti, extracts from *Crowds and Power* (1960), trans. Carol Stewart, (New York: Farrar, Straus and Giroux, 1984) 16–19, 20–22.

Jodi Dean
Crowds and Party//2016

The Enduring Crowd
Elias Canetti's study of the crowd is a theory of collective desire. The crowd assembles libidinal and affective intensities into the force of a longing irreducible to the crowd's emotion, to the specific excitement or event that calls it together. Canetti classifies crowds with respect to their prevailing emotion – the baiting crowd out for the kill, the flight crowd in which everyone flees, the prohibition crowd that refuses, the reversal crowd turning against those who command or oppress it and the feast crowd that enjoys in common. What we might think of as the unconscious structure and processes of the crowd, the crowd's economy of enjoyment, persists through or underneath these different types of crowds. [T]his crowd unconscious has four attributes: a desire to grow, a state of absolute equality (which Canetti defines as the 'discharge'), a love of density and a need of direction.

These crowd attributes dynamically generate collective *jouissance*. The desire to increase, expand, accumulate, and extend infuses even the crowd enclosed in an institution. The urge to grow is ineliminable, a primary impulse of the crowd. Crowds can be open or closed, but even spatial limitations can be breached by the crowd's desire to grow. Consider, for example, the odd obviousness of majority rule. The weight of number forces itself as the push of the crowd. It exerts as pressure, no matter whether right or wrong, reasonable or not. Even those who object and resist encounter this pressure. Going against the crowd is hard. The crowd wants to pull everything into itself, to take on more and increase itself. Canetti writes, 'the crowd never feels itself saturated.'[1]

With the discharge, Canetti offers a view of equality fundamentally different from the psychoanalytic association of equality with envy. Equality in the crowd is de-differentiation, de-individuation, the momentary release from hierarchy, closure, and separation. 'It is for the sake of this equality that people become a crowd and that they tend to overlook anything which might detract from it', Canetti writes. 'All demands for justice and all theories of equality ultimately derive their energy from the actual experience of equality familiar to anyone who has been part of a crowd.' The press for equality comes not from ressentiment. It's not born of weakness or deprivation. It comes from the strength of many as it amplifies itself, reinforces itself, and pushes itself back upon itself. With shouts, exclamations, and noise – the spontaneous 'utterance in common' – the crowd expresses the equality that is its substance.

The crowd's density is its indivisibility or degree of solidarity. Understood physiologically, density manifests itself in commonality of feeling, for example, the excitement that passes through the crowd, amplifying and feeding into itself. Close proximity helps here. Canetti pairs equality and density, telling us that in the dancing crowd they coincide. The 'skillful enactment of density and equality' engenders the crowd feeling.

The crowd's direction is its goal. When common, the goal 'strengthens the feeling of equality.' The stronger the common goal is, the weaker the individual goals that threaten the crowd's density. Whereas [Gustav] Le Bon and [Sigmund] Freud attribute the crowd's need for direction to its need for a leader, Canetti makes direction into a process internal to the crowd: direction, common cause, subordinates individual preferences. Everyone belonging to a crowd 'carries within him a small traitor who wants to eat, drink, make love and be left alone.' When the crowd has a direction, when it is moving toward a goal, it can remain dense. Without its goal, the crowd disintegrates into individuals pursuing their own private ends. The goal is outside the crowd, that toward which it is oriented. The goal is not the discharge, although the discharge is the aim.

Canetti's crowd processes resemble psychoanalytic dynamics of desire and drive. Growth and direction point outwards. Equality and density turn back in. Together they form the knot of intensities I am referring to as the crowd unconscious. The crowd isn't structured like a language. It isn't a discursive formation. Rather, it's the dynamic press of many, the force exerted by collectivity. It doesn't have a politics any more than does an anthill, forest, or heap of stones. Canetti's crowds include dancing warriors and swarms of insects, spermatozoa and the dead, production and inflation. The real press of many takes and disrupts multiple forms: material, institutional, imaginary, symbolic. It also occurs in varying temporalities: quick or slow, momentary or enduring. The multiplicity of forms and tempos overlap and intersect, flowing together into a crowd of crowds. What the crowd wants most of all – what it lacks – is endurance.

Canetti writes: 'The tendency of all human crowds to become more and more – the blind, reckless, dynamic movement which sacrifices everything to itself and which is always present in a gathering crowd – this tendency is *transferable*.' He doesn't explicate the concept. Instead he gives multiple examples: hunters transfer the growth tendency to their prey, farmers transfer it to their crops, modern Europeans transfer it to money, using the word 'million' as the basic unit for counting population and money – 'the abstract number has become filled with a crowd-meaning contained by no other number today.' The mechanisms of transference matter little to Canetti. He blurs together rituals, symbols, and processes. All enable the transmission or displacement of the crowd's desire to increase from the crowd onto something else. Wheat, mountains, and sea can become crowd symbols because they can carry the desire for increase.

Practical Optimism

Although Canetti doesn't make this point, the party, too, can carry the desire for increase as well as other attributes of the crowd unconscious. As it gathers and generates power, the party, especially the communist party, operates as a transferential object – a symbol and combination of rituals and processes – for the collective action of the many.

The crowd wants to endure. The party provides an apparatus for this endurance. Marxist discussions of the party typically focus on the organisational and ideological aspects of the party apparatus: vanguard versus mass, covert versus legal, revolutionary versus reformist. Left out is the affective infrastructure of the party, its reconfiguration of the crowd unconsciousness into a political form. Gavin Walker shifts discussion toward this reconfiguration. He describes the party as a 'material substratum' that 'allows the reverberations or 'overtone' of the event to remain at the core of a consistency.'[2] As the body that turns the subjectivising crowd event into a moment in a subjective process of politicising the people, the party is tasked with transmitting the event's overtone. It can't simply declare an event to be an action of the heroic working class or revolutionary people. The party has to defend this declaration in a hostile setting. Even more, it has to ensure its truth, conducing the affective intensity of the crowd discharge in the wake of its dissipation.

Under contemporary conditions of communicative capitalism, nonstop ubiquitous media offer a never-ending supply of disasters, invasions, shootings, and protests. Scandals and epidemics displace one another as the most important issue of the day, their measure in tweets testimony to their inability to produce a gap in the dominant order. Anyone can issue an interpretation of an event, calling it this or that and attempting to push discussions in one direction rather than another. Moreover, a certain reflexivity, a self-consciousness about media, is a constitutive feature of communicative capitalism. Hashtags, slogans, memes, images, and phrases or manners of speech that briefly achieve a kind of recognisable currency before becoming outmoded or forgotten all point to the multiple, distributed ways in which communicative acts are less about meaning than circulation, less about use value than exchange value.[3] This setting poses particular problems for left politics: how can acts remain intelligible as acts of a collective subject? How do the people prevent their acts from being absorbed back into communicative capitalism?

The party provides an affective infrastructure that can help address these problems. Rather than ceding the transmission of the overtone to intellectuals, particularly those individualised within academic or journalistic career paths, and instead of requiring fragmented activists working along multiple separate trajectories to produce their alliance event by event, issue by issue, the party is a form for concentration and endurance. In a capitalist setting, the party provides communism with a body – one that is heterogeneous, porous, and polymorphous.

By the end of the twentieth century, this body was present primarily as memory, fear, bureaucracy, or sect, as former necessity and current impossibility. The perspective it provides became so many scattered inclinations to political correctness, no less righteous and insistent for all their fragmentation into weakness. Indeed, the superegoic effects of righteous injunction seem all the more intense precisely because there is no party that can anchor them, no program to which one might appeal for justification and relief. Circulating as insults and directives in social media, these effects rage as an incessant urge to police and punish, whipping the Left into the frenzy of its own failure. The Left can see differences, but no longer pull them together into a politics. […]

1   [Footnote 2 in source] Elias Canetti, *Crowds and Power*, trans. Carol Stewart, (New York: Farrar, Straus and Giroux, 1984) 22. Originally published in German in 1960.

2   [6] Gavin Walker, 'The Body of Politics: On the Concept of the Party', *Theory & Event*, vol. 16, no. 4, (2013).

3   [7] See my discussion in *Democracy and Other Neoliberal Fantasies* (Durham, NC: Duke University Press, 2009) chapter one.

Jodi Dean, extract from *Crowds and Party* (London and New York: Verso, 2016) 214–218. (Some footnotes omitted).

Eyal Weizman and Matthew Fuller
Investigative Aesthetics: Conflicts and Commons in the Politics of Truth//2021

[…] Any contestation of the strategies of denial and obfuscation must contend with the reality that there is no longer any immediately universal standard or norm that we can turn to and make absolute measurements with. In that respect, an investigative aesthetics must take on part of the challenge of post-truthers, while combating others. Investigative aesthetics must go on questioning the mainstream institutions of state-sanctioned authority, but crucially it proposes something else, an alternative, and rigorous, collective and diverse set of truth practices.

To some extent society might have itself to blame for elevating scientific authority over truth, rendering it unquestionable. Nuclear power, racist algorithms, the domination of disciplines such as geology by oil companies, the endless 'accidental' devastations of pollution, the epidemic mayhem of intensive farming and science's too eager siding with whomever offers research funds, all play their part in the slackening of trust. Though the scientific process is conceived to be open and collective, when used as political currency, scientific truth often tends to be presented as too complex to be contributed to or questioned by the 'general public'. This results in the institutions of science sometimes taking on something of the guise of their theological predecessors – inherently true, beyond reproach, with transcendental qualities.

It is thus no wonder that what we today see across widespread locations of many kinds is a sense of inchoate rebelliousness. If the institutions of truth demand belief in the form of simple allegiance, then no doubt opposition will be articulated as heretical. The rebellion against scientific experts and the institutions that buttress facts thus resembles, in some aspects, the Reformation's rebellion against Rome. Indeed, few of the current crop of anti-epistomologists have been slow to cast themselves in the image of insurgent speakers of truth to power. It is a fight for power that deserves a few incredulous giggles, but it has its merits.

Over the presumed ruins of institutional truth, 'anti-epistemologists' present truth as simple and given, ready at hand, its weight coming from mere pronouncement. Rejection of a given authority is simply replaced by affirmation of another. In this struggle perhaps the current push to passive scepticism towards expertise can be taken as a prompt to look for other ways of producing and disseminating knowledge. [...] A different line would be to embrace the challenge to institutional authorities of power knowledge, while opposing and combating the methods of anti-epistemologists. It is precisely when the value of truth is unstable that we need to question both facts and fact-making: when we cannot rely on the authority of experts and their institutions of knowledge that are debated and decided upon outside the public domain and outside public scrutiny. Then, we must find ways to bring this debate to the public, perhaps meaning in turn to take part in *making* publics, seeing them as active entities that gather around specific issues as sociologist Noortje Maares suggests.

Models are awkward. Calculations come with caveats. For those in power it has often seemed far better to emphasise truth merely as an exercise of power on the one hand (theirs) or as a matter of a point of view in the hands of the other, where it is essentially trivial, rather than something that has to be struggled for and worked at. Investigative aesthetics can act against this tendency by insisting that truth is something with which one is careful. As the philosopher Isabelle Stengers argues in her 'Manifesto for Slow Science', it is necessary to carefully recognise the tensile interrelations of emergent facts, the knowledge and positions that make them credible and the penumbra of possibilities that surround them.

An aesthetic of truth reduced to certainty offers *veritas* a quasi-religious ideal of cognitively affordable simplifications that rise toweringly above the everyday muddle. Veritas, though by its nature impossible to state, is seen as *that which is simply the case*. Here, fear of the complexity of the world is answered by an elated simplification of it, manifesting as a farcical remake of the defensive corrals of species, gender, race, nation and the pre-eminence of capital. This is the opposite of the aesthetics that revels in, and struggles with, complexity in the world. In a sense, then, investigative aesthetics bears the traces of a conflict within and between different definitions of aesthetics. It points to an inter-aesthetic conflict – tending, in certain inflections, perhaps, towards an aesthetic civil war. This struggle is as much about what aesthetics might be, what its boundaries are, and how they might expand. [...]

Eyal Weizman and Matthew Fuller, extract from *Investigative Aesthetics: Conflicts and Commons in the Politics of Truth* (London and New York: Verso, 2021) 22–25. (Footnotes omitted).

T.J. Demos
Decolonising Nature: Contemporary Art and the Politics of Ecology//2016

[...] Decolonising nature entails transcending human-centred exceptionalism, no longer placing ourselves at the centre of the universe and viewing nature as a source of endless bounty. Fields of inquiry that have recently investigated the terms of such a move include speculative realism, new materialism, ecosophical activism, object-oriented ontology, elementary politics, and post-humanism, each variously proposing innovative methodologies of post-anthropocentric analysis. This diverse and at times conflictual movement represents nothing less than a paradigm shift in the humanities, constitutionally preoccupied in the past with the human, its histories, epistemologies, ethics, and aesthetics. [...] There are indeed many critical resources newly available for political-ecology analysis. At the forefront of this convergence, art figures as a central platform for the creative practice of speculative realisms, linking with further philosophical inquiry and conceptual experimentation, as well as exploring, for instance, what a 'world-without-us' would be like, or what 'zoe-egalitarianism' would mean and 'becoming-Earth' entail. But there are many potential rifts and discontinuities in this theoretical confluence. Along with [Bruno] Latour, theorists like [Timothy] Morton have gone to great lengths to criticise the traditional Western concept of nature by mobilising post-anthropocentric terms that are also post-natural. Long positioned as an ahistoric monolith in a separate realm apart from the human, nature's conventional definition appears to critics faulty for its basis in ontological objectification and dualistic thinking, the conceptual platform for extractivist practice. It is also opposed for its ideological manipulations, particularly where it acts as a force of naturalisation, fixation, and domination. 'Ecology without nature', then, promises to dissolve representational forms that allow for exploitation of a vast realm by agents who exist in the unnatural zone of culture.[1] Yet, in my view, rejecting the term nature is not an option, even while I agree with efforts geared toward its conceptual reorientation in order to undo nature's objectification and ontological isolation. Even more, it's crucial to acknowledge nature's significance as a rallying cry within the contemporary resurgence of Indigenous and environmentalist activism, which also insists that humans are fully integrated in and part of the natural realm. An additional obstacle with some of these approaches is that proposals for new sociopolitical compositions, modelled on a cosmopolitical scenography of global governance, as in Latour's work, often lack a structural critique of neoliberalism (indeed, this absence helps explain Latour's problematic support for techno-fixes and geoengineering projects, a position directly challenged in [Naomi] Klein's recent work).[2] For there's little in Latour's 2004 book *Politics of Nature*, or in his recent writings about the Anthropocene, that attends to the WTO, free trade arrangements, the World Economic Forum in Davos, or the political economy of petro-capitalism – a complex actor-institutional network that motors the global fossil-fuel ecologies of unsustainability. As a result, we are invited to overlook the manifold violence that is climate change. In this regard, Latour's silence, or lack of direct engagement with corporate globalisation, parallels speculative realism's characteristic political diffidence, its general withdrawal from the political sphere of human activities, swept aside in its eagerness to theorise object-oriented ontologies. Given these tendencies, it's necessary to bring these formations into relation with key accounts of political and social ecology; that is, if they are to gain critical use value. For me, these include, but are not limited to, the work of postcolonial and Marxist theorists and activists (for instance, Vandana Shiva, David Harvey, Neil Smith, and Jason Moore), along with the direct political analysis of groups like the International Forum on Globalization, the International Rights of Nature Tribunal, and the Indigenous movement Idle No More, in addition to a more socially engaged eco-criticism (such as that of Rob Nixon, Ashley Dawson, and Ursula Heise), all of which focus on the crises and conflicts of actual environmental struggles. As well, environmental concerns in the Global South need to be addressed, and here I've considered what Madhav Gadgil and Ramachandra Guha call the 'environmentalism of the poor'. Doing so helps to avoid continuing the Global North's legacy of provincialism, prejudice, and privilege regarding ecology, which has led to the multifaceted violence toward the West's colonised peoples, as well as toward its own poor, disenfranchised, and Indigenous populations – part and parcel of what Gadgil and Guha term an 'environmentalism of affluence', which also might be said to characterise some of the recent theorisations of the speculative turn.[3] [...]

1   [Footnote 46 in source] Timothy Morton, *Ecology without Nature: Rethinking Environmental Aesthetics* (Cambridge, Massachusetts, and London: Harvard University Press, 2007).

2   [47] Bruno Latour, 'Love Your Monsters', in *Love Your Monsters: Postenvironmentalism and the Anthropocene*, eds. Ted Nordhaus and Michael Shellenberger (Oakland, CA: Breakthrough Institute, 2011) 17–25, http://thebreakthrough.org /index.php/journal/past-issues/issue-2/love-your-monsters; and Naomi Klein, *This Changes Everything* (New York: Simon & Schuster, 2015) 279.

3   [50] Madhav Gadgil and Ramachandra Guha, 'Ideologies of Environmentalism', in *Ecology and Equity: The Use and Abuse of Nature in Contemporary India* (London: Routledge, 1995) 98.

T.J. Demos, extract from *Decolonizing Nature: Contemporary Art and the Politics of Ecology*, (Berlin: Sternberg Press, 2016) 19–22. (Some footnotes omitted)

Catherine Flood and Gavin Grindon
Disobedient Objects//2014

[…] Disobedient objects have a history as long as social struggle itself. Ordinary people have always used them to exert 'counterpower'. Objects have played a key role in social change alongside performance, music and the visual arts. Here the focus is on the previously under-examined area of the art and design of object-making within social movements, a people's history of art and design from below. Yet the imagination and creativity of making within social movements has played a key role in achieving social change; upending the terms of public debates; and directly influencing more familiar commercial art and design. The role of material culture in social movements is a mostly untold story. […]

Making Trouble: Swarm Design and Ecologies of Agency

Disobedient objects are most commonly everyday objects appropriated and turned to a new purpose, from the wooden shoe of the saboteur (from *sabot*, French for wooden shoe) thrown into a factory machine to the shoe thrown at President Bush by an Iraqi journalist during a press conference with the words, 'This is a farewell kiss from the Iraqi people, you dog'. Collective appropriation can be found in the noisemaking pots and pans first used in Chile's *cacerolazos* in the 1970s, in which the archetypal objects of domestic design sounded a counter public sphere, or the mass jingling of keys, which unlocked the air of public space during the 1989 Czech Velvet Revolution. But disobedient objects are about making as much as breaking. Disobedience can involve DIY hacking and alteration, and also the design of whole new ways of disobeying. The re-use of easily accessible objects, like the shipping barrels composing nineteenth century barricades (from *barrique*, French for barrel), implicate these objects in unfinished dialectics of social struggle and make them one means of the global circulation of struggles. For example, wooden pallets, the structural foundation of one unit load, were produced by the mid-twentieth-century standardisation of international container shipping. They were brought about by efficiency drives rooted in de-skilling and breaking the power of unionised longshoremen's labour. But these mass-produced wooden frames, designed for disciplining labour and circulating commodities, became, around the world, a shared infrastructural basis for the first 1970s tree-sits in New Zealand; furniture and barricade elements in 1970s Kabouter squats in the Netherlands, or those of Okupa in Spain; and more recently the base of 123 Occupy's designs to support the protest-unit of Occupy Wall Street tents.

Disobedient objects are not mere props. Or rather, as disability scholars have observed, democracy has always relied on prostheses. The system of voting, for example, has always been propped up by objects, from the Chartists' call for the democratising impairment of secret ballots, where paper cards replace voices, to the pushbutton electronic voting machines introduced in India in the 1980s, which facilitated voting for illiterate citizens. Social movements, too, have their own props and they can fall down without them. (Even though, in British ecological movements, the key material infrastructures of protest events are referred to, self-depreciatingly, as 'activist tat'.) Though we have avoided the term, we might think of these as 'activist objects' in the sense that they are active, bound up with the agency of social change. The objects do not possess agency in themselves, but make change as part of ecologies composed also of other objects, music, performing bodies, technology, laws, organisations and affects. A weaker, less resourced power can triumph through asymmetrical innovation, and since the 1980s the strategic advantages of smallness and mobility have increased. So while disobedient objects are often appropriated, they also often appropriate their context of existing architecture or situations, unlocking them to reframe a situation or produce new relationships. As many have argued, the best response to a powerful enemy can be a more powerful story. Eclectic Electric Collective's inflatable cobblestones thrown at the police playfully destabilise relations between police and protesters. The Book Bloc implicates the police in a dance with demonstrators. The police's attempt to control the streets using violence is reframed as an attack on access to education. The holes wrought in the shields by the police's truncheons are part of their provenance, a certifying signature of their unwitting co-authorship.

While their social and geographical contexts vary widely, disobedient objects share common modes of production, lines of communication and influence. History from below entails multiplicity, and we focus on the interweaving of different historical moments. These objects don't move from producer to market in a circulation of commodities, as in Marx's scheme of Money-Commodity-Money, but are one means of a circulation of struggles (perhaps, Movement-Object-Movement). Making a new world is always an experiment, but it doesn't happen in an isolated laboratory. The objects involved are prototypes that exist in the wild, to be modified and reworked to meet the needs of different times and places. They have a distributed collective authorship, involving multiple reappropriations and reworkings as movements learn from each other and develop each other's tactics, or solve similar problems with parallel approaches.

Tripods

Tripods, objects that augment the body's ability to blockade, are an archetypal example of this swarm design. On 26 March 1974, loggers arrived in the village of Reni in Uttarakhand, northern India. Female villagers, after trying to reason with them, explaining that they relied on the trees for their livelihood, were threatened with guns. In response, they extended Ghandian methods to *chipko*: hugging the trees in a bodily blockade. Their successes in forest conservation became a strategic rallying point for the nascent ecological movement. In 1978 in New Zealand, as part of anti-logging protests that led to the foundation of Pureora Forest Park, activists extended such blockades by moving out of easy reach, building platforms using wooden pallets high up in the trees to blockade the felling with 'tree-sits', a tactic also adopted in Australia's Terrania Creek in 1979 (in what became national park land, including the picturesque Protesters Falls), and in the US in 1985 to prevent logging in Willamette National Forest, Oregon. As the tactic spread, tree surgery businesses or industrial rope access firms were sometimes hired in the United States and Britain to assist police and bailiffs in extracting protesters from trees. But protesters out-designed the authorities once again. In 1989, during huge anti-logging blockades in Coolangubra State Forest, Australia, activists raised a three-legged tripod about six metres high that blocked the single logging road into the forest: a tree-sit without a tree. The first tripod was a metal scaffold, pulled into place by a vehicle, but others there and at the parallel Chaelundi forest blockades used wooden logs. One person sat atop the tripod, so that removing any of its legs would cause him or her to fall and be injured.[1] Some of these forests later became national parks. The North East Forest Alliance's 1991 *Intercontinental Deluxe Guide to Blockading* spread tripod (and lock-on) designs to the UK and US (some individual activists travelled between Australian, American and British actions, too). In the US, wooden tripods first appeared in 1992 blockades protecting the Cove Mallard wilderness. In Britain, the tripod was adopted by Reclaim the Streets, where urban activists with strong ties to earlier British tree-sits scavenged steel scaffolding poles to make tripods. In an urban context they constituted 'intelligent barricades' that closed a road to cars but left it open for pedestrians and bicycles. Beginning on Angel High Street, London, in 1994, these tripods made Reclaim the Streets parties possible. The design spread through the how-to guide *Road Raging* (c.1996). Bipod and even unipod designs, alongside complex multi-tripod architectural arrangements using overlapping legs, sometimes in response to the development of specialised police removal units, proliferated in the United States, Asia-Pacific and Europe. Groups invested in lighter, more quickly erected aluminium (and even bamboo) poles over steel scaffolding. From the 2006 British Climate Camp protests, the tripod became a graphic icon of protest and was sometimes erected at camp entrances for purely symbolic reasons. […]

Context is everything. We should be wary of any uncritical affirmation of the power of making, 'creative' activism or transversal innovation in the context of the neoliberal relations of the 'creative industries'. Rather, the contradiction remains open: to produce any value at all capital relies on the same capacity to be creative that is always also escaping and refusing. Even the most ultra-left or experimental politics are indebted to the creativity of social movement cultural traditions. This creativity can come from mobilising folk-traditions and religious or spiritual values: for example, in British labour union banners' dense iconography; Indonesian group Taring Padi's protest puppets' adaptation of the traditions of wayang puppet theatre; Muneteru Ujino's neo-folk metal Mikoshi used in the 2003 demonstrations in Japan against the invasion of Iraq; the carved Maori *pouwhenua* (pre-European land marker post) made for carrying at the head of the 1975 Maori land rights march and subsequent protests; or the avatar of the Broom-Wielding Goddess of Good Governance. (Swachha Narayani) protecting street hawkers in Sewa Nagar market in Delhi, who, in her many arms, holds a video camera to film the police. […]

Disobedient objects also lead us to think about how movements produce new forms of knowledge and strategy that help us see from below. While they may find footholds in various disciplines, they also draw from popular global and local traditions of making, outside professional art and design or academia. Some of these are evoked by the many how-to publications which instruct their readers on the design of disobedience: the barricade diagrams of Auguste Blanqui's 1866 *Instructions for an Insurrection*; Bread and Puppet Theater's *68 Ways to Make Really Big Puppets*; Dave Foreman's *Ecodefense: A Field Guide to Monkeywrenching*; *The Squatter's Handbook*; *The Activist Tat Collective Recipe Book* for camps and convergences, or the recent collection *Beautiful Trouble*. These objects embody knowledge and skills. They are not formed from nothing. We might consider the section of [Karl] Marx's *Grundrisse*, in which he argues that the fixed capital of factory machines materially embodies the 'general intellect' of workers – their aggregate skill and knowledge – in order to replace them. This might prompt us to wonder what other anti-capitalist machines the general intellect might imagine and embody itself in. We might think of the objects and performances of social movements as just such machines, embodying knowledge otherwise. There is certainly a mutiny of professional knowledge, including design, in these objects. But they are also moulded by the collective, informal, experiential knowledge of local laws around protest; how to negotiate with police; political meeting and street protest dynamics. Additionally, they spring from a base in leisure and domestic skills that become political tools, from camping to knitting and sewing. Behind the design of tripods stand other changes in leisure and education, for example, the growth of climbing as a sporting activity and the growth of indoor walls in the 1980s, often appearing first in university gyms. Such knowledges are one example of what [Stefano] Harney and [Fred] Moten call 'the undercommons'. [...] Its appearance in the museum echoes its role in the university: It cannot be denied that the university is a place of refuge and it cannot be accepted that the university is a place of enlightenment. In the face of these conditions one can only sneak into the university and steal what one can. To abuse its hospitality, to spite its mission, to join its refugee colony, its gypsy encampment, to be in but not of — this is the path of the subversive intellectual in the modern university. [...]

1   [Footnote 29 in source] Although this design spread, it was pre-dated or paralleled by similar architectural design solutions to resisting eviction, for example, the nets and scaffold towers of the anti-road building actions of Claremont Road, London, in 1994; the Sharpness nuclear train blockade of 1980 in Britain, or the wooden towers and barriers of the anti-nuclear Free Republic of Wendland, Germany, in 1980. Ian Cohen, *Green Fire* (Pymble, 1997) 199, Iain McIntyre (ed), *How to Make Trouble and Influence People* (Oakland, 2013) 154.

Catherine Flood and Gavin Grindon, extracts from 'Introduction' in *Disobedient Objects*, eds. Catherine Flood and Gavin Grindon, (London: V&A Publishing, 2014) 9, 14–19.

Judith Baca
Whose Monument Where? Public Art in a Many-Cultured Society//1996

[...] Using the term 'public art' in an audience of many cultures brings different images to mind in each of us. Perhaps some of us envision the frescoes and statues of the Italian Renaissance or Christo's umbrellas, while others see the murals of Los Tres Grandes or the ritual sand paintings and totems of Native peoples. Someone said that the purpose of a monument is to bring the past into the present to inspire the future. Monuments may be like the adobe formed from the mud of a place into the building blocks of a society; their purpose may be to investigate and reveal the memory contained in the ground beneath a 'public site', marking our passages as a people and re-visioning official history. As artists creating the monuments of the 90s, the ultimate question for us to consider is, what shall we choose to memorialise in our time?

Over the past twenty years as a public artist, I have been struck by how our common legacy in public art is derived from the 'cannon-in-the-park' impulse, which causes us to drag out the rusty cannons from past wars, polish them up, and place them in the park for children to crawl over at Sunday picnics. The purpose was to evoke a time past in which the 'splendid triumphs' and 'struggles of our forefathers' shifted the course of history. These expositions were meant to inspire an awe of our great nation's power to assert its military will and prevail over enemies. Running our hands over the polished bronze, we shared in these victories and became enlisted in these causes. Never mind if for us as people of colour they were not our forefathers, or even if the triumphs were often over our own people. [...]

From the triumphant bronze general on horseback – the public's view of which is the underside of galloping hooves – to its more contemporary corporate versions, we find examples of public art in the service of dominance. By their daily presence in our lives, these artworks intend to persuade us of the justice of the acts they represent.

The power of the corporate sponsor is embodied in the sculpture standing in front of the towering office building. These grand works, like their military predecessors in the parks, inspire a sense of awe by their scale and the importance of the artist. Here, public art is unashamed in its intention to mediate between the public and the developer. In a 'things go down better with public art' mentality, the bitter pills of development are delivered to the public. While percent-for-art bills have heralded developers' creation of amenable public places as a positive side effect of 'growth', every inch of urban space is swallowed by skyscrapers and privatised into the so-called public space of shopping malls and corporate plazas. These developments predetermine the public, selecting out the homeless, vendors, adolescents, urban poor, and people of colour. Planters, benches, and other 'public amenities' are suspect as potential hazards or public loitering places. [...]

No single view of public space and the art that occupies it will work in a metropolis of multiple perspectives. While competition for public space grows daily, cultural communities call for it to be used in dramatically different ways. What comes into question is the very different sensibilities of order and beauty that operate in different cultures. When Christo, for example, looked for the first time at El Tejon Pass, he saw potential. He saw the potential to create beauty with a personal vision imposed on the landscape – a beauty that fit his individual vision of yellow umbrellas fluttering in the wind, marching up the sides of rolling hills. The land became his canvas, a backdrop for his personal aesthetic.

Native people might look at the same landscape with a very different idea of beauty, a beauty without imposition. [...] Or perhaps Native peoples could not think of this area without recalling Fort Tejon, one of the first California Indian reservations established near this site in the Tehachapi Mountains, placed there to 'protect' Indians rounded up from various neighbouring areas, most of whose cultures have been entirely destroyed. In Christo's and the Native visions we have two different aesthetic sensibilities, as divergent as the nineteenth-century English manicured garden is from the rugged natural New Mexican landscape of the Sangre de Cristo Mountains. [...]

At this time the conditions of our communities are worse than those that precipitated the civil rights activism of the 60s and 70s. 52% of all African American children and 42% of all Latino children are living in poverty. Dropout rates exceed high school graduation rates in these communities. What, then, is the role of a socially responsible public artist? As the wealthy and poor are increasingly polarised in our society, face-to-face urban confrontations occur, often with catastrophic consequences. Can public art avoid coming down on the side of wealth and dominance in that confrontation? How can we as artists avoid becoming accomplices to colonisation? If we chose not to look at triumphs over nations and neighbourhoods as victories and advancements, what monuments could we build? How can we create a public memory for a many-cultured society? Whose story shall we tell?

Of greatest interest to me is the invention of systems of 'voice giving' for those left without public venues in which to speak. Socially responsible artists from marginalised communities have a particular responsibility to articulate the conditions of their people and to provide catalysts for change, since perceptions of us as individuals are tied to the conditions of our communities in a racially unsophisticated society. We cannot escape that responsibility even when we choose to try; we are made of the 'blood and dust' of our ancestors in a continuing history. Being a catalyst for change will change us also.

We can evaluate ourselves by the processes with which we choose to make art, not simply by the art objects we create. Is the artwork the result of a private act in a public space? Focusing on the object devoid of the creative process used to achieve it has bankrupted Eurocentric modernist and postmodernist traditions. Art processes, just as art objects, may be culturally specific, and with no single aesthetic, a diverse society will generate very different forms of public art.

Who is the public now that it has changed colour? How do people of various ethnic and class groups use public space? What ideas do we want to place in public memory? Where does art begin and end? Artists have the unique ability to transcend designated spheres of activity. What represents something deeper and more hopeful about the future of our ethnically and class-divided cities are collaborations that move well beyond the artist and architect to the artist and the historian, scientist, environmentalist, or social service provider. Such collaborations are mandated by the seriousness of the tasks at hand. They bring a range of people into conversations about their visions for their neighbourhoods or their nations. Finding a place for those ideas in monuments that are constructed of the soil and spirit of the people is the most challenging task for public artists in this time.

Judith Baca, extracts from 'Whose Monument Where? Public Art in a Many-Cultured Society', in Suzanne Lacy (ed.), *Mapping the Terrain: New Genre Public Art* (Seattle: Bay Press, 1996) 131–138.

Sethembile Msezane
It's Coming Down Today//2015

I was born in the 90s, but I'm not a Born Free; it was before South Africa became a democracy. Many believe that my generation doesn't have anything to protest against. Given that police threw stun grenades at a student protest outside parliament last month, that is far from the truth.

I believe that South Africa's memorialised public spaces are barren of the black female body, so last year I started doing performance art (I'm a fine arts student at the University of Cape Town) to draw attention to the issue. I performed as Lady Liberty on Freedom Day, Rosie the Riveter on Women's Day. The character I'm portraying here depicts the statue of the Zimbabwe bird that was wrongfully appropriated from Great Zimbabwe by the British colonialist Cecil Rhodes. It currently sits in his Groote Schuur estate.

The Rhodes Must Fall protests had been going on for a month, kickstarted by an activist smearing his statue with excrement. During a lecture, students were asked whether they were for or against. Most said 'for', that it was a painful reminder of our colonial past, but one student – with a piece of paper that said '#procolonialism' on her chest – called protesters neanderthals, and said, 'If you're against the statue you're against enlightenment and education, and you shouldn't be at university.'

I knew it was only a matter of time before the statue fell, but at 11am on 9 April my supervisor said: 'It's coming down today'. I'd prepared my costume for the occasion and rushed to get ready. A friend helped me transport my plinth and wings. I arrived just before 2pm and was up on the plinth by quarter past. It was a little nerve-racking to be so high up because I was wearing high heels.

I looked at people's phones and sunglasses, trying to see the reflection of the statue coming down. I saw the shadow move and thought, 'This is the moment'. That's when I lifted my wings.

I was up there for four hours. I would hold up my wings for about two minutes, take a 10-minute break and then put them up again. My legs hurt, but I didn't realise how sore my arms were until I came down – they were shaking. My feet were blue, I was sunburnt; I had heat stroke and blurry vision from looking directly into the sun. I went home, had a shower and went straight to sleep. I felt like we were beginning to question this idealistic 'rainbow nation'.

I first saw the picture the next day on Facebook. When someone told me it was all over the global news, I was surprised.

I'm not
sure that
we need

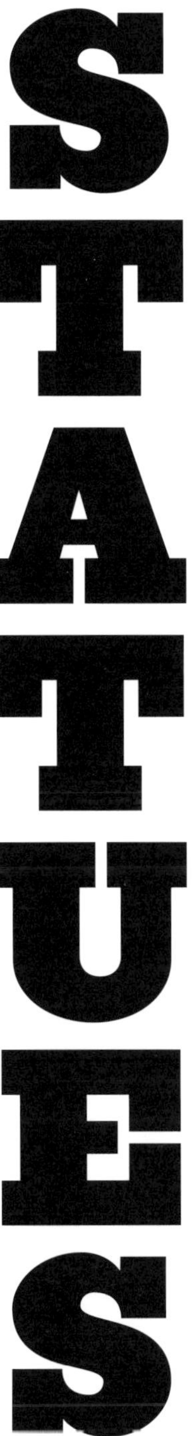

at all

Sethembile Msezane, 'It's Coming Down Today', 2015

Since the fall of the statue, I think people are still in disbelief. I haven't been back yet, but I imagine students stand where the statue was and admire the landscape and the view of the whole of Cape Town.

I'm not sure that we need statues at all – it's a colonialist thing, like marking territory. My work is a response, to get people to look at the landscape with a different eye. People haven't forgiven or forgotten, they're still harbouring hatred. That's why the statue needed to fall. It fostered the kind of thinking that is dangerous to a country in healing.

Sethembile Msezane interviewed by Erica Buist, 'Sethembile Msezane Performs at the Fall of the Cecil Rhodes Statue', *The Guardian* (15 May, 2015) (https://www.theguardian.com/artanddesign/2015/may/15/sethembile-msezane-cecil-rhodes-statue-cape-town-south-africa).

Allora & Calzadilla
In Conversation with Stephanie Smith//2005

Allora & Calzadilla […] Vieques is an island off the mainland of Puerto Rico used for the past 60 years by the US Military and NATO forces to practice military bombing exercises. The civil disobedience movement on the island, along with the active protest movement and various civic initiatives by Viequenses and an international network of support, led in May of 2002 to the stopping of the bombing, the removal of the US military forces from the island and the beginning of the process of demilitarisation, decontamination and future development. When the civil disobedience movement succeeded in removing the US military from the island in 2003, the land changed ownership from US military property to the ownership and management by the US Department of Interior, Fish, and Wildlife Services. This shift in management has created a stalemate for the civic initiative organisations on the island, who are demanding that their land be decontaminated of all toxic substances and unexploded ordnance and ultimately be restored to municipal jurisdiction and management.

[…] *Returning a Sound* was made after the military lands were finally opened to the public in May 2003. We were thinking about how this celebratory moment, in which the civic movement enjoyed a momentous victory, was also quite a precarious time, as the ultimate fate of the land was still uncertain. We became interested in the idea of an anthem as a commemorative structure, but we were not satisfied with the conservative connotations of the word, its uses and abuses. We preferred the more open set of associations that the Greek etymology of the word offered: *antiphonos*, sounding in answer, and *anti-*, in return. We wanted to create a gesture that would at once proclaim loudly the achievement of the civic initiatives yet would call to attention the new stakes of the movement.

Our video, *Returning a Sound*, follows the path of Homar, a civil disobedient, moving throughout the island on his moped. The muffler of his bike has been altered from an apparatus used to silence the noise produced by the motor to an instrument, a trumpet, used to produce a loud resounding call, a call to attention and to action, as the island now is entering a transitional period between destruction and recovery and a new era of imagining its future development.

Stephanie Smith What about *Under Discussion*?

Allora & Calzadilla The present state of the land in Vieques is under discussion. Facing challenges in many ways far greater and complex than the demilitarisation campaigns, the citizens of Vieques are currently entrenched in a mire of bureaucratic, administrative, legal, and political debates concerning the fate of their island. This film follows the son of a local fisherman involved in the Fisherman's Movement, a key movement in the 1970s that initiated the civil disobedience movement on the island. He has converted the discussion table, by turning it upside down, into a boat, and is driving it along the coastal areas of the island where the land status is still contested. Mobilising the discussion table through its conversion into a fishing boat, the protagonist takes the debate into new, unexpected directions.

Smith Under Discussion was just included in the Venice Biennale. Was it your choice to show the piece? If so, why did you select it for that context?

Allora & Calzadilla Yes, we chose to show the work for a number of reasons, starting first with the site of the Biennale in the Italian Naval Arsenale. Shown in that context, the video opens up to crosscultural and transhistorical references, as the subject of militarism, conquest, and empire have played a central role throughout civilisations and histories. The video considers what happens to former military land. Showing it in the context of a large-scale international art exhibition housed in a former navy property confronts the viewer with one possible outcome, a site for cultural production, while hopefully critically opening that space up to its own form of interrogation, perhaps leading the viewer to question, among other things, the role culture plays in such transitional spaces, what it permits and what it excludes. Another, more pragmatic interest of ours was to expose the situation in Vieques to a large international public. With no interest in instrumentalisation, we hope this work expands the network of solidarity and support for the people of Vieques and the global demilitarisation movement in general. One of the reasons for the success of the peace and justice campaign in Vieques was its ability to reach out to a global network of supporters who have both contributed to and learned from the initiatives in Vieques. So for example, you find people in a village in South Korea who call their town 'The Vieques of Korea' and are using tactics similar to those that were used in Vieques in their own resistance to bombing exercises in Maehyang-ri. Or a conference organised in Glasgow, Scotland, entitled 'Lessons from Vieques – a Conference Celebrating Peace, Resistance and a Commitment to a Military-free Scotland' (April 2005). There were also 9,000 protesters marching in Fretzdorf, Germany, on 27 March, 2005, for the struggle in Vieques. Our intention in showing *Under Discussion* in Venice was to establish yet another link in this larger global network of solidarity and support. [...]

Smith The central figure in each video makes a perambulation around the island: either by land or by sea he ends up right back where he started. That seems a bit pessimistic: it suggests a condition of stasis that runs counter to the trumpet's call for action although perhaps is more in keeping with the protagonists' roles as witnesses/observers.

Allora & Calzadilla We see this cyclical movement a bit differently. The idea for the protagonists' particular trajectory was for it to function as a kind of mapping. In *Returning a Sound*, Homar travels through those tracts of land that in his lifetime and in the generation before him had never been accessible. In the expropriations of the 1940s, thousands of families living throughout the island were forced off of their land and made to either leave together or to settle in a small wedge of land in the island's centre. The military occupation of the island divided the geography into three sections. In the west was the ammunition storage facility and in the east was the life-firing range. In between was the civilian population. So in *Returning a Sound*, Homar begins his journey in the civilian area in the central northern town of Isabel II and then moves in a clockwise direction around the entire island. With his modified bike, he starts in the town and then moves into the military lands. A similar logic holds true for *Under Discussion*. In this instance, Diego starts in the central southern town of Esperanza and moves eastward along the fishing routes that were the contested grounds of the Fisherman's Movement, which initially bore witness to the devastating effects of the bombing. Since both of their actions took place within a certain temporality, we understand that the protagonists do not really arrive exactly where they started. Time has passed – both the protagonist and his environment in which his action took place are somehow, even if only slightly, different. It is more of a spiral than a circular movement. This understanding of time and transformation, in a certain manner, reflects the ecological nature of the peace and justice movement in Vieques, in which change happens slowly, across generations, yet also respects and acknowledges the contribution of all actions, however great or small, in the eventual transformation of place.

Smith These works followed another project in Vieques, an interrogative design, intervention, and photography project called *Land Mark*, which you made prior to the military pullout from the island.

Allora & Calzadilla The photography project – which we have shown in various exhibition contexts – is an extension of a series of actions that took place in Vieques in 2001–2002. We worked in collaboration with activist groups involved with protest actions in the disputed US Navy bomb testing range.

Initially our project consisted of designing custom-made soles that were added onto the shoes of people involved with the land reclamation campaign. The shoes were used in civil disobedience actions in which people seeking to reclaim the land entered the range and, as a result of walking in that landscape, marked their presence in the form of a stamp on the terrain. The images on the bottom of the shoes, chosen by each individual user, depicted territories (geographical, bodily, linguistic, etc.) that functioned as counter-representations of the site's function at that time as well as what it is still to become.

[…] Our works […] look at the question of environmental justice – what and who counts as an endangered species – and how this discourse reconceptualises the relationships between nonhuman and human nature and, as a result, fosters new forms of environmentalism. The land-rights struggle in Vieques extends the parameters of the term sustainability to include the very survival of the indigenous civilian population of the island, and, as a result, complicates and broadens mainstream notions of environmentalism and sustainability to include questions of social justice that affect how people live in their environments. The recent transition of the contaminated naval grounds into a wildlife refuge administered by the US Department of the Interior and the rapid development of mostly North American tourist initiatives further complicate this debate. The former mask grave health problems caused by the release of toxic chemicals from the hundreds of thousands of bombs dropped over the past 60 years on this small island and the latter continues a long history of colonisation and systematic exclusion of the local population from the natural and productive resources of the island.

Stephanie Smith, extracts from 'An Interview with Allora & Calzadilla' in *Beyond Green: Towards Sustainable Art*, (Chicago and New York: Smart Art Museum and iCI, 2005) 34–39.

Amar Kanwar
On The Sovereign Forest: In Conversation with Ute Meta Bauer and Anca Rujoiu//2020

The Sovereign Forest (2012–ongoing), a multilayered project, focusses on struggles over the resource-rich land of Odisha (formerly Orissa), in East India – a land marked since the 1990s by conflicts between local communities, the Indian government and international corporations. *The Sovereign Forest*, a long-term collaboration between artist Amar Kanwar, Sudhir Pattnaik/Samadrusti and Sherna Dastur, initiates a creative revision of our understanding of crime, politics, human rights and ecology. A constellation of films, texts, photographs and seeds are brought together in the project's investigation of the validity of poetry as evidence in a trial, discourses on vision, compassion and justice, and the determination of the self.

Ute Meta Bauer and Anca Rujoiu The Sovereign Forest is a long term commitment to the resistance of indigenous communities and farmers in Odisha against industrial corporations, local organised crime and the government since 1999.
　　What brought you there first?

Amar Kanwar In the mid 1990s, during the first wave of the so-called New Economic Policy, it was difficult for any ordinary person to get a sense of the scale of the operations. At that time, I decided to collect newspaper reports of the previous two years – of visits, transactions, Memoranda of Understanding and statements by various government and industrial leaders. Most of these news reports were brief and did not have much detail. It was a simplistic way to do research but I didn't want to ask anyone and I wanted information that was factual and had no spin.
　　Plotting this research and the areas of interest on a map of India became an obvious course of action. Corporations and cartels that were well known internationally had several reasons to come here. They were all targeting the coastal zones, especially Gujarat but also other states, the alpine regions of the lower and middle Himalayas, and all along the mineral seams of the Eastern Ghats, which is where Odisha is located. I then travelled extensively for a couple of years in these three regions, researching, meeting various people – villagers, activists, ecological groups, journalists, scientists, bureaucrats and others – trying to understand what was happening. I also filmed in all these areas. I made many friends and learnt a lot from these travels. In Odisha, I met Sudhir Pattnaik

and worked with him. I worked in different ways with other groups and NGOs, taught film-making informally and filmed in many areas more or less at the same time. I saw several remarkable small villages and hamlets resisting against very powerful multinational industrial cartels, local politicians and mafias. These resistances were inspiring. There was also a history and experience that I came across there. I had no plans of an exhibition at that time; I was interested in multiple ways of responding to these experiences and was trying to find alternative ways of making, showing and relating.

Bauer and Rujoiu For industrial corporations, land is a money-making resource; for central and local government, land is a commodity. For the people, it's their home, their livelihood. On this disputed territory, the interests of corporations intersect with the corrupt apparatus of state while violently hitting the lives and land rights of farmers and indigenous communities. However, in your work, land is not reduced to a single image or definition. Is *The Sovereign Forest* a way to look at land again and again?

Kanwar For some, land is water. Water is a part of these people, and they can talk only when it flows. For some land is memory without which you cannot think. For some land is food without which there is no taste. For some it is miles underground, a site of labouring in the dark. For many it offers an embrace that calms them from deep inside. Just as I keep trying to understand life, I keep trying to understand land. At one point land, for me, had become words – words about information, anger, protest, the cycle of brutality and the response to it. Over time I felt the need to find a way to look again, not only at the land but at life, its meaning. Not just at the life of others but mine too. So I tried many things to shift the way I look – to slow down and think, to increase the awareness of every breath, to see every imperceptible movement: the shift of a blade of grass, the sound of a fishing net hitting water, light moving. I even tried to empty the image of emotion, distance the human form and then look and look again at the land, so as to be able to sense and see its inner narratives. I wanted to find the fluidity and interchangeability of these narratives so that any story of any being in any language from any memory could seep seamlessly inside any form or object, living or non-living, in any landscape. Finally, it became necessary to step back and look at the scene of the crime in order to prepare oneself, rather than researching the land. To prepare to enable, to increase capacity, to see the signs of what was no longer there, or of what was about to be erased. To see the enormous sorrow that perhaps had seeped into the soil and was now out of sight. […]

Bauer and Rujoiu [...] One of the components of *The Sovereign Forest* is a handmade book with projection dedicated to Shankar Guha Niyogi, the late workers' leader. Another book, *Memory Of* (2012–14), remembers and names each of the farmers in Odisha who lost their lives fighting against the dispossession of their land. You situate their individual experiences and memory in a wider narrative of collective struggle. You also highlight how these communities denounce crimes and express knowledge of their rights in order to demand justice. You bring to the fore the creativity of these communities' resistance and resilience, expressed through songs, poetry, craft and theatre, and, last but not least, through your own work as a film-maker and an artist.

Kanwar [...] To fully account for the story of Niyogi's life and that of the Chhattisgarh Mukti Morcha ('Chhattisgarh Liberation Front'), in the state of Chhattisgarh (earlier Madhya Pradesh) in East India, an organisation of workers, farmers and indigenous communities in the Indian state of Chhattisgarh, will perhaps take several books and oral narratives. In the context of this discussion I am reminded of a perspective that Niyogi himself put forward, not just as a slogan or stated vision but as a prerequisite for any form of social-political action. His call was to 'Create and Struggle or Create as You Struggle'. Whenever I lose track or am overwhelmed by the negativity around, I recall this vision. Regardless of how small or insignificant a work I may be doing. It is the act of making, of creating something for one's self or for others, of contributing to a collective, of generosity alongside or even entwined with resistance that makes life more meaningful.

In *The Prediction* (1991–2012), a part of *The Sovereign Forest*, the story of a murder trial that took place over two decades is presented. Those who conspired to kill were first convicted, but all were finally acquitted. Justice was supposedly delivered. And so *The Prediction* presents a counterpoint from the past, to the present unfolding of crimes in Odisha. [...] Niyogi predicted his assassination, but didn't tell anyone about his apprehension. He knew that for the companies to get full access to the land, and the mineral seams, his organisation would need to be destroyed first. He anticipated a severe attack on the local populations, on all kinds of people's organisations and on the land and forests of the region after his death. All of which has come true unfortunately. But at that time no one knew why he was asking for a filmmaker to be around. In hindsight we can see his logic. He wanted the events to be filmed, for a witness to be there, to record the onslaught on Guha lands and the experience of the people. He was killed in 1991. I was a young filmmaker. It was a very disturbing experience but also one that opened up, for me, a world of solidarity and resistance that I hadn't seen before. [...] At different times I had several discussions with Sudhir Pattnaik and Sherna Dastur and we began to add elements to the film as and when the opportunity arose. Stories, more films, books, texts, seeds, different ways of reading, knowing and looking and exhibiting in and outside Odisha. *The Scene of Crime* became central to *The Sovereign Forest* and we grew around it a spectrum of evidence. Sudhir and Sherna have both co-created and nurtured *The Sovereign Forest* over a long time, in too many ways to list here. They usually also don't talk much about their work, so I interviewed both of them. These texts can be read in the book on *The Sovereign Forest* and will give a deeper idea of the range of this collaboration.

Two months after first presenting the exhibition at dOCUMENTA (13), we installed it in Bhubaneswar and it was then open to the public for four years, until we had to let go of the building. If it had no meaning it would not have lasted more than a month. If it has and is felt to be of some use, then it will reincarnate, improve and resurface. The next possible location in Odisha is still being worked on, most likely in a rural space, in collaboration with a rural trust/organisation. It will perhaps change quite a bit so as to relate more deeply with more issues around agriculture. Everything is always tentative. We move ahead a bit, discuss with as many people as we can, think more and then try again. We are under no illusions – about ourselves, about our impact or about the communities involved. We are in a terrain of conflict, of depravation, of ecological and livelihood destruction, and acting in this terrain is fraught with contradictions and dilemmas. We try to address these, and to do the best we can without harming anyone, supporting as many people as we can, and are always learning through the process. [...]

Amar Kanwar, Ute Meta Bauer and Anca Rujoiu, extracts from 'On *The Sovereign Forest*: In Conversation with Amar Kanwar', in *Afterall*, no. 49 (Spring/Summer 2020), 7–13.

The open crowd is the true crowd, the crowd abandoning itself freely to its natural urge for growth.

Elias Canetti, 'The Open and the Closed Crowd', 1960 (see pages 193–196)

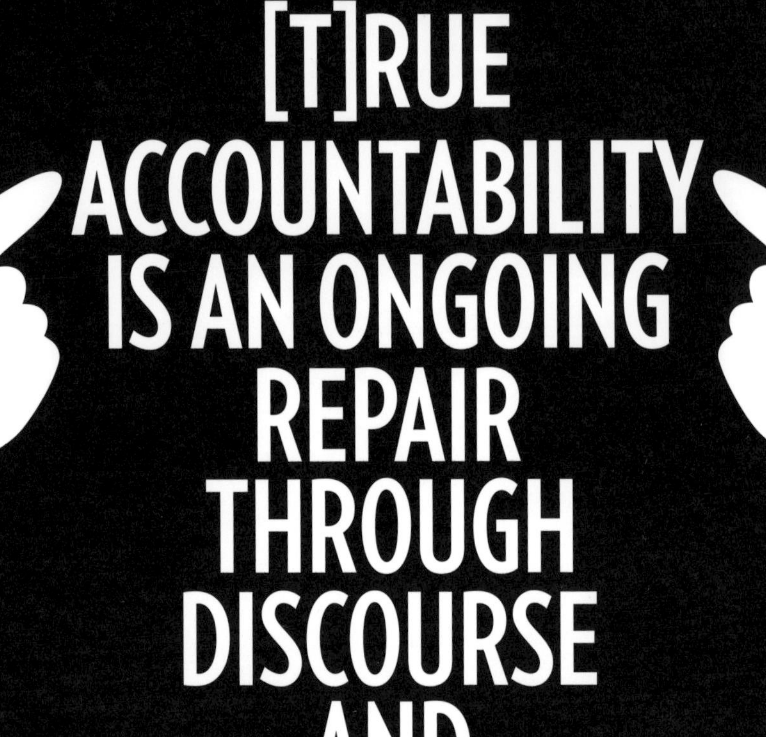

Michael Rakowitz, 'Letter to an Encyclopedic Museum Curator', 2022

CODA

Michael Rakowitz
Letter to an Encyclopedic Museum Curator//2022

[…] Dear Encyclopedic Museum Curator,

My apologies for being late to reply. When you wrote, I was laid up with the flu, and after a few days of travel, I received some difficult news about my mother's health.

The reliefs from Room F that you inquired about will be on view at the Nasher Sculpture Center until early May, so it will certainly be possible for the work to be shown at your museum in the context of the Assyrian reliefs during the time you've proposed.

But I wonder if we may think more audaciously and provocatively about how to do this. As you know, Daesh's destruction of the Northwest Palace of Nimrud was followed in late 2018 by the auctioning of a relief that was in the possession of the Virginia Theological Seminary. The price paid for this relief – $31 million by an anonymous private collector – was enhanced by the demolition of the palace three years before, and while the money will be used for the admirable purpose of funding a scholarship at VTS, the auction bolstered further the narrative of Iraq as a site of extraction and speculation.

I am hoping my work can impact and support efforts to interrupt this cycle. In the past few years, I have been focusing more on institutional responsibility and my commitments as an artist, descended from an Iraqi Jewish mother forced to depart her homeland. A desire to return, despite its impossibilities, fuels so much of my practice. A multitude of Iraq's cultural heritage now exists outside of its borders, away from its people, and what remains has been targeted for destruction. But what perishes is not just the monumental reliefs of colossal figures of deities like the Lamassu, it is the communities of people who live alongside them. The DNA of those lives cannot be 3D printed and replaced. That is why I have come to call my works not reconstructions, but reappearances or ghosts of the originals. An imperfect and vulnerable offering that will one day also disappear.

Let me say without hesitation that it would be a pleasure to collaborate with you on this project. But in order to do this, I'd like to up the ante and create a more complex agreement. I'd like to gift to the museum the entirety of Room F, Section 1, free of charge, in exchange for the return to Iraq of Panel F-[number withheld], currently in the museum's collection.

Given all that has been destroyed in Iraq, and the intersection of that destruction with the west's insatiable appetite for the objects of the east while not always, if ever, extending that concern to its people, this return of an original would be more than just restitutive. It would be restorative. So much is missed when our conversations around decolonisation rest only on questions of repatriation. I liken this to the inadequacy of apology versus accountability. Apology, when uttered, unburdens the person saying it more than it heals the person to whom it was directed. But true accountability is an ongoing repair through discourse and reckoning. It is never finished. Restoration exists as a practice within every museum that I have known. In fact, when I visited your museum in January, the director took me to the area where some of the reliefs were being restored. I was so moved to see the backs of the reliefs. In that moment, the Apkallu were like figures in the round. I was seeing the relief as if it had turned its back on me, as if it were walking away. Going home.

Please understand the absolute sincerity of my proposal here, and please do not perceive this as a vilification of the museum, the work you do, or some unkind purity judgement of the museum's collections. The best one can hope for in doing any kind of work is that it will continue to teach and that we will be open to learning. We know that museums are important, and at their best, they can be based on a mutual curiosity among the world's cultures. But we cannot ignore the cultural traumas caused by the extraction of many of these objects, nor the imperative to break this cycle and restore dignity and humanity to the people that have been parted from their cultural heritage.

For a long time, I thought I was making these reappearances to replace what was destroyed in Iraq. I imagined that one day, perhaps, my reappearances might end up in places like Nineveh, Nimrud, Mosul, or Baghdad. Yet what was destroyed in Iraq was disappeared in part because the west valued it so much. And so I wish to complicate my work even more by acknowledging that a ghost needs to haunt. It is not, however, the Iraqis who need to be haunted. It is us.

I thank you for reading this and hope you and the museum will think seriously with me on this proposal.

Sincerely,
Michael

Michael Rakowitz, extract from 'Letter to an Encyclopedic Museum Curator', in *Grey Room*, no. 87 (Spring, 2022) 111–113.

Biographical Notes

Basel Abbas and **Ruanne Abou-Rahme** are a collaborative duo of visual artists who live and work between Ramallah, Palestine and New York, USA.

Nora Al-Badri is a multi-disciplinary and conceptual media artist.

Allora & Calzadilla are a collaborative duo of visual artists who live and work in San Juan, Puerto Rico.

Doug Ashford is an artist and a visiting Associate Professor for the MFA Program in Painting at The Yale School of Art.

Judith Baca is a Chicana artist, professor, arts administrator, community leader and social and cultural activist.

Ute Meta Bauer is a Professor of Art at NTU's School of Art, Media, and Design.

Dave Beech is an artist and writer and a Reader in Art and Marxism at Chelsea College of Art.

Franco 'Bifo' Berardi is a writer, media theorist and media activist.

Tania Bruguera is an artist and activist who focuses on installation and performance art.

Christoph Brunner is Assistant Professor for Philosophy of Media and Technology at Erasmus University Rotterdam.

Erica Buist is a writer, playwright, author and journalist living in London.

Judith Butler is Distinguished Professor in the Graduate School at the University of California, Berkeley and works in philosophy and gender studies.

Amílcar Cabral (1924–1973) was a writer, agronomic engineer, political organiser and diplomat from Guinea-Bissau.

Elias Canetti (1905–1994) was a German novelist, essayist, sociologist and playwright, who was awarded the Nobel Prize for Literature in 1981.

Jessica Cooley is a scholar-curator and the ACLS Emerging Voices Fellow for the University of Minnesota's Liberal Arts Engagement Hub.

Douglas Crimp (1944–2019) was an art critic and Fanny Knapp Allen Professor of Art History and Professor of Visual and Cultural Studies at the University of Rochester, New York.

Jodi Dean is a political theorist based in Geneva, NY, and the author of editor of 14 books, most recently *Comrade: An Essay on Political Belonging*, published by Verso.

Chto Delat is a collective of artists, critics, philosophers and writers.

Gilles Deleuze (1925–1995) was a poststructuralist French philosopher.

T.J. Demos is Professor of History of Art and Visual Culture at the University of California, Santa Cruz, and Director of its Center for Creative Ecologies.

Nika Dubrovsky is an artist and an author who grew up in the unofficial cultural scenes of squats and samizdat of the late USSR. She has written for e-flux, artnet, colta, ХЖ and others, and has exhibited her work worldwide.

Süreyyya Evren is a Turkish writer and cultural theorist.

Mark Fisher (1968–2017) was an English writer, political and cultural theorist, philosopher and teacher based in the Department of Visual Cultures at Goldsmiths, University of London.

Catherine Flood is an independent curator and writer who works with historical collections and contemporary art and design on social and ecological themes.

Ann M. Fox is an independent curator and a Professor of English at Davidson College, where she specialises in literary and cultural disability studies, graphic medicine, and modern and contemporary drama.

Andrea Fraser is an artist and a Professor in the Department of Art at the University of California Los Angeles (UCLA) School of the Arts and Architecture.

Matthew Fuller is a writer, artist and Professor of Cultural Studies at the Department of Media, Communications and Cultural Studies at Goldsmiths, University of London.

Nan Goldin is an American photographer and activist.

David Graeber (1961–2020) was an American anthropologist and anarchist activist.

Gavin Grindon is Senior Lecturer in Curating and Art History at the University of Essex, where he writes and teaches on activist-art.

Félix Guattari (1930–1992) was a French psychoanalyst, philosopher and political activist.

The Guerrilla Girls are a collective of political feminist artists.

Global Ultra Luxury Faction (G.U.L.F.) is an autonomous direct-action wing of Gulf Labor.

Gulf Labor is a coalition of artists and activists based in New York.

Stuart Hall (1932–2014) was a Jamaican-born British sociologist and cultural theorist.

David Harvey is a British geographer and the Distinguished Professor of Anthropology at the Graduate Center of the City University of New York (CUNY).

Tom Holert is an art historian, writer, curator and artist based in Berlin.

Brian Holmes is an essayist, artist and activist working on political ecology.

Darcus Howe (1943–2017) was a British writer, broadcaster and racial justice campaigner.

Sanja Iveković is a Croatian photographer, performer, sculptor and installation artist.

Amar Kanwar is a visual artist and social activist based in New Delhi.

Lina Khatib is Head of the Middle East and North Africa Programme at Chatham House.

Leslie Labowitz is a Los Angeles artist and entrepreneur.

Suzanne Lacy is an American artist, educator, writer and professor at the USC Roski School of Art and Design, California.

Carrie Lambert-Beatty is a Professor in the Department of History of Art and Architecture and the Department of Visual and Environmental Studies at Harvard University.

Aude Launay is an independent researcher, writer and curator trained as a philosopher.

Marc James Léger is a Marxist cultural theorist living in Montreal.

Liberate Tate is an art collective based in London.

Lucy Lippard is an American art historian, curator, writer and activist.

Achille Mbembe is a Research Professor of History and Politics at the Wits Institute for Social and Economic Research in Johannesburg, South Africa.

Yates McKee is an art critic and PhD candidate in Art History at CUNY Graduate Center.

MTL Collective is a collective based in New York that combines research, aesthetics, organizing, and action.

Chantal Mouffe is an Emeritus Professor of Political Theory at the Centre for the Study of Democracy at the University of Westminster, London.

Sethembile Msezane is a South African visual artist, public speaker and performer.

Zanele Muholi is a South African visual activist and photographer.

Antonio Negri is an Italian political philosopher and sociologist.

Jan Nikolai Nelles is an artist and technologist whose artistic research deals with resilience through creativity and the limits of human consciousness.

Roberto Nigro is full Professor of Philosophy at the Leuphana University of Lüneburg in Germany, where he holds the Chair of Continental Philosophy and is Dean of the Faculty of Kulturwissenschaften (Social and Cultural Sciences).

Not An Alternative is a collective and non-profit that works at the intersection of art, activism and critical theory.

Katarzyna Pabijanek is a curator, critic and lecturer in the Gender Studies program at the Institute of Literary Research of the Polish Academy of Sciences.

Vivian Paulissen is Head of Programmes at European Cultural Foundation.

Michael Rakowitz is an Iraqi-American artist living and working in Chicago.

Gerald Raunig works at the eipcp (European Institute for Progressive Cultural Policies) as one of the editors of the multilingual publishing platform transveral texts, and at the Zürcher Hochschule der Künste as professor for philosophy.

Oliver Ressler is an artist and filmmaker who lives and works in Vienna.

Adam Rolston is an American contemporary visual artist.

Martha Rosler is a Brooklyn-based artist, theorist and educator.

Anca Rujoiu is a curator and editor who was a member of the founding team of the NTU Centre for Contemporary Art in Singapore.

Salman Rushdie is an author and a Fellow of the British Royal Society of Literature.

Gregory Sholette is a New York-based artist, writer, teacher and activist.

Stephanie Smith is an affiliate faculty member of the Department of Visual Art at the University of Chicago, and a founding member of its Open Practice Committee.

Tidal Magazine was born during the occupation of Wall Street in 2011.

Françoise Vergès is a writer, political theorist and decolonial feminist from Reunion Island. *Scent* publication (2023, forthcoming in English, 2024) *Program of Absolute Disorder: Decolonize the Museum* (2023).

Peter Weiss (1916–1982) was a German playwright, dramatist, visual artist, filmmaker and novelist.

Eyal Weizman is a Professor of Spatial and Visual Cultures and Director of the Centre for Research Architecture at Goldsmiths, University of London.

Deborah Willis is a University Professor and Chair of the Department of Photography & Imaging at the Tisch School of the Arts at New York University.

Bibliography

Abbas, Basel and Ruanne Abou-Rahme, (in conversation with Tom Holert), 'The Archival Multitude', in *Journal of Visual Culture*, vol. 12, no. 3 (December, 2013) 345–363

Abou-Rahme Nasser, Jayyusi, *May The will to revolt and the spectre of the real: Reflections on the Arab moment*, City vol. 15 no.6, (December, 2011) 625–630

Abujbara, Juman, Andrew Boyd, David Mitchell and Marcell Taminato, eds. *Beautiful Rising: Creative Resistance from the Global South* (New York: OR Books, 2018)

Ai Weiwei, *Conversations: Ai Weiwei* (New York: Columbia University Press, 2021)

Al-Badri, Nora and Jan Nikolai Nelles, 'Interview with Aude Launay', *ZéroDeux*, no. 84 (Winter 2017/2018)

Araeen, Rasheed, *Art Beyond Art - Ecoaesthetics: A Manifesto for the 21st Century* (London: Third Text Publications, 2010)

Athanasiou, Athena and Judith Butler. *Dispossession: The Performative in the Political* (London: Polity Press, 2013)

Ault, Julie, ed. *Show and Tell: A Chronicle of Group Material* (London: Four Corners Books, 2010)

Badiou, Alain, *The Rebirth of History: Times of Riots and Uprisings* trans. Gregory Elliot (London and New York: Verso, 2012)

Badovinac, Zdenka, Eda Čufer, Anthony Gardner, eds. *NSK From Kapital to Capital: Neue Slowenische Kunst, an Event of the Final Decade of Yugoslavia* (Cambridge and London: The MIT Press, 2015)

Beech, Dave, 'To Boycott or Not to Boycott', *Art Monthly*, no. 380 (October, 2014) 380–382

Bishop, Claire, 'Antagonism and Relational Aesthetics,' in *October*, vol. 110 (Fall, 2004) 51–79

Bookchin, Murray, *The Next Revolution: Popular Assemblies and the Promise of Direct Democracy* (London and New York: Verso, 2015)

Boyd, Andrew, and Dave Oswald Mitchell, eds. *Beautiful Trouble: A Tool Box for Revolution* (New York: OR Books, 2016)

Bradley, Will, and Charles Esche, eds. *Art and Social Change: A Critical Reader* (London: Tate Publishing and Afterall, 2007)

Bruguera, Tania and Immigrant Movement International, 'Migrant Manifesto', (2011) (http://immigrant-movement.us/wordpress/migrant-manifesto/)

Brunner, Christoph, Roberto Nigro, Gerald Raunig, 'Post-Media Activism, Social Ecology and Eco-Art', *Third Text*, vol. 21, no. 1, (January 2013) 10–16

Burger, Peter, *Theory of the Avant-Garde*, trans. Michael Shaw (Minneapolis: University of Minnesota Press, 1984)

Cabral, Amílcar, 'National Liberation and Culture' (1970), *Transition*, no. 45 (1974)

Canetti, Elias, *Crowds and Power* (1960), trans. Carol Stewart, (New York: Farrar, Straus and Giroux, 1984)

Chto Delat, extracts from 'A Declaration on Politics, Knowledge, and Art on the Fifth Anniversary of the Chto Delat Work Group', in *Chto Delat? Newspaper, #special issue: When Artists Struggle Together* (November, 2008)

Cockburn, Alexander, Jeffrey St. Clair, eds. *5 Days That Shook the World* (London and New York: Verso, 2000)

Cooley, Jessica A. and Ann M. Fox, 'Crip Curation as Care: *A Manifesto*', *Theater*, vol. 52 no. 2 (2022), 5–17

De Cauter, Lieven, Ruben De Roo & Karel Vanhaesebrouck, eds. *Art and Activism in the Age of Globalization* (Rotterdam: NAi Publishers, 2011)

Dean, Jodi, *Crowds and Party* (London and New York: Verso, 2016)

Deleuze, Gilles, *Negotiations, 1972–1990*, trans. Martin Joughin (New York: Columbia University Press, 1997)

Demos, T.J., *Decolonizing Nature: Contemporary Art and the Politics of Ecology* (Berlin: Sternberg Press, 2016)

______. *Against the Anthropocene: Visual Culture and Environment Today* (Berlin: Sternberg Press, 2017)

______. *Beyond the World's End: Art of Living at the Crossing* (Durham and London: Duke University Press, 2020)

______. *Radical Futurisms: Ecologies of Collapse, Chronopolitics, and Justice-to-Come* (London: Sternberg Press, 2023)

Downey, Anthony, ed. *Uncommon Grounds: New Media and Critical Practices in the Middle East* (London and New York: I.B. Tauris, 2014)

______. *Dissonant Archives: Contemporary Visual Culture and Contested Narratives in the Middle East* (London and New York: I.B. Tauris, 2015)

______. *Futures Imperfect: Contemporary Art Practices and Cultural Institutions in the Middle East* (Berlin: Sternberg, 2016)

D'Souza, Aruna, *Whitewalling: Art, Race & Protest in 3 Acts* (New York: Badlands Unlimited, 2018)

Edwards, Steve, 'Commons and Crowds: Figuring Photography from Above and Below,' in *Third Text*, vol. 23, no. 4 (July 2009) 447-464

Dubrovsky, Nika and David Graeber, 'Another Art World, Part 1: Art Communism and Artificial Scarcity', *e-flux journal*, no. 102, (September, 2019); 'Another Art World, Part 3: Policing and Symbolic Order', *e-flux journal*, no. 113, (November, 2020)

Eshun, Kodwo and Anjalika Sagar, eds. *The Ghosts of Songs: The Film Art of the Black Audio Film Collective, 1982-1998* (Liverpool: Liverpool University Press, and FACT, 2007)

Evans, Mel, *Artwash: Big Oil and the Arts* (London: Pluto Press, 2015)

Evren, Süreyyya, 'Gezi Resistance in Istanbul: Something in Between Tahrir, Occupy and a Late Turkish 1968', *Anarchist Studies*, vol. 21, no. 2 (2013) 7–10

Feher, Michel, Gaëlle Krikorian and Yates McKee, eds. *Nongovernmental Politics* (New York: Zone Books, 2007)

Fisher, Mark and Franco 'Bifo' Berardi, 'Give Me Shelter', *Frieze*, no. 152, (2003) 150–152

Flood, Catherine and Gavin Grindon, eds. *Disobedient Objects* (London: V&A Publishing, 2014)

Foster, Hal, *Recodings: Art, Spectacle, Cultural Politics* (Seattle: Bay Press, 1985)

Freire, Paulo, *Pedagogy of the Oppressed*, trans. Myra Bergman Ramos (London: Penguin Books, 1996 edn.)

Goldin, Nan, *Artforum*, vol. 56, no. 5 (January 2018), 128

Graeber, David, *The Democracy Project: A History, A Crisis, A Movement* (London: Allen Lane, 2013)

Groys, Boris, 'On Art Activism', *e-flux journal*, no. 56 (June 2014)

Guattari, Félix, *The Three Ecologies* (1989), trans. Ian Pindar and Paul Sutton (London: Athlone Press, 2000)

Guerrilla Girls, *Confessions of the Guerrilla Girls* (New York: HarperCollins, 1995)

Gulf Labor, 'Petition', (16 March, 2011) (https://gulflabour.org/sign-the-petition/)

Harney, Stefano and Fred Moten, *The Undercommons: Fugitive Planning and Black Study* (Wivenhoe, New York and Port Watson: Minor Compositions, 2013)

Harvey, David, *Rebel Cities: From the Right to the City to the Urban Revolution*, (London and New York: Verso, 2012)

Helguera, Pablo, *Education for Socially Engaged Art* (New York: Jorge Pinto Books, 2012)

Hlavajova, Maria and Simon Sheikh, eds. *Former West: Art and the Contemporary After 1989* (Utrecht, Cambridge and London: BAK, basis voor actuele kunst and The MIT Press, 2016)

Iveković, Sanja and Pabijanek, Katarzyna, '"Women's House": Sanja Iveković Discusses Recent Projects (Interview)' in *Art Margins* (20 December, 2009) (https://artmargins.com/qwomenshouseq-sanja-ivekovic-discusses-recent-projects-interview/)

Iveković, Sanja, *Public Cuts* (Ljubljana: Zavod P.A.R.A.S.I.T.E., 2006)

Holmes, Brian, *Unleashing the Collective Phantoms: Essays in Reverse Imagineering*, (New York: Autonomedia, 2008)

______. *Escape the Overcode: Activist Art in the Control Society* (Eindhoven: Van Abbemuseum, 2009)

Meta Bauer, Ute, and Anca Rujoiu, 'On *The Sovereign Forest*: In Conversation with Amar Kanwar', in *Afterall*, no. 49 (Spring/Summer 2020)

Kester, Grant H., ed. *Art, Activism & Oppositionality: Essays from Afterimage* (Durham and London: Duke University Press, 1998)

Kester, Grant H., *The One and the Many: Contemporary Collaborative Art in a Global Context* (Durham and London: Duke University Press, 2011)

Khatib, Lina and Ellen Lust, ed. *Taking to the Streets: The Transformation of Arab Activism* (Baltimore: John Hopkins University Press, 2014)

Khatib, Lina, *Image Politics in the Middle East: The Role of the Visual in Political Struggle* (London: I.B. Tauris, 2013)

Kim, David D., *Reframing Postcolonial Studies: Concepts, Methodologies, Scholarly Activisms* (Cham: Springer Nature, 2021)

Kwon, Miwon, 'One Place after Another: Notes on Site Specificity', in *October*, vol. 80 (Spring 1997) 85–110

Laclau, Ernesto and Chantal Mouffe, *Hegemony and Socialist Strategy: Towards a Radical Democratic Politics* (London and New York: Verso, 1985)

Lacy, Suzanne, ed. *Mapping the Terrain: New Genre Public Art* (Seattle: Bay Press, 1996)

Lacy, Suzanne, *Leaving Art: Writings on Performance, Politics, and Publics, 1974-2007* (Durham and London: Duke University Press, 2010)

Lambert-Beatty, Carrie, 'Twelve Miles: Boundaries of the New Art/Activism', in *Signs*, vol. 33, no. 2 (Winter, 2008) 309–327

Liberate Tate, 'Disobedience as Performance', *Performance Research*, vol. 17, no. 4 (2012) 135–140

Lichtenfels, Peter and John Rouse, *Performance, Politics and Activism* (Basingstoke: Palgrave Macmillan, 2017)

Madoff, Steven Henry, ed. *What about Activism?* (Berlin: Sternberg Press, 2019)

Martin, Stewart, 'Critique of Relational Aesthetics' in *Third Text*, vol. 21, no. 4 (July, 2007) 369–386

Mbembe, Achille, 'Interview with Vivian Paulissen, African Contemporary Art: Negotiating the Terms of Recognition', *Africultures* (1 December, 2009) (https://africultures.com/african-contemporary-art-negotiating-the-termsof-recognition-9030/)

McKay, George, *Senseless Acts of Beauty:Cultures of Resistance since the Sixties* (London and New York: Verso, 1996)

McKee, Yates, *Strike Art: Contemporary Art and the Post-Occupy Condition* (London and New York: Verso, 2016)

McLagan, Meg and Yates McKee, eds. *Sensible Politics: The Visual Culture of Nongovernmental Activism* (New York: Zone Books, 2012)

Memou, Antigoni, *Photography and Social Movements: From the globalisation of the movement (1968) to the movement against globalisation (2001)* (Manchester and New York: Manchester University Press, 2013)

Milstein, Cindy, ed. *Rebellious Mourning: The Collective Work of Grief* (Chico, California: AK Press, 2017)

Mitchell, W.J.T., Bernard E. Harcourt, and Michael Taussig. *Occupy: Three Inquiries in Disobedience.* Chicago and London: The University of Chicago Press, 2013.

Mouffe, Chantal, 'Artistic Activism and Agonistic Spaces', *Art & Research: A Journal of Ideas, Contexts and Methods*, vol. 1, no. 2 (Summer 2007) 1–5

______. *Agonistics: Thinking the World Politically* (London: Verso, 2013)

Msezane, Sethembile, 'Sethembile Msezane Performs at the Fall of the Cecil Rhodes Statue', *The Guardian* (15 May, 2015) (https://www.theguardian.com/artanddesign/2015/may/15/sethembile-msezane-cecil-rhodes-statue-cape-town-south-africa)

MTL Collective, 'From Institutional Critique to Institutional Liberation? A Decolonial Perspective on the Crises of Contemporary Art', *October*, no. 165, (Summer, 2018) 192–227

Muholi, Zanele and Deborah Willis, 'Zanele Muholi's Faces & Phases', *Aperture Magazine*, (April, 2015) 59-62

Not An Alternative, 'Institutional Liberation', *e-flux journal*, no. 77 (November, 2016)

Parker, Rozsika, and Griselda Pollock, eds. *Framing Feminism: Art and the Women's Movement 1970-1985* (London: Pandora, 1987)

Rakowitz, Michael, 'Letter to an Encyclopedic Museum Curator', in *Grey Room*, no. 87 (Spring, 2022) 111–113

Raunig, Gerald, *Art and Revolution: Transversal Activism and the Long Twentieth Century*, trans. Aileen Derieg (Los Angeles: Semiotext(e), 2007)

Raunig, Gerald, and Gene Ray, eds. *Art and Contemporary Critical Practice: Reinventing Institutional Critique* (London: MayFly Books, 2009)

Ressler, Oliver and Marc James Léger, 'From Reaching Heiligendamm: An Interview with Oliver Ressler', in *Art Journal*, vol. 67, no. 1 (2008), 101–111

Roberts, John, *Revolutionary Time and the Avant-Garde*, (London and New York: Verso, 2005)

Rockhill, Gabriel, *Radical History & The Politics of Art* (New York: Columbia University Press, 2015)

Rosler, Martha, 'Out of the Vox: Art's Activist Potential', *Artforum* (September, 2004) 218–220

Ross, Andrew, ed. *The Gulf: High Culture/Hard Labor* (New York and London: OR Books, 2015)

Ross, Kristin, *May '68 and its Afterlives* (Chicago and London: University of Chicago Press, 2002)

Schulman, Sarah, *Let the Record Show: A Political History of Act Up New York, 1987-1993* (2021)

Sholette, Gregory, *Dark Matter: Art and Politics in the Age of Enterprise Culture* (London: Pluto Press, 2010)

______. *Delirium and Resistance: Activist Art and the Crisis of Capitalism* (London: Pluto, 2017)

______. *The Art of Activism and the Activism of Art* (London: Lund Humphries, 2022)

Sholette, Gregory, and Oliver Ressler, eds. *It's the Political Economy, Stupid: The Global Financial Crisis in Art and Theory* (London: Pluto Press, 2013)

Smith, Stephanie, *Beyond Green: Towards Sustainable Art*, (Chicago and New York: Smart Art Museum and iCI, 2005)

Smith, Terry, *Contemporary Art: World Currents* (London: Lawrence King Publishing, 2011)

Snow, Tom, 'Art as Activism', in *Art Monthly*, no. 472 (June 2019) 6–10

Stimson, Blake and Gregory Sholette, eds. *Collectivism After Modernism: The Art of Social Imagination After 1945* (Minneapolis: University of Minnesota Press, 2007)

Stracey, Frances, *Constructed Situations: A New History of the Situationist International* (London: Pluto Press, 2014)

Tancons, Claire, 'Occupy Wall Street: Carnival Against Capital? Carnivalesque as Protest Sensibility,' in *e-flux journal*, no. 30 (December 2011)

Thompson, Nato, *Culture as Weapon: The Art of Influence in Everyday Life*, (New York: Melville House, 2017)

Thompson, Nato, ed. *The Interventionists: Users' Manual for the Creative Disruption of Everyday Life*, (Cambridge, Massachusetts and London, England: The MIT Press, 2004)

Tidal Magazine, eds. *Tidal Magazine: Occupy Theory, Occupy Strategy*, no. 2 (March 2012)

Verges, Francoise, 'Let's Decolonise the Arts! A Long, Difficult and Passionate Struggle', trans. Adriano Hundhausen, *Artalk Revue*, Winter (2020) 1–9

Wallis, Brian, ed. *Art After Modernism, Rethinking Representation*, (New York: New Museum of Contemporary Art, 1984)

Warner, Michael, *Publics and Counterpublics* (New York: Zone Books, 2002)

Warsza, Joanna, ed. *I Can't Work Like This: A Reader on Recent Boycotts and Contemporary Art* (Berlin: Sternberg Press, 2017)

Weibel, Peter, ed. *Global Activism: Art and Conflict in the 21st Century*, (Karlsruhe, Cambridge and London: ZKM Centre for Art and Media and The MIT Press, 2014)

Weiss, Peter, *The Aesthetics of Resistance, Volume I* (1975), trans. Joachim Neugroschel (Durham and London: Duke University Press, 2005)

Whitney Museum, *Whitney Biennial 2012* (New York and New Haven: Whitney Museum of Art and Yale University Press, 2012)

ACKNOWLEDGEMENTS

Editor's acknowledgements

As editors of this volume, we would like to acknowledge and recognise the collective effort that contributes to any and every publication. Here, we express thanks and solidarity with artists whose works are surveyed in the texts, whether in their own words or the words of others, together with the writers, interviewers, and interviewees. We are additionally indebted to colleagues at Whitechapel Gallery, particularly Sofia Victorino who we first discussed the possibility of a volume on *Activism* with, and Anthony Iles and Evie Tarr who we worked with to bring this collection to completion. Our gratitude is also owed to countless friends, figures, and colleagues that we have learnt from, participated in public discussions and debates with over a number of years on many of the concerns addressed in this book, including T.J. Demos, Sarah E. James, Briony Fer, Tamar Garb, Stephanie Schwartz, Mignon Nixon, Anthony Gardner, Julian Stallabrass, Simon Sheikh, Anthony Downey, Steve Edwards, Gail Day, Ros Gray, Mark Fisher, Chantal Mouffe, Hannah Baader, Tobias Wendl, Gavin Grindon, Antigoni Memou, Vasıf Kortun, Burak Delier, Warren Carter, Eray Çaylı, Andrew Witt, Andy Murray, Larne Abse Gogarty, Marcus Verhagen, Mike Cooter, Juliet Hacking, Pierre Saurisse, Filipa Lowndes Vicente, Mariana Pinto dos Santos, and Martim Ramos.

Publisher's acknowledgements

Whitechapel Gallery is grateful to all those who gave their generous permission to reproduce the listed material. Every effort has been made to secure all permissions and we apologise for any inadvertent errors or omissions. If notified, we will endeavour to correct these at the earliest opportunity.

Whitechapel Gallery

whitechapelgallery.org

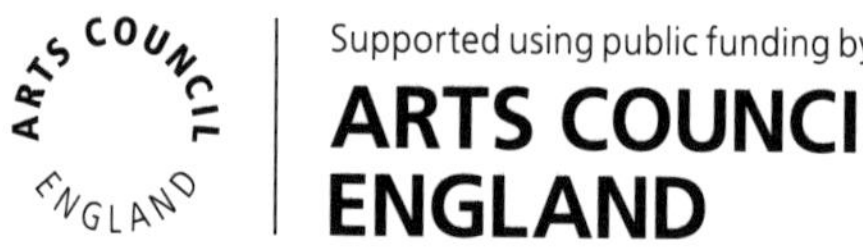

Supported using public funding by

ARTS COUNCIL ENGLAND